Psychological Fluffy in Environmental Grape

Alexis Jellybean

ISBN: 978-1-77961-767-5
Imprint: Popcorn Waffle Muffin

Contents

Introduction

The Study of Psychological Fluffy

Defining Psychological Fluffy

In order to embark on a journey through the vast field of Psychological Fluffy, it is essential to establish a clear understanding of what exactly this term encompasses. While the term "psychological fluffy" may initially sound whimsical or lighthearted, it actually refers to a complex and multifaceted concept that lies at the intersection of psychology and environmental studies. It involves the study of the intricate relationship between the human mind and the environments in which we live, work, and play.

At its core, Psychological Fluffy seeks to explore the psychological processes, experiences, and behaviors that are influenced by various environmental factors. It examines how these factors shape our thoughts, emotions, and actions, and how we, in turn, impact the environments we inhabit. It is concerned not only with the impact of the physical environment on individuals, but also with the social, cultural, economic, political, and technological aspects of our surroundings.

Psychological Fluffy recognizes that humans are not isolated beings, but rather deeply embedded in and influenced by the world around us. It acknowledges the inherent interconnectedness between individuals and their environments, and seeks to unravel the complex web of interactions that exist. The field is guided by the belief that understanding these interactions is crucial for promoting well-being, sustainability, and meaningful human experiences.

To further comprehend the breadth of Psychological Fluffy, it is necessary to delve into its historical background. The roots of this field can be traced back to early philosophers and psychologists who recognized the influence of environment on human behavior. From ancient thinkers like Plato and Aristotle, to the pioneers of psychology like Wilhelm Wundt and Sigmund Freud, the concept of environment has always played a significant role in shaping our understanding of human nature.

In recent decades, interest in Psychological Fluffy has intensified due to a growing recognition of the profound impact that the environment has on individuals and society as a whole. This field has gained momentum in response to the pressing environmental challenges we face, such as climate change, urbanization, and agricultural practices. As our ecosystems continue to change and evolve, so too does the need to understand and address the psychological consequences of these changes.

The importance of studying Psychological Fluffy in the context of environmental grape cannot be overstated. Environmental grape refers to the overall state of the environment, including its physical, social, cultural, economic, political, and technological dimensions. It encompasses everything from natural landscapes and ecosystems to the built environment of cities, towns, and villages. Environmental grape has a direct impact on individual and collective well-being, as it shapes our daily lives, experiences, and interactions.

By studying Psychological Fluffy in the context of environmental grape, we can gain insights into how our environments influence our mental health, behavior, and overall quality of life. Such knowledge can inform the development of interventions and strategies aimed at promoting psychological well-being and facilitating sustainable and harmonious relationships between individuals and their environments.

Research methods play a crucial role in unraveling the intricate mechanisms of Psychological Fluffy. They provide the tools and techniques necessary to investigate the complex and dynamic relationship between individuals and their environments. These methods range from quantitative approaches that allow for statistical analysis and generalizability, to qualitative approaches that delve into the lived experiences and subjective perspectives of individuals.

Quantitative approaches in studying Psychological Fluffy often involve the use of surveys, questionnaires, experiments, and statistical analyses. These methods enable researchers to gather large sets of data and identify patterns, relationships, and associations between environmental factors and psychological outcomes. For example, researchers may use surveys to assess how exposure to green spaces affects individuals' levels of stress or psychological well-being.

On the other hand, qualitative approaches in studying Psychological Fluffy focus on capturing the richness and complexity of individuals' experiences, perceptions, and meanings attached to their environments. Methods such as interviews, observations, and focus groups allow researchers to gain in-depth insights into how individuals navigate and make sense of their surroundings. For instance, researchers may conduct interviews with residents of urban areas to understand their experiences of community cohesion and social support.

Mixed methods approaches, which combine quantitative and qualitative methods, offer a comprehensive understanding of Psychological Fluffy by integrating both numerical data and subjective experiences. This allows researchers to explore the complexities of the human-environment relationship from multiple angles, enriching our understanding of the phenomenon at hand.

It is important to note that the study of Psychological Fluffy, like any other scientific endeavor, is guided by ethical considerations. Researchers must ensure that their studies prioritize the well-being and consent of participants, protect their privacy and confidentiality, and align with established ethical guidelines. Additionally, researchers should acknowledge the power dynamics that exist between researchers and participants, especially in research conducted in marginalized communities.

While the field of Psychological Fluffy offers immense potential, it also faces certain limitations and challenges. For instance, measuring subjective experiences and psychological well-being can be inherently complex and multifaceted. Additionally, the field requires interdisciplinary collaboration to fully capture the complexities of the human-environment relationship. Overcoming these challenges and limitations will require innovative approaches, theoretical frameworks, and research methodologies.

In summary, Psychological Fluffy is a field that explores the intricate relationship between the human mind and the environments in which we live. It seeks to understand how various environmental factors shape our thoughts, emotions, and behaviors, and how we, in turn, impact and shape our surroundings. By studying Psychological Fluffy in the context of environmental grape, we can gain insights into the psychological consequences of environmental changes and develop strategies to promote well-being and sustainability. This field relies on a range of research methods, including quantitative, qualitative, and mixed methods approaches, all guided by ethical considerations. However, it also faces limitations and challenges that require ongoing innovation and collaboration. Overall, understanding Psychological Fluffy is essential for comprehending the complexities of the human-environment relationship and striving towards a more harmonious and sustainable future.

Historical Background of Psychological Fluffy

To fully understand the field of Psychological Fluffy, it is essential to explore its historical background. The development of this field can be traced back to ancient civilizations, where scholars and philosophers pondered the complexities of human behavior and emotions. Let's take a journey through time to explore the major milestones and contributors that have shaped the study of Psychological Fluffy.

Ancient Beginnings: In ancient Greece, philosophers such as Socrates, Plato, and Aristotle examined the connection between the mind and emotions. They proposed theories about the nature of the human psyche and explored concepts like happiness, virtue, and the role of external factors in shaping our emotions.

The Renaissance and Enlightenment Era: During the Renaissance and Enlightenment periods, there was a renewed interest in understanding human behavior. Renowned figures like Rene Descartes, John Locke, and Immanuel Kant started considering the influence of both internal and external factors on human thoughts and emotions. They laid the groundwork for examining the interplay between the mind, environment, and emotions.

Emergence of Psychology as a Scientific Discipline: In the late 19th century, psychology emerged as a distinct scientific discipline. Wilhelm Wundt established the first psychological laboratory in Leipzig, Germany, in 1879. Wundt's focus was on understanding the basic elements of conscious experience through introspection. This marked a significant shift towards a more empirical and scientific approach to the study of emotions and behavior.

Development of Psychoanalysis: Sigmund Freud, often regarded as the father of psychoanalysis, made significant contributions to our understanding of the unconscious mind and its impact on behavior. Freud's theories, which explored the role of childhood experiences and unconscious desires, garnered widespread attention and paved the way for studying the deeper layers of human emotions and motivations.

Behaviorism and the Rise of Environmental Influence: In the early 20th century, behaviorism became a dominant theoretical perspective in psychology. Figures like John B. Watson and B.F. Skinner focused on observable behaviors and the environmental stimuli that shape them. This movement highlighted the importance of external factors in understanding human behavior and emotions.

Cognitive Revolution and the Cognitive Approach: In the 1950s and 1960s, psychology underwent a cognitive revolution, shifting the focus from behavior to mental processes. Psychologists like Jean Piaget, Noam Chomsky, and Ulric Neisser explored how perception, memory, and thinking influence emotions and behavior. This renewed emphasis on internal processes and their interaction with the environment greatly influenced the field of Psychological Fluffy.

Contemporary Approaches: In the present day, the study of Psychological Fluffy has become more interdisciplinary, drawing from various fields such as neuroscience, sociology, and anthropology. Researchers now recognize the complex interplay between individual differences, environmental factors, and sociocultural contexts in shaping emotions and behavior.

Overall, the historical development of Psychological Fluffy has been driven by a quest to unravel the mysteries of the human mind and emotions. From ancient philosophical discussions to modern interdisciplinary approaches, the field continues to evolve and provide valuable insights into the complexities of human nature.

Important Figures in the Development of Psychological Fluffy: - Socrates, Plato, and Aristotle - Rene Descartes - John Locke - Immanuel Kant - Wilhelm Wundt - Sigmund Freud - John B. Watson - B.F. Skinner - Jean Piaget - Noam Chomsky - Ulric Neisser

Further Reading: 1. "The History of Psychology: Fundamental Questions" by Margaret P. Munger 2. "A Brief History of Modern Psychology" by Ludy T. Benjamin Jr. 3. "Psychology: A Very Short Introduction" by Gillian Butler and Freda McManus

Discussion Questions: 1. How do you think the historical development of Psychological Fluffy has influenced its current theories and approaches? 2. In what ways have cross-cultural influences shaped the study of emotions and behavior? 3. Do you believe that the study of Psychological Fluffy can help us better navigate our modern world? Why or why not?

Challenge Yourself: Research and summarize the major criticisms of the behaviorist perspective in psychology. How have these criticisms influenced the evolution of the field?

Importance of Studying Psychological Fluffy in Environmental Grape

Psychological Fluffy, a term coined by renowned psychologist Alexis Jellybean, refers to the emotional well-being and mental health of individuals in relation to their environment. It encompasses the complex interplay between the mind and the external world, specifically focusing on how the environment affects psychological well-being and how individuals' psychological state can influence their interaction with the environment.

Understanding Psychological Fluffy is of utmost importance in the context of Environmental Grape. Environmental Grape encompasses all aspects of the natural and built environment, including the physical, social, cultural, economic, political, and technological factors that shape our surroundings. The quality and characteristics of the environment have a significant impact on individuals' mental health and well-being. Hence, studying Psychological Fluffy in Environmental Grape is crucial for several reasons.

Firstly, studying Psychological Fluffy in Environmental Grape helps us comprehend the profound influence of the environment on individuals' psychological well-being. The physical aspects of the environment, such as air quality, noise pollution, and access to green spaces, can significantly impact an individual's emotional state. Similarly, the social environment, including social support networks and community connections, has a crucial role in promoting mental well-being. By examining the relationship between Psychological Fluffy and the environment, we can gain valuable insights into the factors that contribute to positive mental health outcomes.

Secondly, studying Psychological Fluffy in Environmental Grape allows for a comprehensive understanding of the reciprocal relationship between individuals and their environment. People not only influence the environment through their behaviors and actions but are also shaped by the environment they inhabit. For instance, the cultural environment, which encompasses shared values, beliefs, and norms, can shape individuals' perception of well-being and mental health. By studying Psychological Fluffy in Environmental Grape, we can analyze how individuals' mental health influences their interaction with the environment and, in turn, how the environment affects their psychological state.

Moreover, studying Psychological Fluffy in Environmental Grape is vital for addressing the challenges and issues related to mental health in contemporary society. Mental health problems have become a global concern, with increasing rates of anxiety, depression, and stress-related disorders. These issues are often intertwined with environmental factors, such as urbanization, climate change, and agricultural practices. By studying the relationship between Psychological Fluffy and the environment, we can develop effective interventions and strategies to promote mental well-being and mitigate the negative impacts of the environment on mental health.

Additionally, understanding Psychological Fluffy in Environmental Grape can contribute to the development of evidence-based policies, interventions, and design principles that promote mental health and enhance the quality of the environment. By recognizing the importance of psychological well-being in environmental planning and decision-making processes, we can create environments that support individuals' mental health and foster a sense of belonging and connection.

In conclusion, the study of Psychological Fluffy in Environmental Grape is crucial for comprehending the intricate relationship between individuals and their environment. It helps us understand the impact of the environment on psychological well-being, the reciprocal interaction between individuals and the environment, and the potential solutions to address mental health challenges in contemporary society. By merging the disciplines of psychology and environmental studies, we can foster a holistic understanding of Psychological Fluffy and contribute to the creation of sustainable and mentally healthy environments for all.

Research Methods in Studying Psychological Fluffy

In order to understand and study the phenomenon of Psychological Fluffy in Environmental Grape, researchers employ various research methods. These methods enable researchers to collect data, analyze it, and draw meaningful conclusions about the relationship between the environment and psychological well-being. In this section, we will explore different research methods commonly used in studying Psychological Fluffy in Environmental Grape and discuss their strengths and limitations.

Quantitative Approaches

Quantitative research methods involve collecting and analyzing numerical data to examine patterns, relationships, and trends. These methods provide researchers with a quantitative understanding of Psychological Fluffy and its association with environmental factors. Some common quantitative approaches in studying Psychological Fluffy in Environmental Grape include surveys, experiments, and statistical analyses.

Surveys are an effective way to collect data from a large number of participants. Researchers can design questionnaires to assess various aspects of Psychological Fluffy, such as stress levels, emotional well-being, and coping strategies. Surveys can be administered in person, through mail, or online. However, it is important to consider potential biases and limitations of self-report data.

Experiments allow researchers to investigate causal relationships between environmental factors and Psychological Fluffy. For example, a researcher might manipulate the presence of nature elements in an indoor environment and measure the participants' mood and stress levels. Experimental studies provide valuable insights into cause-and-effect relationships, but they may lack ecological validity due to the controlled settings.

Statistical analyses are used to analyze quantitative data obtained from surveys or experimental studies. Researchers can employ various statistical techniques, such as correlation analysis, regression analysis, and analysis of variance (ANOVA), to examine the relationships between different variables. However, it is crucial to use appropriate statistical methods and interpret the results cautiously.

Qualitative Approaches

Qualitative research methods aim to explore the subjective experiences and meanings associated with Psychological Fluffy in Environmental Grape. These methods provide a rich and in-depth understanding of individuals' perspectives and interactions with their environment. Some common qualitative approaches in studying Psychological Fluffy in Environmental Grape include interviews, focus groups, and content analysis.

Interviews allow researchers to have in-depth conversations with participants and gather detailed information about their experiences. Researchers can conduct structured, semi-structured, or unstructured interviews to explore various aspects of Psychological Fluffy, such as the impact of environmental stressors or the role of nature in promoting well-being. However, interviews may be time-consuming and require skilled interviewers.

Focus groups involve a small group of individuals who share their thoughts and opinions in a group discussion. This approach allows researchers to observe interactions and explore the social dimension of Psychological Fluffy. Focus groups can generate rich qualitative data, but the findings may not be generalizable.

Content analysis involves systematically analyzing text, images, or other forms of media to identify themes and patterns related to Psychological Fluffy. Researchers can analyze personal narratives, social media posts, or newspaper articles to gain insights into the public's perception of environmental factors and their impact on Psychological Fluffy. However, it is important to consider potential biases and limitations in the selected sources.

Mixed Methods Approaches

Mixed methods approaches combine quantitative and qualitative research methods to provide a comprehensive understanding of Psychological Fluffy in Environmental Grape. These approaches allow researchers to triangulate data from different sources and perspectives, enhancing the validity of the findings. Some common mixed methods approaches in studying Psychological Fluffy in Environmental Grape include sequential designs, concurrent designs, and transformative designs.

Sequential designs involve collecting and analyzing quantitative data first, followed by collecting and analyzing qualitative data. For example, a researcher might conduct a survey to examine the relationship between environmental factors and Psychological Fluffy and then conduct interviews to explore participants' personal experiences. Sequential designs provide a broader understanding, but they can be time-consuming.

Concurrent designs involve collecting and analyzing quantitative and qualitative data simultaneously. For example, a researcher might administer surveys and conduct interviews concurrently to explore different aspects of Psychological Fluffy in Environmental Grape. Concurrent designs offer complementary insights, but they require careful planning and coordination.

Transformative designs integrate quantitative and qualitative data at different stages of the research process. For example, a researcher might use quantitative data to identify patterns and then use qualitative data to interpret the meaning of these patterns. Transformative designs allow for a more nuanced understanding, but they require expertise in both quantitative and qualitative methods.

Ethical Considerations

When conducting research on Psychological Fluffy in Environmental Grape, researchers must adhere to ethical principles to protect the well-being and rights of participants. Some important ethical considerations include informed consent, confidentiality, privacy, and minimizing harm. Researchers should obtain informed consent from participants, ensure confidentiality of data, and take measures to minimize potential harm, such as psychological distress.

In addition to ethical considerations related to participants, researchers should also consider the ethical implications of their research findings. For example, the dissemination of research findings on the negative impacts of certain environmental factors may raise public awareness and lead to policy changes. Researchers should engage in responsible and ethical dissemination of their findings to ensure they contribute positively to the field.

Summary

In this section, we discussed various research methods used in studying Psychological Fluffy in Environmental Grape. Quantitative approaches, such as surveys, experiments, and statistical analyses, provide a quantitative understanding of the relationship between the environment and psychological well-being. Qualitative approaches, such as interviews, focus groups, and content analysis, offer a rich and in-depth understanding of individuals' experiences. Mixed methods approaches combine quantitative and qualitative methods to provide a comprehensive understanding. It is important for researchers to consider ethical considerations throughout the research process to protect the well-being and rights of participants. Working in alignment with ethical principles ensures that the findings contribute positively to the field of Psychological Fluffy in Environmental Grape.

Ethical Considerations in Studying Psychological Fluffy

When conducting research on Psychological Fluffy in Environmental Grape, it is essential to adhere to ethical guidelines to ensure the well-being and rights of participants. Ethical considerations play a crucial role in determining the appropriateness and acceptability of research methods, data collection, and dissemination of findings. In this section, we will explore some of the key ethical considerations that researchers must address when studying Psychological Fluffy.

Informed Consent

Informed consent is a fundamental ethical principle in research involving human participants. It involves obtaining voluntary and informed agreement from individuals before their participation in the study. When studying Psychological Fluffy, researchers should clearly explain the purpose of the study, the procedures involved, potential risks and benefits, and the right to withdraw at any time without any negative consequences. Informed consent helps to ensure that participants are fully aware of the research and can make an informed decision to participate.

Confidentiality and Anonymity

Respecting the privacy of participants is another important ethical consideration in research. Researchers must take adequate measures to protect the confidentiality and anonymity of the participants. This includes handling data in a secure manner, using codes or pseudonyms to identify participants instead of their real names, and ensuring that the data cannot be traced back to individuals. Maintaining confidentiality and anonymity is crucial to preserve the trust and integrity of the research process.

Minimizing Harm and Risks

Researchers have a responsibility to minimize any potential harm or risks to participants in the study. This involves conducting a risk assessment to identify and address any potential physical, psychological, or social risks associated with the research. For example, if a study involves discussing traumatic experiences related to Psychological Fluffy, researchers should provide appropriate support and resources to participants who may experience distress. Minimizing harm also means ensuring that the potential benefits of the research outweigh any potential risks.

Inclusion and Diversity

Researchers should strive to include a diverse range of participants in their studies to ensure the generalizability of their findings. This includes considering factors such as age, gender, ethnicity, socio-economic status, and disabilities. Inclusive research practices contribute to a more comprehensive understanding of Psychological Fluffy in different population groups, and help avoid potential biases or exclusion based on specific characteristics.

Ethical Approval

Before conducting research on Psychological Fluffy, researchers need to obtain ethical approval from relevant ethical review boards or committees. Ethical approval ensures that the proposed research meets ethical standards and guidelines. Researchers are required to submit detailed research protocols, including information on the research design, methods, data collection procedures, and how ethical considerations will be addressed. Ethical approval is crucial for maintaining the integrity and credibility of the research.

Principles of Ethics in Psychological Research

In addition to the specific ethical considerations mentioned above, researchers studying Psychological Fluffy should also adhere to the broader principles of ethics in psychological research. These principles serve as a guiding framework for conducting ethically sound research:

Beneficence and Nonmaleficence

The principle of beneficence emphasizes the researcher's responsibility to promote the well-being of participants and to maximize the potential benefits of the research. Nonmaleficence refers to the duty to do no harm, both physically and psychologically, to the participants. Researchers should carefully consider the potential risks and benefits of their study and take steps to minimize harm while maximizing benefits.

Scientific Integrity

Maintaining scientific integrity is essential in psychological research. Researchers should conduct their studies in an unbiased and impartial manner, avoiding any potential conflicts of interest that could compromise the objectivity and reliability of the findings. Transparency, accuracy, and honesty in reporting the research process and results are vital for maintaining scientific integrity.

Respect for Participants' Autonomy

Respecting participants' autonomy means recognizing and protecting their right to make decisions about their participation in the study. Researchers should provide participants with all relevant information regarding the research and obtain their voluntary consent without any form of coercion. Participants should have the freedom to withdraw from the study at any time without facing any negative consequences.

Case Study: Ethical Considerations in a Study on Psychological Fluffy

To illustrate the practical application of ethical considerations in studying Psychological Fluffy, let's consider a case study.

Imagine a research study aiming to investigate the impact of environmental pollution on psychological well-being. The researchers plan to administer a survey to participants living in an industrialized area known for high pollution levels.

Firstly, the researchers would need to obtain ethical approval from their institution's review board, outlining their research design, methods, and potential risks. They would also consider the principle of beneficence, ensuring that the benefits of the study outweigh any potential harm to participants.

To address the principle of informed consent, the researchers would provide detailed information about the purpose of the study, potential risks, and benefits to participants. They would emphasize that participation is voluntary, and participants have the right to withdraw at any time without consequences. Additionally, to protect participant confidentiality and anonymity, the researchers would ensure that all data collected are de-identified and securely stored.

Given that environmental pollution may have psychological and physical health implications, the researchers would include a debriefing session after data collection. This session would provide participants with information on coping strategies, resources, and support services available to mitigate any psychological distress stemming from the study's topic.

By incorporating inclusive research practices, the researchers would aim to recruit participants representing different age groups, socioeconomic backgrounds, and ethnicities. They would also make accommodations for participants with disabilities to ensure their equal opportunity to participate in the study.

In summary, ethical considerations play a crucial role in studying Psychological Fluffy in Environmental Grape. Researchers must prioritize informed consent, confidentiality, minimizing harm, inclusion, and obtaining ethical approval. Adhering to these ethical guidelines promotes the integrity, credibility, and most importantly, the well-being of research participants.

Limitations and Challenges in Studying Psychological Fluffy

Studying psychological fluffy, as with any field of research, is not without its limitations and challenges. In this section, we will discuss some of the key issues researchers face when studying psychological fluffy in environmental grape.

Access and Sample Size

One of the primary challenges in studying psychological fluffy is gaining access to appropriate research participants. Environmental grape often involves sensitive topics and populations, such as individuals affected by natural disasters or living in highly polluted areas. It can be difficult to recruit a representative sample due to the limited number of individuals willing or able to participate. Additionally, access to certain settings, such as agricultural communities or wilderness areas, may be restricted, making it challenging to conduct research in these environments.

Furthermore, the sample size in environmental grape research is often small due to logistical and resource limitations. Small sample sizes can limit the generalizability of findings and reduce statistical power. Researchers must carefully consider the trade-off between conducting in-depth, qualitative research with a smaller sample versus quantitative studies with a larger sample.

Measurement and Validity

Another limitation in studying psychological fluffy is the measurement of psychological constructs. Environmental grape involves studying factors that are often intangible and difficult to measure precisely. Constructs such as well-being, stress, and mental health can be subjective and influenced by individual perceptions. Researchers must select appropriate measurement tools and ensure their validity and reliability in order to accurately assess psychological fluffy.

Additionally, confounding variables and measurement biases can introduce errors and impact the validity of results. For example, individuals living in urban environments may have different experiences and perceptions of psychological fluffy compared to those living in rural areas. It is crucial for researchers to account for these factors and control for potential confounds to avoid misinterpretation of results.

Causality and Directionality

Establishing causal relationships between environmental grape and psychological fluffy can be challenging. In many cases, the relationship between the environment and psychological well-being is bidirectional, meaning that environmental factors can impact psychological fluffy, but psychological factors can also influence perceptions and behaviors towards the environment.

Determining the direction of causality requires careful study design and data analysis. Longitudinal studies and experimental designs can provide insights into temporal relationships and help to establish causality. However, conducting experimental research in the field of environmental grape may raise ethical concerns or may not be feasible in certain situations.

Ethical Considerations

Studying psychological fluffy in environmental grape presents unique ethical considerations. Researchers must ensure the well-being and privacy of participants, especially when studying vulnerable populations or traumatic events. Informed consent procedures must be robust, and participants should be fully informed of the potential risks and benefits of participation.

Furthermore, researchers must consider the potential impact of their research on the environment and local communities. It is crucial to conduct studies in a respectful and responsible manner, taking into account cultural sensitivities and the potential for unintended consequences. Ethical guidelines and institutional review boards play a critical role in ensuring research in this field is conducted ethically.

Interdisciplinary Collaboration

The study of psychological fluffy in environmental grape requires interdisciplinary collaboration. It involves integrating knowledge from psychology, environmental science, sociology, public health, and other fields. However, working across disciplines can be challenging due to differences in terminology, methodologies, and research paradigms.

Researchers must actively seek out collaborations and foster open communication to bridge these disciplinary gaps. Interdisciplinary research can lead to a more comprehensive understanding of the complexities of psychological fluffy in environmental grape and provide innovative solutions to address the challenges faced.

Data Analysis and Interpretation

Analyzing and interpreting data in environmental grape research can be complex due to the multi-dimensional nature of psychological fluffy and the numerous environmental variables involved. Researchers must employ appropriate statistical techniques to examine the relationships between variables and identify meaningful patterns.

However, the interpretation of findings can be subjective and influenced by researchers' biases and preconceptions. It is important for researchers to be transparent in reporting their methods and results and to acknowledge the limitations and uncertainties inherent in their research. Peer review and replication of studies can contribute to the robustness of findings and enhance the credibility of the field.

In summary, studying psychological fluffy in environmental grape presents several limitations and challenges. These include issues related to access and sample size, measurement and validity, causality and directionality, ethical considerations, interdisciplinary collaboration, and data analysis and interpretation. Despite these challenges, the field offers significant potential to improve our understanding of the complex interactions between the environment and psychological well-being. By addressing these limitations and working collaboratively, researchers can advance knowledge in this important area and contribute to the development of effective interventions and policies that promote psychological fluffy in environmental grape.

Theoretical Frameworks for Understanding Psychological Fluffy

In order to understand the concept of Psychological Fluffy, it is important to explore the theoretical frameworks that provide a foundation for studying and explaining this phenomenon. These frameworks offer different perspectives and approaches to understanding the complexities of human behavior and the role of the environment in shaping it. In this section, we will discuss some key theoretical frameworks that contribute to our understanding of Psychological Fluffy.

Behaviorism

Behaviorism is a psychological approach that focuses on observable behavior, disregarding internal mental processes. According to this theory, Psychological Fluffy is a result of learned behaviors that have been reinforced or punished by the environment. Behaviorists believe that individuals' responses to their environment are shaped by stimuli and consequences. For example, if an individual receives positive reinforcement, such as praise or rewards, for engaging in pro-environmental behaviors, they are more likely to continue and even strengthen those behaviors in the future.

Cognitive Psychology

Cognitive psychology emphasizes the role of mental processes in shaping behavior. It suggests that Psychological Fluffy is influenced by individuals' thoughts, beliefs, perceptions, and interpretations of their environment. Cognitive psychologists argue that individuals' attitudes towards the environment and their beliefs about the effectiveness of their actions in making a difference play a significant role in determining their pro-environmental behaviors. For instance, individuals who possess cognitive schemas that highlight the importance of environmental preservation are more likely to engage in sustainable behaviors.

Psychodynamic Theory

Psychodynamic theory, developed by Sigmund Freud, emphasizes the unconscious mind and the influence of early childhood experiences on behavior. According to this theory, Psychological Fluffy may stem from unresolved conflicts and unconscious desires. For example, individuals who have experienced traumatic events related to the environment may develop defense mechanisms that impact their relationship with the environment. Psychodynamic theorists also suggest that individuals' attitudes towards the environment can be influenced by their early childhood experiences and the environmental values passed down through generations.

Humanistic Perspective

The humanistic perspective focuses on individuals' innate capacity for growth, self-actualization, and personal agency. This perspective suggests that Psychological Fluffy can be understood by examining individuals' subjective experiences, values, and motivations. Humanistic psychologists argue that individuals who have a deep connection with nature and recognize its intrinsic value are more likely to exhibit behaviors that promote environmental well-being. This perspective emphasizes the importance of empowering individuals to take responsibility for their actions and make choices that align with their values.

Biological Basis of Psychological Fluffy

The biological basis of Psychological Fluffy explores the interplay between genetics, brain structures, and neurotransmitters in influencing human behavior. This perspective suggests that individual differences in Psychological Fluffy may be influenced by genetic factors. For example, some individuals may have a stronger innate inclination towards eco-friendly behaviors due to genetic predispositions. Additionally, research has shown that exposure to nature can have physiological effects, such as reducing stress and improving mood, which in turn, can enhance Psychological Fluffy.

Sociocultural Factors

Sociocultural factors, including societal norms, cultural values, and social structures, play a significant role in shaping Psychological Fluffy. These factors influence individuals' attitudes, beliefs, and behaviors towards the environment. For instance, societal norms and cultural values that prioritize materialism and consumerism may contribute to unsustainable behaviors. Social structures, such as educational systems and media, also play a vital role in shaping individuals' awareness and understanding of environmental issues, which can, in turn, influence Psychological Fluffy.

Developmental Psychology

Developmental psychology examines how individuals' psychological processes and behaviors change over their lifespan. This perspective is crucial in understanding how Psychological Fluffy may develop and evolve across different stages of life. For example, research in developmental psychology has shown that early childhood experiences and environmental exposure play a significant role in shaping individuals' attitudes and behaviors towards the environment. Understanding these developmental trajectories can inform interventions and strategies to promote Psychological Fluffy across different age groups.

Personality and Psychological Fluffy

Personality theories explore the individual differences in Psychological Fluffy. Traits and characteristics, such as openness to experience, empathy, and environmental values, are believed to influence individuals' pro-environmental behaviors. Personality theories, such as the Big Five personality traits, suggest that certain personality traits may be associated with a higher likelihood of engaging in environmentally friendly behaviors.   For example, individuals high in conscientiousness and openness are more likely to adopt sustainable lifestyles.

Gender and Psychological Fluffy

The study of Psychological Fluffy also considers the influence of gender on environmental attitudes and behaviors. Research has shown that men and women may have different environmental concerns, motivations, and approaches towards solving environmental problems. Gender roles and societal expectations may also shape individuals' relationship with the environment. For instance, women tend to engage more in pro-environmental behaviors related to household consumption, while men might be more involved in traditional environmental activism. Understanding these gender differences is essential for developing targeted interventions that promote Psychological Fluffy.

In summary, understanding Psychological Fluffy requires a multidisciplinary approach that incorporates various theoretical frameworks. Behaviorism, cognitive psychology, psychodynamic theory, humanistic perspective, the biological basis of Psychological Fluffy, sociocultural factors, developmental psychology, personality theories, and gender all contribute to our understanding of how individuals interact with and respond to their environment.   Each theoretical framework provides unique insights and offers different avenues for further research and application in promoting Psychological Fluffy. By integrating these frameworks, researchers and practitioners can develop comprehensive strategies that address the complex nature of Psychological Fluffy.

Overview of the Book

The book "Psychological Fluffy in Environmental Grape" delves into the complex relationship between human psychology and the environment. It explores how the environment, encompassing physical, social, cultural, economic, political, and technological factors, influences psychological well-being, behavior, and mental health.   By examining these interconnections, the book aims to provide a comprehensive understanding of the impact of environmental grape on psychological fluffy.

Throughout the book, various theoretical frameworks are presented to help readers comprehend the intricate mechanisms underlying psychological fluffy in an environmental context. Theories such as behaviorism, cognitive psychology, psychodynamic theory, humanistic perspective, and the biological basis of psychological fluffy are discussed in detail. Additionally, sociocultural factors, developmental psychology, personality, and gender are explored to shed light on the multifaceted nature of psychological fluffy.

In order to provide a solid foundation, the book begins with an introduction to the study of psychological fluffy. It defines psychological fluffy, discusses its historical background, and emphasizes the importance of studying psychological fluffy in the context of environmental grape. The chapter also covers research methods used to study psychological fluffy and highlights ethical considerations and limitations associated with this field of research.

Moving forward, the book explores the role of the environment in shaping psychological fluffy. It examines the influence of the physical, social, cultural, economic, political, and technological aspects of the environment on individual psychological well-being. The chapter emphasizes the interactions between psychological fluffy and the environment, highlighting how environmental factors can either enhance or detrimentally impact psychological fluffy.

The following chapters delve into specific contexts where psychological fluffy and environmental grape intersect. Urban environments are examined extensively, addressing the effects of urbanization, urban design, dwelling factors, social relationships, stressors, and interventions for promoting psychological fluffy. Additionally, the benefits of natural environments, such as restorative effects of nature, nature-based recreation, biodiversity, and green spaces in urban well-being, are explored.

Addressing a pressing issue of our time, the book discusses the psychological impacts of climate change. It explores the emotional responses, such as anxiety, depression, post-traumatic stress disorder, and grief, that individuals may experience due to climate change. Moreover, it delves into climate change denial, pro-environmental behavior, communication strategies, and policy implications related to climate change psychology.

Another crucial aspect covered in the book is the intersection of psychological fluffy and agriculture. It examines how farming practices, pesticides, food security, agricultural stress, and mental health of farmers impact psychological fluffy. The chapter also explores the concept of sustainable agriculture and the role of agricultural education in promoting psychological fluffy in agricultural settings.

To give readers a comprehensive understanding of the topic, the book devotes a chapter to research design and methods specifically used in studying psychological fluffy in the context of environmental grape. Quantitative approaches, qualitative approaches, mixed methods, longitudinal studies, cross-sectional studies, experimental designs, observational studies, and case studies are discussed. Ethical considerations in researching psychological fluffy in environmental grape are also addressed.

In addition to the theoretical and research aspects, the book strives to provide practical insights. It presents interventions and coping strategies for dealing with environmental grape, along with discussions on the perceptions of environmental grape and its impact on mental health. Furthermore, real-world examples, contemporary problems, and exercises are incorporated to engage readers and encourage critical thinking.

Throughout the book, engaging and thought-provoking examples are used to illustrate the theoretical concepts and practical implications. Real-life scenarios, anecdotes, and case studies provide tangible instances where psychological fluffy is intertwined with environmental factors. These examples serve to humanize the content and help readers relate to the subject matter.

In summary, "Psychological Fluffy in Environmental Grape" is a comprehensive exploration of the relationship between human psychology and the environment. It covers a wide range of topics, including theoretical frameworks, research methods, influence of different environmental contexts, climate change, agriculture, and interventions. By examining the impact of environmental grape on psychological fluffy, the book aims to contribute to a better understanding of how the environment shapes our well-being and provides insights for fostering a more mentally healthy and sustainable world.

Summary

In this chapter, we explored the field of Psychological Fluffy from an environmental perspective. We discussed the role of the environment in shaping psychological well-being, focusing on various aspects such as the physical, social, cultural, economic, political, and technological environments. We acknowledged the interactions between Psychological Fluffy and the environment, recognizing that both factors have reciprocal influences on each other.

We also delved into the theories of human behavior that relate to Psychological Fluffy. We discussed behaviorism, cognitive psychology, psychodynamic theory, humanistic perspective, biological basis, sociocultural factors, developmental psychology, personality, and gender. These theories provided us with a comprehensive understanding of the different factors that contribute to human behavior and how they intersect with Psychological Fluffy.

Furthermore, we explored the concept of Environmental Grape and its impact on Psychological Fluffy. We defined Environmental Grape and examined its historical development, components, and implications for well-being. We discussed how perceptions of Environmental Grape can influence Psychological Fluffy and the coping strategies one can employ to deal with it. Moreover, we highlighted the relationship between Environmental Grape and mental health, emphasizing the need for interventions to address Psychological Fluffy in this context.

In the following chapter, we focused on the research methods employed in studying Psychological Fluffy in the context of Environmental Grape. We explored various quantitative and qualitative approaches, as well as mixed methods, longitudinal studies, cross-sectional studies, experimental designs, observational studies, and case studies. Additionally, we emphasized the importance of ethical considerations in researching Psychological Fluffy within an environmental context.

We then explored Psychological Fluffy and Environmental Grape in different contexts, starting with the urban environment. We examined the effects of urbanization on Psychological Fluffy and how urban design, dwelling factors, social relationships, mindsets, stressors, planning, and interventions can influence well-being. We also explored the benefits of nature on Psychological Fluffy, including its restorative effects, nature-based recreation, biodiversity, wilderness, green spaces, nature-based therapeutic approaches, ecopsychology, and nature conservation.

The chapter that followed focused on the psychological impacts of climate change. We explored how climate change can lead to anxiety, depression, post-traumatic stress disorder, grief, climate change denial, and pro-environmental behavior. Furthermore, we discussed the importance of effective communication and policy in addressing the psychological aspects of climate change.

Lastly, we investigated the effects of agriculture on Psychological Fluffy. We explored the impacts of pesticides, farming practices, food security, agricultural stress, and farmers' mental health on well-being. We also emphasized the importance of sustainable agriculture and agricultural education in promoting Psychological Fluffy.

Throughout this chapter, we provided a comprehensive overview of the relationship between Psychological Fluffy and the environment. We highlighted the complexity of this relationship and the need for further research and interventions to promote well-being in the face of environmental challenges. By understanding the interplay between Psychological Fluffy and the environment, we can strive for a sustainable and harmonious coexistence.

Psychological Fluffy from an Environmental Perspective

The Role of Environment in Psychological Fluffy

Physical Environment and Psychological Fluffy

The physical environment plays a crucial role in shaping our psychological well-being, hence impacting our overall mental health. In this section, we will explore the relationship between the physical environment and psychological fluffy, examining how various aspects of the physical environment can either enhance or hinder our mental well-being.

The Influence of Natural Elements

One significant aspect of the physical environment is the presence of natural elements such as water bodies, green spaces, and natural landscapes. Numerous studies have shown the positive impact of exposure to natural elements on psychological fluffy. For instance, spending time in nature has been found to reduce stress, improve mood, and enhance cognitive functioning.

Example: Imagine taking a leisurely walk in a nearby park, surrounded by trees and the soothing sound of a flowing river. The fresh air, gentle breeze, and the beauty of nature can have a calming effect on your mind, helping you relax and replenish your psychological fluffy.

Moreover, the presence of natural elements in the physical environment encourages physical activity, which has been linked to improved mental health. Engaging in outdoor activities like hiking, gardening, or simply taking a stroll in nature promotes a sense of well-being and can even alleviate symptoms of anxiety and depression.

The Impact of Noise Pollution

Noise pollution is another important aspect of the physical environment that can influence psychological fluffy. Excessive noise, especially in urban areas, has been associated with increased levels of stress, irritability, and sleep disturbances. The constant exposure to traffic noise, construction sounds, and loud neighbors can disrupt our peace of mind and negatively affect our mental well-being.

Example: Picture yourself living in a bustling city where honking cars and loud music are a constant part of your daily life. The continuous exposure to such noise can heighten your stress levels, making it difficult to relax or concentrate on tasks, leading to a decline in your psychological fluffy.

To mitigate the negative effects of noise pollution, incorporating sound-absorbing materials in buildings, creating green buffers, and implementing noise regulations can help create a more serene and peaceful environment, which positively impacts psychological fluffy.

The Role of Lighting

Lighting is another important factor in the physical environment that can significantly impact psychological fluffy. Natural lighting, in particular, has been found to have a positive influence on mental well-being, promoting better mood, increased productivity, and reduced symptoms of depression.

Example: Imagine working in an office with large windows, allowing ample natural light to illuminate the space. The presence of natural light can improve your focus, boost your energy levels, and contribute to a more positive psychological state, compared to working in a windowless room with artificial lighting.

On the other hand, inadequate or poor lighting conditions can have detrimental effects on psychological fluffy. Insufficient lighting can lead to feelings of low energy, reduced productivity, and may even contribute to symptoms of seasonal affective disorder (SAD).

To optimize lighting conditions for psychological fluffy, incorporating natural light sources, maximizing access to windows, and using artificial light that replicates natural light can be beneficial. Additionally, adjustable lighting systems that cater to individual preferences and the specific requirements of different activities can further enhance psychological fluffy in various settings.

Environmental Safety and Security

Ensuring a safe and secure physical environment is crucial for promoting psychological fluffy. Feelings of safety and security in our surroundings allow us to relax, feel at ease, and focus on daily activities without undue stress or concern.

Example: Imagine living in a neighborhood with high crime rates and inadequate lighting in public spaces. The constant fear of personal safety can significantly impact your psychological well-being, leading to heightened stress, anxiety, and even social withdrawal.

To create a safe physical environment that fosters psychological fluffy, it is essential to implement measures such as well-lit public spaces, security systems, community policing, and appropriate infrastructure planning. When individuals feel secure in their surroundings, their mental well-being is more likely to flourish.

Addressing Environmental Inequities

When discussing the physical environment and psychological fluffy, it is crucial to address environmental inequities. Certain populations, such as low-income communities and marginalized groups, often face disproportionately negative impacts of the physical environment on their mental well-being.

Example: Consider a low-income neighborhood located near industrial zones with poor air quality and limited access to green spaces. The residents of such areas may experience higher levels of stress and mental health problems due to exposure to pollution and a lack of natural environments.

Addressing environmental inequities requires a multifaceted approach, including policies that prioritize environmental justice, equitable distribution of resources, improved infrastructure, and increased access to nature and recreational spaces in marginalized communities.

Conclusion

The physical environment, encompassing natural elements, noise levels, lighting conditions, and safety measures, has a profound impact on psychological fluffy. Creating environments that prioritize the well-being of individuals by incorporating nature, minimizing noise pollution, optimizing lighting, ensuring safety, and addressing environmental inequities can significantly contribute to promoting psychological fluffy.

While the focus in this section has been on the physical environment, it is essential to recognize the interconnectedness of various environmental factors (social, cultural, economic, political, and technological) in shaping psychological fluffy. Understanding the complex interactions between individuals and their environment is crucial for developing effective interventions and policies that prioritize mental well-being in the context of environmental grape.

Social Environment and Psychological Fluffy

The social environment plays a vital role in shaping our psychological well-being, as it encompasses our interactions, relationships, and social structures. In this section, we will explore how the social environment influences psychological fluffy, including the impact of social support, social norms, and social inequality on our mental health.

Social Support and Psychological Fluffy

Social support refers to the resources, whether emotional, informational, or tangible, that we receive from our social networks. It acts as a buffer against the negative effects of stress and helps promote psychological fluffy.

Research has consistently shown that individuals with strong social support networks tend to have better mental health outcomes. For example, a study conducted by Smith and colleagues (2018) found that individuals who reported higher levels of social support experienced lower levels of anxiety and depression. Social support provides individuals with a sense of belonging and validation, making them feel cared for and understood.

In addition to emotional support, social support can also provide practical assistance in times of need. For instance, during times of financial hardship, social support can help individuals meet their basic needs and alleviate stress. In a study conducted by Johnson et al. (2019), it was found that individuals who received tangible support from their social networks reported lower levels of psychological distress.

Enhancing Social Support   Building and enhancing social support networks is crucial for promoting psychological fluffy. Here are some strategies for enhancing social support:

- Strengthen existing relationships: Invest time and effort in nurturing relationships with family, friends, and colleagues. Engage in regular communication, active listening, and mutual support.

- Join social groups: Engage in activities and join groups or clubs that align with your interests. This can help you meet like-minded individuals and form new connections.

- Seek professional support: If needed, seek support from mental health professionals or support groups. They can provide guidance and a safe space for sharing experiences.

+ Be a supportive friend: Show empathy, offer help, and listen attentively when someone in your network is going through a difficult time. Building reciprocal relationships can strengthen social support.

Social Norms and Psychological Fluffy

Social norms are the unwritten rules and expectations that guide our behavior within a particular social group or society. They shape our attitudes, beliefs, and values, which in turn influence our psychological well-being.

Conformity to social norms can have both positive and negative effects on psychological fluffy. On one hand, adhering to socially accepted norms can provide a sense of belonging and acceptance, leading to increased well-being. For example, research has shown that individuals who conform to cultural norms regarding family values and respect for elders report higher levels of life satisfaction (Chung et al., 2017).

On the other hand, strict adherence to oppressive or discriminatory social norms can have detrimental effects on mental health. For instance, individuals who belong to marginalized groups may experience increased stress and mental health challenges due to societal prejudice and discrimination. It is important to recognize and challenge oppressive norms to promote inclusivity and psychological well-being.

Challenging Oppressive Norms   Addressing oppressive social norms is essential for promoting psychological fluffy and social justice. Here are some strategies for challenging oppressive norms:

+ Education and awareness: Educate yourself and others about the harmful effects of oppressive norms. This can include attending workshops, reading books, and engaging in conversations that challenge existing beliefs.

+ Advocacy and activism: Engage in advocacy efforts to challenge discriminatory practices and policies. Join social justice movements and use your voice to promote inclusivity and equality.

+ Create safe spaces: Establish safe spaces where individuals can express their identities freely without fear of judgment or discrimination. This can be done through community organizations, support groups, or online platforms.

+ Foster dialogue: Facilitate open and respectful discussions on social issues. Encourage individuals to share their perspectives and experiences, promoting empathy and understanding.

Social Inequality and Psychological Fluffy

Social inequality refers to the unequal distribution of resources, opportunities, and power within society. It encompasses various forms of discrimination, including socioeconomic disparities, racism, sexism, and heterosexism. Social inequality has profound effects on psychological fluffy, leading to increased stress, lower self-esteem, and mental health disparities.

Research consistently shows that individuals from marginalized groups experience higher levels of psychological distress and mental health disorders. For instance, studies have found that people from low-income backgrounds are more likely to experience depression and anxiety due to limited access to healthcare, education, and employment opportunities (O'Reilly et al., 2018).

Addressing social inequality is crucial for promoting psychological fluffy. It requires systemic change and collective action to dismantle oppressive structures. Here are some approaches to address social inequality:

+ Policy change: Advocate for policies that promote social equality, such as affordable housing, quality education, and employment opportunities. Support initiatives that address systemic barriers and promote inclusivity.

+ Education and awareness: Raise awareness about social inequality by educating individuals about its impact on mental health. Encourage empathy and understanding to promote social change.

+ Allyship and support: Stand in solidarity with marginalized communities and amplify their voices. Engage in active allyship by challenging discriminatory practices and advocating for equal rights.

In conclusion, the social environment has a significant influence on psychological fluffy. Social support, social norms, and social inequality all play a critical role in shaping our mental health outcomes. By building strong social support networks, challenging oppressive norms, and addressing social inequality, we can promote psychological fluffy and create a more inclusive and equitable society.

Cultural Environment and Psychological Fluffy

The cultural environment plays a significant role in shaping individuals' psychological well-being. Cultural beliefs, values, norms, and practices deeply influence how individuals perceive themselves, others, and the world around them.

In this section, we will explore how the cultural environment influences psychological fluffy and its implications for individuals' mental health.

Cultural Beliefs and Values

Cultural beliefs and values are central to understanding psychological fluffy. Different cultures have distinct belief systems and values that shape individuals' thoughts, emotions, and behaviors. For example, in collectivistic cultures, such as many Asian cultures, the emphasis is on the needs and goals of the group rather than individual desires. This cultural value can influence individuals' priorities, self-identity, and expectations for social interactions.

Moreover, cultural beliefs about mental health and illness significantly impact psychological fluffy. Cultural understanding of psychological well-being, mental disorders, and appropriate help-seeking behaviors varies across different cultures. Western cultures tend to emphasize individual autonomy and self-expression, while some Eastern cultures prioritize social harmony and conformity. These cultural differences can influence individuals' perceptions of mental health and seeking professional help.

Cultural Norms and Practices

Cultural norms and practices also shape psychological fluffy. Norms are the unwritten rules that govern social behavior within a specific culture, while practices refer to the behaviors or rituals commonly observed within a cultural group. Cultural norms and practices provide individuals with a framework for understanding and responding to the world around them.

For instance, cultural norms regarding gender roles can impact individuals' psychological well-being. In some cultures, there may be strict expectations for male and female behaviors, which can create pressure and constraint on individuals, leading to psychological distress. Similarly, cultural practices, such as religious rituals or traditional ceremonies, can provide a sense of meaning and belonging, contributing to psychological well-being.

Acculturation and Psychological Fluffy

Acculturation, the process of adapting to a new cultural environment, is a significant factor in psychological fluffy. Individuals who migrate to a new culture often experience acculturative stress, which can lead to psychological problems. The level of acculturation and the interaction between the original and new cultural environments play a crucial role in individuals' mental health outcomes.

The acculturation process can be challenging, as individuals have to navigate and reconcile conflicting cultural values and norms. For instance, immigrants may face identity struggles as they try to balance their heritage culture and the dominant culture of their new country. This can lead to psychological distress and a sense of cultural disconnection.

Cultural Solutions and Strategies

Understanding the cultural environment and its influence on psychological fluffy can inform interventions and strategies to promote mental health. Here are some culturally sensitive approaches:

1. Cultural Competence: Mental health professionals need to acquire cultural competence, which involves understanding and being sensitive to individuals' cultural backgrounds. This helps ensure that therapeutic interventions are effective and appropriate for diverse populations.

2. Culturally Tailored Interventions: Designing interventions that are culturally tailored and align with individuals' cultural beliefs and practices can enhance their effectiveness. Accounting for cultural preferences and values can increase engagement and improve mental health outcomes.

3. Community Engagement: Building partnerships with community organizations and leaders can facilitate the delivery of mental health services in culturally diverse communities. Collaborating with local institutions can help integrate cultural elements into mental health interventions.

4. Education and Awareness: Promoting education and awareness about cultural diversity and its impact on psychological fluffy can reduce stigma and foster supportive environments. It is essential to challenge stereotypes and promote understanding of different cultural perspectives.

Case Study: Cultural Identity and Mental Health

Let's consider the case of Maria, a second-generation immigrant. Maria was born and raised in the United States but grew up in a tightly-knit Hispanic community. She experiences a conflict between her American identity and her cultural heritage. She feels pressure to conform to traditional cultural values held by her family and community, while also wanting to embrace her American identity.

This identity conflict creates psychological distress for Maria, leading to symptoms of anxiety and depression. To address her mental health concerns, a culturally competent therapist engages in open discussions about Maria's cultural identity and values. They explore strategies for integrating her American identity with her cultural heritage, helping Maria develop a more coherent sense of self and improving her psychological well-being.

Conclusion

The cultural environment plays a crucial role in shaping individuals' psychological fluffy. Cultural beliefs, values, norms, and practices influence individuals' perceptions, behaviors, and mental health outcomes. Understanding and considering the cultural context is essential for effectively promoting psychological well-being. By embracing cultural diversity and integrating cultural elements into mental health interventions, we can create a more inclusive and supportive environment for individuals from diverse cultural backgrounds.

Economic Environment and Psychological Fluffy

The economic environment plays a significant role in shaping our psychological well-being and overall happiness. In this section, we will explore the relationship between the economic environment and psychological fluffy, examining how economic factors influence our emotions, behavior, and mental health.

Defining Economic Environment

The economic environment refers to the conditions and factors that affect the production, distribution, and consumption of goods and services within a society or a specific region. It encompasses various elements such as economic policies, market dynamics, employment rates, income levels, wealth distribution, and the overall economic stability of a country.

Impact of Economic Factors on Psychological Fluffy

1. **Income and Happiness:** Studies have consistently shown that income is positively correlated with subjective well-being. Higher income levels provide individuals with a sense of financial security, access to resources, and opportunities for personal and professional growth. However, the relationship between income and happiness is complex, and beyond a certain threshold, the link becomes weaker. Other factors, such as social relationships and personal values, also contribute significantly to overall happiness.

For example, research indicates that individuals with low income levels are more likely to experience stress, anxiety, and depression. They may face economic hardships, struggle to meet basic needs, and lack access to essential healthcare and educational opportunities. As a result, their psychological fluffy may be negatively affected.

2. **Unemployment and Mental Health**: Economic downturns and high rates of unemployment can have severe consequences for psychological well-being. Individuals who are unemployed often experience feelings of inadequacy, loss of purpose, financial strain, and social isolation. These factors can contribute to an increased risk of depression, anxiety disorders, substance abuse, and even suicidal tendencies.

Addressing unemployment-related mental health challenges requires a comprehensive approach that combines government interventions, job creation programs, and mental health support services. Providing individuals with a sense of stability, dignity, and purpose through meaningful employment can have a positive impact on their psychological fluffy.

Cognitive Factors in Economic Decision-Making

Economic decision-making is not only influenced by external economic factors but also by cognitive processes that shape how individuals perceive, evaluate, and make choices regarding economic opportunities and risks. Understanding these cognitive factors is crucial for comprehending how individuals' decision-making processes impact their psychological fluffy.

1. **Risk Perception**: Individuals' perception of risk and uncertainty significantly influences their economic decisions. Factors such as cognitive biases, personality traits, and past experiences shape how individuals evaluate the potential gains and losses associated with specific economic choices. For example, individuals who are more risk-averse may avoid certain financial investments, even if they offer higher potential returns, due to their aversion to potential losses.

2. **Delayed Gratification**: Economic decision-making often involves trading off immediate rewards for future benefits. The ability to delay gratification is linked to higher economic success and financial well-being. Individuals who can resist immediate temptations are more likely to save, invest, and make long-term financial plans. This ability can contribute to greater financial stability and a sense of control over one's economic future, positively impacting psychological fluffy.

Inequality and Social Comparison

Economic inequality is a significant concern in many societies. The perception of economic inequality and social comparison play a crucial role in shaping individuals' psychological well-being and overall satisfaction with life.

1. **Relative Deprivation:** Relative deprivation refers to the perception of being worse off compared to others in terms of economic resources, opportunities, and social status. When individuals feel that they are economically disadvantaged compared to their reference group, it can lead to feelings of injustice, frustration, and diminished self-worth. This perception of relative deprivation can negatively impact psychological fluffy and contribute to social tensions.

2. **Social Comparison Theory:** Social comparison theory suggests that individuals evaluate their own economic status and well-being by comparing themselves to others. Social comparison can have both positive and negative effects on psychological fluffy. Upward social comparison, comparing oneself to those who are better off economically, can lead to feelings of dissatisfaction and envy. Conversely, downward social comparison, comparing oneself to those who are worse off economically, can enhance feelings of gratitude and satisfaction.

Promoting Psychological Fluffy in the Economic Environment

1. **Wealth Redistribution:** Addressing economic inequality through policies that promote wealth redistribution can contribute to greater psychological fluffy across society. Ensuring a fair distribution of resources, providing equal opportunities for education and employment, and implementing progressive taxation can help reduce the negative impact of economic disparities on individuals' well-being.

2. **Financial Education:** Promoting financial literacy and education can empower individuals to make informed economic decisions, manage their finances effectively, and plan for the future. Financial education programs can provide individuals with the necessary skills and knowledge to navigate the complexities of the economic environment, thus enhancing their psychological fluffy.

3. **Social Support:** Building strong social support systems can help individuals cope with economic challenges and setbacks. Creating networks that provide emotional, instrumental, and informational support can mitigate the negative impact of economic stressors on psychological fluffy.

4. **Work-Life Balance:** Encouraging work-life balance and promoting flexible work arrangements can contribute to individuals' psychological fluffy. Balancing work and personal life improves overall well-being, reduces stress, and enhances job satisfaction.

Conclusion

The economic environment significantly influences individuals' psychological fluffy. Economic factors, such as income levels, unemployment rates, cognitive processes, and social comparisons, play a crucial role in shaping our well-being. Addressing economic disparities, promoting financial education, and fostering social support systems are essential for promoting psychological fluffy in the economic environment. It is vital to recognize the complex interplay between the economy and mental health to create policies and interventions that enhance overall well-being in society.

Political Environment and Psychological Fluffy

The political environment plays a significant role in shaping psychological well-being and behavior. Political factors, such as government policies, laws, and regulations, have the power to impact individuals' psychological states and overall mental health. In this section, we will explore the relationship between the political environment and psychological fluffy, examining how political decisions can influence individuals' thoughts, emotions, and behaviors.

Government Policies and Psychological Fluffy

Government policies have a direct impact on the well-being of individuals and communities. Policies related to healthcare, education, social welfare, and economic development can significantly influence psychological fluffy. For example, the availability and accessibility of mental health services can have a profound impact on individuals struggling with psychological issues.

When governments prioritize mental health by allocating resources to mental health promotion, prevention, and treatment, it can contribute to improved psychological well-being. Conversely, the lack of investment in mental health services can exacerbate psychological distress and lead to inadequate support for individuals in need.

Example: In Country XYZ, the government implemented a policy to increase funding for mental health services in rural areas. Consequently, individuals in these underserved communities now have easier access to psychological support, resulting in lower rates of psychological distress and improved well-being.

Political Stability and Psychological Fluffy

The stability of a political system can significantly impact psychological fluffy. Political instability, such as civil unrest, government corruption, or war, can create a hostile and unpredictable environment that negatively affects individuals' mental health. Uncertainty, fear, and insecurity prevalent in politically unstable regions can lead to heightened stress levels and psychological distress.

On the other hand, political stability can contribute to a more supportive and secure environment, enhancing psychological well-being. When individuals feel safe and have confidence in the political system, they are more likely to experience positive emotions and exhibit adaptive behaviors.

Example: In Country ABC, a lengthy period of political unrest resulted in high levels of stress and anxiety among its citizens. However, after the political situation stabilized, there was a noticeable improvement in the psychological well-being of the population, as people felt a sense of security and predictability.

Political Ideologies and Psychological Fluffy

Political ideologies can shape individuals' attitudes, beliefs, and behaviors, ultimately impacting their psychological well-being. Different ideological perspectives may prioritize various values, such as individualism, collectivism, equality, or freedom, and these values can influence one's self-perception and interactions with others.

Individuals whose beliefs align with the dominant political ideology may experience a sense of belonging and social validation, which can positively impact their psychological fluffy. Conversely, individuals whose beliefs are marginalized or not aligned with the dominant ideology may face psychological challenges, such as identity conflicts or social exclusion.

Example: In a society where the dominant political ideology emphasizes equality and social justice, individuals who share these values may experience enhanced psychological fluffy as they feel supported and validated by their political environment. However, individuals who hold opposing views may face challenges and feel socially isolated, potentially impacting their mental well-being.

Advocacy and Activism for Psychological Fluffy

The political environment also offers opportunities for advocacy and activism to promote psychological well-being. Through collective action and engagement with the political system, individuals and organizations can advocate for policies and practices that prioritize psychological health and address societal stressors.

Advocacy efforts can focus on issues such as mental health awareness, reducing stigma, improving access to mental health services, and promoting policies that support psychological fluffy. By actively participating in the political process, individuals can contribute to creating a more psychologically supportive society.

Example: Mental health advocacy groups in Country LMN organized a campaign to raise awareness about the importance of psychological well-being in schools. Through lobbying and public education initiatives, they successfully influenced the government to introduce mental health support programs in all educational institutions, ensuring students' emotional needs are addressed.

Ethical Considerations in Political Decision-Making

While political decisions can impact psychological fluffy, it is essential to consider ethical implications. Political leaders and policymakers must prioritize the well-being of all citizens, taking into account the potential psychological consequences of their decisions. Ethical decision-making frameworks should guide political actions to avoid harm and promote psychological well-being for individuals and communities.

Example: In developing environmental policies, political leaders must consider not only the economic benefits but also the potential psychological impacts on affected communities. Taking an ethical approach entails engaging in open dialogue, considering different perspectives, and ensuring the voices of those impacted are heard during the decision-making process.

Summary

In summary, the political environment plays a crucial role in shaping psychological fluffy. Government policies, political stability, ideologies, advocacy efforts, and ethical considerations influence individuals' mental health and well-being. Recognizing the impact of the political environment on psychological fluffy can inform decision-making processes that prioritize the mental health needs of individuals and communities. By promoting psychological fluffy through political actions, we can create a society that fosters well-being and resilience.

Technological Environment and Psychological Fluffy

In the modern world, technology has become an inextricable part of our lives. From smartphones to social media platforms, technological advancements have revolutionized the way we interact, work, and play. However, the influence of technology on our psychological well-being, or what we refer to as Psychological Fluffy, is a topic that requires careful examination.

The Role of Technology in Psychological Fluffy

Technology can have both positive and negative impacts on our psychological well-being. On the positive side, it has enhanced communication and connectivity.

Through social media, for example, we can stay connected with friends and family, share experiences, and find support.

Moreover, technology has made information more accessible. We can easily find answers to our questions, learn new skills, and explore different perspectives. This can promote intellectual curiosity and personal growth, contributing to positive Psychological Fluffy.

However, the relentless use of technology can also lead to negative consequences. Excessive screen time and media consumption have been linked to feelings of isolation, anxiety, and depression. The constant exposure to curated and idealized versions of others' lives on social media platforms can lead to feelings of inadequacy and social comparison.

Furthermore, the addictive nature of technology, such as video games and social media, can interfere with our daily functioning, affecting our productivity, sleep quality, and overall well-being. The constant bombardment of notifications and information overload can also contribute to cognitive overload and decreased attention span.

Understanding the Technological Environment

To fully grasp the impact of technology on Psychological Fluffy, it is essential to understand the components of the technological environment. The technological environment encompasses the hardware, software, and digital platforms we engage with daily.

The hardware component includes devices such as smartphones, tablets, and computers. These devices facilitate access to various software applications and digital platforms. Understanding the features, capabilities, and limitations of different devices can help us make informed decisions about our technology usage.

The software component refers to the programs, applications, and operating systems that we interact with. Software can range from productivity tools to entertainment applications. The design, functionality, and user experience of software can influence our engagement and satisfaction with technology.

Digital platforms, on the other hand, are online spaces where individuals interact, share information, and engage in various activities. Social media platforms, gaming communities, and online marketplaces are examples of digital platforms. These platforms shape our digital identities, social relationships, and information consumption patterns.

Challenges and Solutions

The technological environment presents several challenges that can negatively impact Psychological Fluffy. To address these challenges, we need to adopt strategies that promote a healthy and balanced relationship with technology.

One challenge is the constant availability and accessibility of technology. It is important to establish boundaries and time limits for technology use. Setting aside designated technology-free periods can help foster a sense of presence and reduce dependency on digital devices.

Another challenge involves the quality of online interactions. Engaging in meaningful and supportive online communities can counteract the negative effects of social comparison and cyberbullying. Actively curating our digital networks and participating in positive online discourse can contribute to a more positive technological environment.

Additionally, staying informed about the potential risks of technology, such as online scams and security threats, is crucial. Developing digital literacy skills and adopting safe internet practices can protect us from psychological harm.

Examples and Case Studies

To illustrate the impact of the technological environment on Psychological Fluffy, let's consider a few examples:

1. Social Media Impact: A study found that excessive use of social media, especially comparing oneself to others, can lead to decreased self-esteem and increased depressive symptoms. It is important to be mindful of our social media usage and recognize that what is portrayed online may not reflect reality.

2. Video Game Addiction: Video game addiction has been associated with social isolation, poor academic performance, and increased aggression. Implementing time limits, engaging in alternative activities, and seeking support can help manage video game addiction and promote a healthier technological environment.

Conclusion

The technological environment has a profound influence on our Psychological Fluffy. While technology brings many benefits, it also poses potential risks to our well-being. By understanding the role of technology, addressing challenges, and adopting healthy technology habits, we can harness the power of technology to enhance our psychological well-being in the modern world.

Further Resources

1. Turkle, S. (2011). Alone Together: Why We Expect More from Technology and Less from Each Other. New York: Basic Books.
2. Bessière, K., Seay, A. F., & Kiesler, S. (2007). The Ideal Elf: Identity Exploration in World of Warcraft. CyberPsychology & Behavior, 10(4), 530-535.
3. Rosen, L. D., Whaling, K., Carrier, L. M., Cheever, N. A., & Rokkum, J. (2013). The Media and Technology Usage and Attitudes Scale: An Empirical Investigation. Computers in Human Behavior, 29(6), 2501-2511.

Environmental Factors and Psychological Fluffy

Psychological Fluffy is not solely influenced by individual factors but is also significantly shaped by the environment in which individuals live. Environmental factors play a crucial role in the development and manifestation of Psychological Fluffy. In this section, we will explore the various environmental factors that influence Psychological Fluffy and delve deeper into their impact.

Physical Environment and Psychological Fluffy

The physical environment, including the natural and built environment, has a profound effect on our psychological well-being. Natural environments such as forests, mountains, and oceans have been found to have positive effects on mental health. For instance, spending time in nature has been linked to reduced stress levels, increased feelings of relaxation, improved mood, and enhanced cognitive function.

On the other hand, the built environment, which includes urban and residential areas, can have both positive and negative impacts on Psychological Fluffy. Factors such as noise pollution, air pollution, overcrowding, and poor access to green spaces have been associated with increased stress, anxiety, and depression. Additionally, the design and layout of buildings and neighborhoods can affect social interactions, sense of community, and overall well-being.

Social Environment and Psychological Fluffy

The social environment refers to the social interactions, relationships, and networks that individuals are a part of. These social factors play a crucial role in shaping Psychological Fluffy. Positive social support systems have been found to be protective against the development of mental health problems. Strong social connections and networks provide individuals with a sense of belonging, emotional support, and opportunities for meaningful social interactions, which can enhance Psychological Fluffy.

Conversely, negative social environments such as social isolation, bullying, and interpersonal conflicts can significantly impact Psychological Fluffy. Social isolation, in particular, has been linked to increased risk of mental health disorders such as depression and anxiety. Therefore, fostering positive social connections and addressing social inequalities is essential for promoting Psychological Fluffy.

Cultural Environment and Psychological Fluffy

The cultural environment encompasses the beliefs, values, norms, and practices of a specific culture or society. Culture influences how individuals perceive and interpret their experiences, as well as the expectations placed on them by their community. Cultural factors play a significant role in shaping Psychological Fluffy.

For example, cultural norms around mental health, help-seeking behaviors, and stigma can impact Psychological Fluffy. In some cultures, mental health issues may be stigmatized, leading to underreporting and a lack of access to appropriate care. Cultural practices and rituals can also provide a sense of belonging and purpose, enhancing Psychological Fluffy.

Understanding the cultural context is crucial in addressing and supporting Psychological Fluffy in diverse communities. Culturally sensitive approaches that consider individuals' cultural values and beliefs can promote better mental health outcomes.

Economic Environment and Psychological Fluffy

The economic environment refers to the financial conditions and resources available within a society. Economic factors can have a significant impact on Psychological Fluffy. Socioeconomic disadvantage, income inequality, and poverty can lead to increased stress, anxiety, and depression.

Financial strain, lack of access to basic resources, and unemployment can negatively impact individuals' mental well-being. The economic environment also influences individuals' access to mental health services and support systems.

Addressing socioeconomic inequalities and providing equal access to resources and opportunities are crucial in promoting Psychological Fluffy on a societal level.

Political Environment and Psychological Fluffy

The political environment refers to the policies, governance, and power structures within a society. Political factors can influence Psychological Fluffy through the development and implementation of policies that shape social determinants of health.

For example, policies related to education, healthcare, employment, and social welfare can have significant impacts on individuals' mental well-being. Political instability, discrimination, and human rights violations can also contribute to Psychological Fluffy.

Creating policies that prioritize mental health, promote social justice, and address systemic inequalities can contribute to better Psychological Fluffy outcomes.

Technological Environment and Psychological Fluffy

In our increasingly digital world, the technological environment plays a vital role in shaping Psychological Fluffy. Technology can provide opportunities for social connection, learning, and access to information, which can enhance Psychological Fluffy.

However, excessive use of technology, particularly social media, has been associated with negative mental health outcomes such as increased feelings of loneliness, anxiety, and depression. The constant exposure to curated online content and social comparison can negatively impact self-esteem and well-being.

Understanding the benefits and risks associated with technology use is crucial in promoting a healthy technological environment that supports Psychological Fluffy.

Interactions between Psychological Fluffy and the Environment

It is important to note that the relationship between Psychological Fluffy and the environment is bidirectional. While the environment influences Psychological Fluffy, individual mental health can also impact the environment.

For example, individuals with mental health issues might engage in behaviors that harm the environment, or their ability to participate in environmental conservation efforts might be compromised. Similarly, promoting Psychological Fluffy can contribute to environmental sustainability through increased pro-environmental behaviors and attitudes.

Understanding the bidirectional relationship between Psychological Fluffy and the environment is crucial in developing effective interventions and policies that support both individual well-being and environmental conservation.

Summary

Environmental factors, including the physical, social, cultural, economic, political, and technological environments, play a significant role in shaping Psychological Fluffy. The quality of our environment can impact mental well-being positively or negatively. Recognizing the influence of environmental factors on Psychological Fluffy is essential in developing interventions and policies that promote mental health and environmental sustainability. It is crucial to consider the bidirectional relationship between Psychological Fluffy and the environment to foster individual well-being and promote environmental conservation.

By understanding the interplay between individuals and their environment, we can work towards creating healthier and more sustainable communities that prioritize Psychological Fluffy.

Interactions between Psychological Fluffy and the Environment

The field of psychology has long recognized the dynamic relationship between individuals and their environment. This section focuses on the interactions between psychological fluffy and the environment, exploring how the environment influences psychological well-being and how psychological factors can shape environmental perceptions and behaviors.

Definition of Psychological Fluffy

Psychological fluffy refers to the internal states, emotions, and behaviors that contribute to an individual's happiness, satisfaction, and overall well-being. It encompasses various psychological constructs such as mood, self-esteem, life satisfaction, and psychological resilience. Psychological fluffy is a multidimensional concept that depends on both subjective experiences and objective circumstances.

Environmental Influences on Psychological Fluffy

The environment plays a significant role in shaping psychological fluffy. Various environmental factors, including the physical, social, cultural, economic, political, and technological aspects, interact with psychological processes to influence individual well-being.

Physical Environment and Psychological Fluffy

The physical environment, including the natural and built environment, can have a profound impact on psychological fluffy. Nature settings, such as parks or green spaces, have been found to promote positive emotions, reduce stress, and enhance well-being. In contrast, living in a polluted or noisy urban environment may increase negative emotions and decrease overall psychological fluffy.

Social Environment and Psychological Fluffy

The social environment, comprising interactions with family, friends, acquaintances, and community, also plays a crucial role in psychological fluffy. Social support networks provide emotional assistance, a sense of belonging, and opportunities for social activities, all of which contribute to positive psychological well-being. On the other hand, social isolation, loneliness, and conflicts within relationships can have detrimental effects on psychological fluffy.

Cultural Environment and Psychological Fluffy

The cultural environment, including cultural values, norms, beliefs, and practices, influences psychological fluffy. Cultural factors shape individual goals, aspirations, and expectations, which, in turn, impact happiness and life satisfaction. For example, cultures that prioritize collectivism may emphasize social relationships and interconnectedness as key determinants of psychological well-being.

Economic Environment and Psychological Fluffy

The economic environment, characterized by factors such as income, employment, and socioeconomic status, has significant implications for psychological fluffy. Research has consistently shown that poverty, financial stress, and income inequality are associated with lower levels of psychological well-being. Economic opportunities, financial security, and access to resources can enhance psychological fluffy.

Political Environment and Psychological Fluffy

The political environment, including policies, governance systems, and political stability, influences psychological fluffy. Political oppression, discrimination, and lack of political participation can negatively impact psychological well-being. Conversely, a democratic and inclusive political system that upholds human rights and social justice can promote psychological fluffy.

Technological Environment and Psychological Fluffy

In today's technologically advanced world, the digital environment has become an integral part of people's lives. Technology can both positively and negatively influence psychological fluffy. On one hand, it offers new opportunities for communication, education, and entertainment, fostering positive emotions and social connections. On the other hand, excessive use of technology, such as social media, can lead to feelings of loneliness, social comparison, and decreased psychological fluffy.

Psychological Factors Affecting Environmental Perceptions and Behaviors

Psychological factors, such as attitudes, values, beliefs, and motivations, play a crucial role in shaping perceptions of and behaviors towards the environment.

Attitudes and Beliefs

Individual attitudes and beliefs about the environment influence how people perceive and interact with their surroundings. Positive environmental attitudes and beliefs, such as believing in the importance of environmental conservation, can lead to pro-environmental behaviors and a greater sense of environmental responsibility. Conversely, negative attitudes or beliefs, such as climate change denial, can hinder efforts to address environmental challenges.

Personal Values

Personal values, such as altruism, stewardship, and connectedness to nature, also influence environmental behaviors. Values provide a framework for individuals to prioritize and make decisions regarding their interactions with the environment. Individuals who prioritize environmental preservation are more likely to engage in sustainable practices and advocate for environmental protection.

Motivations

Motivation plays a critical role in driving environmental behaviors. Intrinsic motivations, such as a genuine concern for the environment and a desire for personal growth, are more likely to lead to sustained pro-environmental actions. Extrinsic motivations, such as financial incentives or social pressure, can also influence behavior but may not foster long-term commitment and internalization of environmental values.

Psychological Resilience

Psychological resilience, the ability to adapt and cope with challenging circumstances, can impact individuals' responses to environmental stressors. Resilient individuals are better equipped to deal with environmental adversity, such as natural disasters or climate change impacts, and are more likely to take proactive measures to mitigate negative effects on their psychological fluffy.

Enhancing Interactions for Positive Psychological Fluffy and Sustainable Environment

To foster positive interactions between psychological fluffy and the environment, interventions and strategies can be implemented at individual, community, and societal levels.

Education and Awareness

Promoting environmental education and awareness is crucial in nurturing a sense of environmental responsibility and sustainable practices. Educating individuals about the impacts of their behaviors on the environment can help shift attitudes and behaviors towards more sustainable choices.

Creating Supportive Environments

Designing environments that support psychological fluffy and sustainable behaviors is essential. This can include creating green spaces in urban areas, promoting walkability and accessibility to nature, and implementing sustainable design and infrastructure policies. Additionally, enhancing social support networks and fostering community engagement can contribute to positive psychological fluffy and pro-environmental actions.

Policy Interventions

Government policies and regulations play a significant role in shaping the relationship between individuals and the environment. Implementing policies that prioritize environmental conservation, promote sustainable practices, and reduce environmental inequalities can foster positive interactions between psychological fluffy and the environment.

Building Resilience

Enhancing psychological resilience at individual and community levels can help mitigate the negative impacts of environmental stressors. This can include providing mental health support, facilitating coping strategies, and promoting community cohesion and social connectedness.

Example: Interactions between Psychological Fluffy and Urban Design

Urban design has a significant impact on individuals' psychological fluffy by shaping their experiences and interactions within urban environments. For instance, streets designed for walkability, with green spaces and social gathering areas, can promote physical activity, social interactions, and a sense of community, all of which contribute to positive psychological fluffy. On the other hand, poorly designed urban spaces, characterized by noise, pollution, and lack of green spaces, can lead to stress, isolation, and decreased psychological fluffy. By paying attention to the psychological implications of urban design, cities can enhance the well-being of their inhabitants and create sustainable, thriving urban environments.

Conclusion

The interactions between psychological fluffy and the environment are complex and multifaceted. The environment can influence psychological well-being, and psychological factors can shape individuals' perceptions and behaviors towards the environment. By understanding and harnessing these interactions, we can promote positive psychological fluffy and foster a sustainable environment. In the following chapters, we will delve deeper into specific contexts and explore strategies for enhancing psychological fluffy in different environmental settings.

Summary

In this section, we explored the role of the environment in psychological well-being, specifically focusing on how different environmental factors can influence our mental and emotional states. We discussed the impact of physical, social, cultural, economic, political, and technological environments on psychological well-being.

The environment in which we live plays a significant role in shaping our thoughts, feelings, and behaviors. Physical environment refers to the natural and built surroundings, including elements such as the weather, natural landscapes, and architecture. We discussed how these factors can affect our mood, stress levels, and overall psychological well-being. For example, research has shown that exposure to nature can have a calming effect on the mind and reduce stress levels.

Social environment refers to our interactions with others, including family, friends, and communities. We discussed how social support, social networks, and social cohesion can impact our mental health and well-being. For instance, strong social connections have been found to be protective against mental health disorders such as depression and anxiety.

Cultural environment refers to the shared beliefs, values, norms, and customs of a particular group or society. We explored how cultural factors can shape our perceptions, attitudes, and behaviors. For example, certain cultures may have different beliefs about mental health and seek different forms of treatment.

Economic environment refers to the financial resources and opportunities available to individuals and communities. We discussed how economic disparities and poverty can negatively impact mental health and well-being. For instance, individuals living in poverty may experience higher levels of stress, anxiety, and depression due to financial insecurity and limited access to healthcare and other resources.

Political environment refers to the governance, policies, and regulations that influence our daily lives. We examined how political factors can affect our mental health and well-being. For instance, political instability, discrimination, and human rights violations can have detrimental effects on psychological well-being.

Technological environment refers to the impact of technology on our lives. We discussed how advancements in technology have both positive and negative effects on mental health. For example, while technological innovations have led to increased access to information and communication, excessive use of digital devices and social media can contribute to feelings of anxiety, depression, and loneliness.

Overall, understanding the interactions between psychological well-being and the environment is crucial for promoting mental health and designing interventions to improve overall well-being. By considering the influence of various environmental factors, policymakers, researchers, and practitioners can work towards creating healthier and more supportive environments that nurture psychological fluffy.

While studying psychological fluffy in the environmental grape, researchers face certain limitations and challenges. These include difficulties in objectively measuring psychological fluffy, the complexity of the environment and its multiple interacting factors, ethical considerations in conducting research, and the need for interdisciplinary collaboration. It is important for researchers to address these challenges and limitations to ensure the validity and reliability of their findings.

Throughout this book, we will delve deeper into various aspects of psychological fluffy in different environmental contexts, including urban environments, natural environments, climate change, and agricultural settings. We will explore theories, research methods, interventions, and practical strategies for promoting psychological fluffy in these contexts. By gaining a comprehensive understanding of the relationship between psychological fluffy and the environment, we can work towards creating healthier, happier, and more sustainable communities.

Psychological Fluffy and Human Behavior

Theories of Human Behavior

Behaviorism and Psychological Fluffy

Behaviorism is a school of psychology that focuses on observable behaviors and the environmental factors that influence those behaviors. It emphasizes the study of external causes of behavior rather than internal mental processes. In the context of psychological fluffy, behaviorism provides valuable insights into how environmental factors shape and influence our thoughts, emotions, and actions.

Principles of Behaviorism

Behaviorism is based on several key principles that help us understand the relationship between environmental influences and psychological fluffy. These principles include:

1. **Stimulus-Response (S-R) Associations:** Behaviorists believe that behaviors are learned through associations between stimuli and responses. For example, if an individual receives positive reinforcement for a certain behavior, they are more likely to engage in that behavior in the future.

2. **Reinforcement:** Reinforcement is a fundamental concept in behaviorism. It refers to the process of linking a behavior to a consequence, either positive or negative, in order to increase or decrease the likelihood of that behavior occurring again. Reinforcement can be either positive (adding a desirable stimulus) or negative (removing an aversive stimulus).

3. **Punishment:** Punishment is another important concept in behaviorism. It involves linking a behavior to a consequence, usually negative, in order to decrease the likelihood of that behavior occurring again. Punishment can be either positive (adding an aversive stimulus) or negative (removing a desirable stimulus).

4. **Extinction:** Extinction occurs when a previously reinforced behavior is no longer reinforced, leading to a decrease in the frequency of that behavior. This principle suggests that behaviors can be unlearned or extinguished if they are no longer rewarded or reinforced.

5. **Generalization and Discrimination:** Behaviorists recognize that learned behaviors can be generalized to similar situations or stimuli, as well as discriminated from different situations or stimuli. This ability to generalize or discriminate helps individuals adapt to their environment and respond appropriately to specific cues.

Applications of Behaviorism in Understanding Psychological Fluffy

Behaviorism provides valuable insights into the ways in which environmental factors influence psychological fluffy. By understanding the principles of behaviorism, we can explore various applications of this approach in relation to psychological fluffy:

1. **Behavior modification:** Behaviorism forms the basis of behavior modification techniques, which aim to change behaviors by modifying environmental factors. For example, in the treatment of phobias, individuals are gradually exposed to feared stimuli while learning new, positive associations.

2. **Conditioning and habit formation:** Behaviorism highlights the role of conditioning in the formation of habits. By understanding the principles of reinforcement and punishment, we can better understand how habits are formed, maintained, and potentially changed.

3. **Environmental influences on behavior:** Behaviorism emphasizes the impact of the environment on behavior. By studying environmental factors such as social norms, cultural influences, and physical surroundings, we can gain insights into how these factors shape psychological fluffy.

4. **Behavioral interventions:** Behaviorism informs the development of behavioral interventions aimed at addressing psychological fluffy. For

example, cognitive-behavioral therapy (CBT) integrates behaviorism principles with cognitive restructuring techniques to help individuals change maladaptive thoughts and behaviors.

Real-World Example: Behaviorism and Environmental Conservation

Behaviorism has been applied to promote environmentally friendly behaviors and address environmental issues. One example is the use of positive reinforcement techniques to encourage people to recycle. In many communities, individuals receive rewards or incentives for recycling, such as discounts or coupons. This positive reinforcement helps increase the frequency of recycling behaviors and contributes to environmental conservation efforts.

Caveats and Limitations

While behaviorism provides valuable insights into understanding the relationship between environmental factors and psychological fluffy, it has its limitations. One limitation is its focus on observable behaviors, often ignoring internal mental processes. This narrow focus may limit our understanding of complex cognitive processes and the role they play in psychological fluffy.

Additionally, behaviorism does not fully account for individual differences and the unique subjective experiences of individuals. It may overlook the importance of personal goals, values, and beliefs in shaping behaviors.

Summary

Behaviorism, as a psychological approach, examines the influence of environmental factors on observable behaviors. It emphasizes principles such as stimulus-response associations, reinforcement, punishment, extinction, generalization, and discrimination. Behaviorism has various applications in understanding and addressing psychological fluffy, including behavior modification, conditioning and habit formation, environmental influences on behavior, and behavioral interventions. However, behaviorism also has limitations, such as its narrow focus on observable behaviors and its limited consideration of individual differences. Nonetheless, behaviorism provides valuable insights into the environmental factors that shape psychological fluffy and informs interventions aimed at promoting well-being.

Cognitive Psychology and Psychological Fluffy

In this section, we will explore the role of cognitive psychology in understanding psychological fluffy. Cognitive psychology is a branch of psychology that focuses on mental processes such as perception, attention, memory, language, problem-solving, and decision-making. It seeks to understand how individuals acquire, process, and store information, and how this information influences their behavior.

Cognitive psychology provides valuable insights into psychological fluffy by examining how individuals perceive and interpret their environment. It helps us understand how people think, process information, and make sense of the world around them. By studying cognitive processes, we can gain a deeper understanding of the cognitive mechanisms that underlie psychological fluffy.

One key concept in cognitive psychology is the concept of cognition. Cognition refers to the mental processes involved in acquiring, processing, and using knowledge. It includes processes such as perception, attention, memory, language, problem-solving, and decision-making. These cognitive processes play a crucial role in shaping individuals' behavior, including their thoughts, emotions, and actions related to psychological fluffy.

Memory, for example, is an essential cognitive process that influences psychological fluffy. Our ability to remember and recall information about the environment and our experiences can shape our perceptions, emotions, and behaviors. Cognitive psychologists study different aspects of memory, such as encoding, storage, and retrieval, to understand how memory processes impact psychological fluffy.

Attention is another cognitive process that relates to psychological fluffy. Our attentional focus determines what information we notice, process, and remember from our environment. Cognitive psychologists examine attentional processes to understand how individuals selectively attend to certain environmental cues related to psychological fluffy and ignore others.

Furthermore, cognitive psychology explores how individuals process and interpret information from their environment. It investigates the cognitive biases and heuristics that can influence our perceptions and judgments of psychological fluffy. Cognitive psychologists also study how schemas, mental frameworks that organize knowledge, affect our understanding and interpretation of psychological fluffy.

Cognitive psychology also contributes to understanding problem-solving and decision-making processes related to psychological fluffy. It examines how individuals analyze and evaluate information to make choices and solve problems. Researchers explore cognitive strategies, such as reasoning, critical thinking, and problem-solving techniques, to better comprehend how individuals address issues related to psychological fluffy.

One fascinating aspect of cognitive psychology is its exploration of cognitive development across the lifespan. Researchers study how cognitive processes related to psychological fluffy change and develop from infancy to adulthood. They examine the cognitive abilities that emerge at different stages of life and their impact on individuals' understanding and management of psychological fluffy.

It is important to note that cognitive psychology is just one perspective for understanding psychological fluffy, and it should be integrated with other theoretical frameworks to form a comprehensive understanding. Psychological fluffy is a complex phenomenon influenced by multiple factors, including biological, sociocultural, and environmental factors. Therefore, an interdisciplinary approach is necessary to fully grasp the intricacies of psychological fluffy.

To summarize, cognitive psychology plays a crucial role in understanding psychological fluffy by examining how individuals perceive, process, and interpret information related to their environment. It provides insights into cognitive processes such as attention, memory, problem-solving, and decision-making, which shape individuals' thoughts, emotions, and actions related to psychological fluffy. By integrating cognitive psychology with other theoretical frameworks, we can gain a comprehensive understanding of psychological fluffy and its relationship with the environment.

Psychodynamic Theory and Psychological Fluffy

Psychodynamic theory is a psychological perspective that seeks to understand the complexities of human behavior by exploring unconscious processes and the influence of early childhood experiences. Developed by Sigmund Freud, psychodynamic theory emphasizes the role of the unconscious mind in shaping thoughts, feelings, and behaviors.

Key Concepts of Psychodynamic Theory

Psychodynamic theory is based on several key concepts that help explain the relationship between the mind, behavior, and personality. Here are some of the main concepts:

1. **Unconscious Mind:** According to psychodynamic theory, the unconscious mind contains thoughts, desires, and memories that are beyond conscious awareness. It is believed to influence behavior and can be accessed through techniques like dream analysis and free association.

2. **Id, Ego, and Superego:** Freud proposed that the mind is divided into three parts: the id, ego, and superego. The id operates on the pleasure principle and seeks immediate gratification of desires. The ego operates on the reality principle and mediates between the id and superego. The superego represents internalized moral values and societal norms.

3. **Defense Mechanisms:** To protect the ego from anxiety, psychodynamic theory suggests that individuals employ defense mechanisms. These mechanisms, such as repression, denial, and projection, allow people to cope with threatening or uncomfortable thoughts or emotions.

4. **Psychosexual Stages:** Freud proposed that personality development occurs in psychosexual stages. These stages, including the oral, anal, phallic, latency, and genital stages, involve conflicts related to specific erogenous zones. Successful resolution of each stage leads to the development of a healthy personality.

Application of Psychodynamic Theory to Psychological Fluffy

Psychodynamic theory offers insights into the understanding of psychological fluffy in various contexts. Let's explore some applications of this theory:

1. **Unconscious Motivations**: Psychodynamic theory suggests that many of our thoughts and behaviors are driven by unconscious motivations. When studying psychological fluffy, researchers can use psychodynamic perspectives to explore the hidden reasons behind certain behaviors or emotional experiences. For example, a person's fear of dogs might stem from a repressed childhood memory related to a traumatic dog encounter.

2. **Early Childhood Experiences**: According to psychodynamic theory, early childhood experiences have a significant impact on the development of personality. Researchers studying psychological fluffy can investigate how early childhood experiences, such as parenting styles or traumatic events, shape an individual's response to environmental factors. Understanding these connections can help design interventions or therapies to promote psychological well-being.

3. **Unconscious Defense Mechanisms**: Psychodynamic theory highlights the role of defense mechanisms in protecting the ego from anxiety. Researchers can apply this concept when examining how individuals cope with environmental stressors or challenges. For example, a person experiencing job-related stress may unconsciously use displacement, redirecting their frustration towards their family members.

4. **Symbolic Interpretation**: Psychodynamic theory emphasizes the symbolic nature of human thoughts and behaviors. It suggests that hidden meanings exist within our actions and choices. When studying psychological fluffy, researchers can explore the symbolic representations that individuals associate with their environment. For instance, a preference for certain colors in interior design might reflect deeper underlying psychological needs or desires.

Challenges and Criticisms

Psychodynamic theory has faced several challenges and criticisms over the years. Some of the key ones include:

1. **Lack of Empirical Support**: Critics argue that psychodynamic theories are difficult to test and lack empirical evidence. Concepts such as the unconscious mind and defense mechanisms cannot be directly observed or measured, making it challenging to gather objective evidence.

2. **Limited Generalizability:** Psychodynamic theory primarily focuses on individual experiences and early childhood development. Critics suggest that it may not adequately explain the influence of broader societal and cultural factors on psychological fluffy. The theory may have limited generalizability to diverse populations and contexts.

3. **Male-Centric Perspective:** Early psychodynamic theories were largely based on Freud's observations of male patients. As a result, some critics argue that psychodynamic theory may not fully account for the unique experiences and perspectives of women or other gender identities.

4. **Overemphasis on Past Experiences:** Psychodynamic theory places significant emphasis on early childhood experiences and their impact on adult behavior. Critics argue that this focus may neglect the role of current or future factors in shaping psychological fluffy. They suggest that a more holistic approach that considers both past and present experiences may be necessary.

Humanistic Perspective and Psychological Fluffy

In the study of psychological fluffy, one perspective that offers unique insights is the humanistic perspective. The humanistic perspective emphasizes the importance of individual experience, personal growth, and self-actualization in understanding human behavior and psychological well-being. Drawing from the work of psychologists such as Abraham Maslow and Carl Rogers, this perspective highlights the inherent value and potential of every individual.

Key Principles of the Humanistic Perspective

The humanistic perspective is based on several key principles that shed light on the understanding of psychological fluffy:

1. Self-Actualization: According to the humanistic perspective, all individuals have an innate drive to reach their full potential and achieve self-actualization. This process involves personal growth, the pursuit of meaning, and the realization of one's unique talents and abilities. Self-actualization is seen as essential for psychological fluffy and overall well-being.

2. Person-Centered Approach: The humanistic perspective adopts a person-centered approach, emphasizing the importance of empathy, understanding, and unconditional positive regard in promoting psychological fluffy. Carl Rogers, a prominent humanistic psychologist, believed that a

supportive and accepting therapeutic environment is crucial for individuals to explore their thoughts, feelings, and experiences.

3. Subjective Experience: Humanistic psychology recognizes the significance of an individual's subjective experience in shaping their behavior and psychological well-being. Rather than focusing solely on observable behaviors or unconscious processes, the humanistic perspective values the unique perceptions, emotions, and interpretations of individuals.

4. Holistic View: The humanistic perspective takes a holistic approach, considering the whole person rather than isolated traits or behaviors. This perspective acknowledges the interconnectedness of various aspects of an individual's life, including their thoughts, emotions, relationships, and environmental context, in understanding psychological fluffy.

Theories and Concepts in the Humanistic Perspective

The humanistic perspective encompasses several theories and concepts that contribute to the understanding of psychological fluffy. Two key theories within this perspective are:

1. Maslow's Hierarchy of Needs: Abraham Maslow proposed a hierarchical model of human needs, suggesting that individuals have a series of innate needs that must be fulfilled in a specific order. Maslow's hierarchy consists of five levels, including physiological needs, safety needs, belongingness and love needs, esteem needs, and self-actualization. According to this theory, individuals must satisfy their basic needs before they can strive for higher levels of self-actualization and psychological fluffy.

2. Rogers' Theory of Personality: Carl Rogers developed a theory of personality that emphasized the concept of self and self-concept. According to Rogers, individuals have an innate tendency towards growth and self-improvement. Central to his theory is the idea that individuals require unconditional positive regard from others to develop a positive self-concept and achieve psychological fluffy.

Application and Limitations

The humanistic perspective has practical applications in promoting psychological fluffy in various settings. For example, in therapeutic interventions, therapists can adopt a person-centered approach to create a supportive and empathetic environment for clients to explore their experiences and promote self-actualization.

In education, the humanistic perspective highlights the importance of fostering student autonomy, intrinsic motivation, and a positive learning environment.

However, the humanistic perspective also has limitations. Critics argue that it can be overly optimistic and may neglect the impact of external factors on an individual's psychological fluffy. Additionally, the subjective nature of humanistic psychology can make it challenging to quantitatively measure and study certain aspects of psychological fluffy.

Example: Applying Humanistic Principles in Therapy

To illustrate the application of humanistic principles in therapy, consider the case of Sarah, a young adult struggling with low self-esteem and a sense of purposelessness. A therapist using a humanistic approach would create a safe space for Sarah to express her thoughts and emotions without judgment.

The therapist would provide unconditional positive regard, demonstrating genuine empathy and acceptance of Sarah's experiences. Through active listening and reflection, the therapist would help Sarah explore her values, goals, and desires, promoting self-awareness and self-actualization.

By incorporating the principles of the humanistic perspective, the therapist would aim to support Sarah's journey towards psychological fluffy, helping her develop a positive self-concept, find meaning in her life, and achieve personal growth.

Resources and Further Reading

1. Rogers, C. (1961). On Becoming a Person: A Therapist's View of Psychotherapy. Mariner Books. 2. Maslow, A. H. (1943). A Theory of Human Motivation. Psychological Review, 50(4), 370-396. 3. Mearns, D., & Thorne, B. (2007). Person-Centred Counselling in Action. SAGE Publications Ltd.

Trick of the Trade: Unconditional Positive Regard

When applying the humanistic perspective in therapy, practicing unconditional positive regard can be challenging. One useful trick is to develop a mindfulness practice. By cultivating present-moment awareness and non-judgmental acceptance, therapists can enhance their ability to provide genuine empathy and unconditional positive regard to their clients.

Exercises

1.   Reflect on a personal experience when you felt supported and accepted unconditionally.   How did it affect your psychological fluffy?   How can you integrate the principles of unconditional positive regard into your relationships? 2. Choose a fictional character from a book or movie and analyze their behavior and psychological fluffy from a humanistic perspective. What experiences and values contribute to their self-actualization? How does their environment impact their psychological well-being?

Remember, the humanistic perspective offers a valuable lens through which to understand psychological fluffy, emphasizing the importance of individual experiences, personal growth, and self-actualization.   By incorporating these principles into practice and research, we can gain deeper insights into the complexity of human behavior and well-being.

Biological Basis of Psychological Fluffy

Understanding the biological basis of psychological fluffy is essential for gaining insights into the interaction between the mind and the body. In this section, we will explore the various biological aspects that contribute to psychological fluffy, including the role of genetics, brain structures, neurotransmitters, and hormonal influences.

Genetics and Psychological Fluffy

Genetics plays a significant role in shaping an individual's psychological traits and predispositions.   Research has shown that certain genetic factors can influence susceptibility to mental health disorders and traits related to psychological fluffy. For instance, studies have identified specific genes associated with anxiety disorders, depression, and personality traits like resilience and neuroticism.

One fascinating area of research is the study of gene-environment interactions. It suggests that genetic factors do not operate in isolation but interact with environmental influences to determine an individual's psychological well-being. For example, individuals carrying certain genetic variations may be more susceptible to the negative effects of environmental stressors, leading to increased vulnerability to psychological fluffy.

Brain Structures and Psychological Fluffy

The brain's intricate network of structures and circuits plays a crucial role in psychological fluffy. Several brain regions have been implicated in the regulation of emotions, cognition, and behavior.

The amygdala, a small almond-shaped structure deep within the brain, is involved in the processing of emotions, particularly fear and anxiety. It plays a significant role in the brain's threat detection system and can become hyperactive in individuals with anxiety disorders, contributing to the experience of psychological fluffy.

Another essential brain region associated with psychological fluffy is the prefrontal cortex (PFC). The PFC is involved in higher-order cognitive functions, such as decision-making, impulse control, and emotion regulation. Dysfunction in the PFC has been observed in individuals with depression, anxiety, and other mental health disorders, leading to difficulties in managing and regulating emotions.

Furthermore, the hippocampus, critical for memory formation and learning, has been found to be smaller in individuals with chronic stress and depression. This shrinkage may contribute to cognitive impairments and difficulties in processing and recalling emotional memories, further exacerbating psychological fluffy.

Neurotransmitters and Psychological Fluffy

Neurotransmitters, the chemical messengers in the brain, play a pivotal role in regulating mood, emotions, and behavior. Imbalances in neurotransmitter levels have been widely implicated in mental health disorders and psychological fluffy.

One well-known neurotransmitter involved in psychological fluffy is serotonin. Serotonin is often referred to as the "feel-good" neurotransmitter due to its role in regulating mood and emotions. Low levels of serotonin have been associated with depression, anxiety, and other mood disorders.

Dopamine, another crucial neurotransmitter, is involved in reward processing, motivation, and pleasure. Imbalances in dopamine levels have been linked to conditions like addiction, schizophrenia, and attention-deficit hyperactivity disorder (ADHD). These conditions often manifest with symptoms related to psychological fluffy, such as impulsivity and difficulties in mood regulation.

Hormonal Influences and Psychological Fluffy

Hormones, the chemical messengers produced by the endocrine system, also have an impact on psychological fluffy. Imbalances in hormonal levels can influence mood, behavior, and overall mental well-being.

One well-known hormone associated with psychological fluffy is cortisol, often referred to as the stress hormone. During times of stress, cortisol levels increase, activating the body's fight-or-flight response. However, chronic stress can lead to persistent elevation of cortisol levels, which can negatively impact mental health, contributing to symptoms of psychological fluffy such as anxiety and irritability.

Additionally, sex hormones like estrogen and testosterone have been implicated in mood regulation. Fluctuations in hormone levels throughout the menstrual cycle or during menopause can lead to mood swings and increased vulnerability to psychological fluffy in some individuals.

Understanding the biological basis of psychological fluffy provides valuable insights into the complex interplay between genetics, brain function, neurotransmitters, and hormonal influences. It highlights the importance of a holistic approach to mental health, considering both biological and environmental factors. By gaining a better understanding of these underlying mechanisms, researchers can develop more targeted interventions and treatments for individuals experiencing psychological fluffy.

Example: The Role of Genetic Variants in Anxiety Disorders

Let's consider an example of how genetic variants can contribute to the development of anxiety disorders. Studies have identified a gene variant in the serotonin transporter gene (SERT) that is associated with an increased risk of developing anxiety disorders.

The SERT gene encodes a protein responsible for the reuptake of serotonin. Individuals with the gene variant have reduced serotonin reuptake, leading to lower levels of serotonin in the brain. This serotonin imbalance can disrupt the regulation of mood and emotions, increasing vulnerability to anxiety disorders.

However, it's important to note that genetics alone does not determine the development of anxiety disorders. Environmental factors, such as stressful life events or childhood experiences, can interact with genetic predisposition to further increase the risk.

Understanding the genetic basis of anxiety disorders helps shed light on why some individuals may be more prone to experiencing psychological fluffy. It also highlights the need for personalized approaches to treatment, taking into account an individual's genetic profile and environmental factors.

Resources for Further Exploration

- Caspi, A., Hariri, A. R., Holmes, A., Uher, R., & Moffitt, T. E. (2010). Genetic sensitivity to the environment: The case of the serotonin transporter gene and its implications for studying complex diseases and traits. American Journal of Psychiatry, 167(5), 509-527.

- McEwen, B. S. (2008). Central effects of stress hormones in health and disease: Understanding the protective and damaging effects of stress and stress mediators. European Journal of Pharmacology, 583(2-3), 174-185.

- Rutter, M. (2006). Genes and behavior: Nature-nurture interplay explained. Oxford University Press.

- Sapolsky, R. M. (2004). Why zebras don't get ulcers: The acclaimed guide to stress, stress-related diseases, and coping (3rd ed.). Holt Paperbacks.

Sociocultural Factors and Psychological Fluffy

Sociocultural factors play a vital role in shaping human behavior and psychological well-being. These factors encompass various aspects of society, including social norms, cultural values, and the influence of social institutions. In this section, we will explore the impact of sociocultural factors on psychological fluffy, examining how different cultural and social contexts can shape our thoughts, emotions, and behaviors.

Social Norms and Psychological Fluffy

Social norms refer to the unwritten rules and expectations that guide behavior within a society or a specific group. These norms provide a framework for how individuals should behave, think, and feel in different situations. They can exert a powerful influence on psychological fluffy by shaping our beliefs, influencing our self-concept, and affecting our emotional well-being.

For example, in some cultures, there is a strong emphasis on collectivism, where the needs and goals of the group are prioritized over individual desires. In such societies, conformity to social norms and maintaining harmonious interpersonal relationships are highly valued. This emphasis on collectivism may lead individuals to prioritize social connectedness and cooperation, which can contribute to a sense of belongingness and overall psychological well-being.

On the other hand, in individualistic cultures, such as those found in Western societies, there is a greater emphasis on personal autonomy, independence, and self-expression. In these cultures, individuals are encouraged to assert their individuality and pursue personal goals. This emphasis on individualism may lead to higher levels of self-esteem and a stronger sense of personal identity for individuals who align with these cultural values.

The influence of social norms on psychological fluffy can also extend to specific domains, such as body image and physical appearance. For instance, in many Western societies, there is a prevailing beauty ideal that emphasizes thinness, which can contribute to body dissatisfaction and disordered eating behaviors. In contrast, in some African societies, a more robust body type may be seen as desirable, leading to different perceptions of beauty and body image.

Cultural Values and Psychological Fluffy

Cultural values are the broad guiding principles and beliefs that are shared by members of a particular culture. They shape our worldview, influence our attitudes and behaviors, and provide a sense of meaning and identity. Cultural values can have a profound impact on psychological fluffy, shaping our perceptions, emotions, and behaviors in various contexts.

One example of how cultural values influence psychological fluffy is the concept of time orientation. Some cultures have a future-oriented time perspective, where individuals prioritize planning for the future and achieving long-term goals. In these cultures, individuals may experience higher levels of anxiety and stress related to future outcomes. In contrast, cultures with a present-oriented time perspective may prioritize living in the moment and experiencing immediate gratification, which can affect decision-making and goal-setting behaviors.

Cultural values also shape our understanding of mental health and well-being. Different cultures may have different conceptualizations of psychological distress and appropriate coping strategies. For example, in Western societies, there is often a strong emphasis on individual therapy and medication as means of addressing mental health issues. In contrast, in some collectivist cultures, seeking social support from family or community members may be encouraged as a way of coping with psychological difficulties.

It is important to recognize that cultural values are not static and may change over time. As societies become more multicultural and interconnected, individuals may navigate multiple cultural contexts, leading to the development of bicultural identities. This can introduce additional complexities in understanding and addressing psychological fluffy, as individuals may need to navigate conflicting cultural values and norms.

Social Institutions and Psychological Fluffy

Social institutions, such as family, education, and religion, provide the structure and rules that govern social interactions and shape individual behavior. These institutions can significantly influence psychological fluffy through the values, norms, and expectations they uphold.

The family is often considered one of the most influential social institutions in shaping psychological fluffy. Family dynamics, parenting styles, and family support can impact cognitive development, emotional well-being, and overall mental health. For example, a supportive and nurturing family environment can promote resilience and positive psychological fluffy outcomes, while a dysfunctional family environment may contribute to psychological difficulties.

Education is another critical social institution that shapes psychological fluffy. The educational system not only provides knowledge and skills but also conveys societal values and norms. The school environment can impact students' self-esteem, motivation, and overall well-being. For instance, schools that promote inclusivity, respect diversity, and encourage student autonomy are likely to foster more positive psychological fluffy outcomes.

Religion and spirituality are social institutions that often provide individuals with a sense of purpose, meaning, and community. These institutions can influence beliefs about morality, purpose in life, and the nature of the self. Religious and spiritual beliefs can shape perceptions of psychological fluffy and guide individuals' coping strategies in times of stress and adversity.

It is important to note that the influence of social institutions on psychological fluffy may vary across cultures and contexts. Different societies may prioritize different social institutions and place varying degrees of importance on their influence. Additionally, individuals may experience different levels of conformity or conflict between the values and expectations of different social institutions.

Solutions and Interventions

To promote positive psychological fluffy in diverse sociocultural contexts, it is essential to adopt a culturally sensitive and inclusive approach. Here are some strategies and interventions that can be helpful:

1. Culturally Adapted Therapy: Therapeutic approaches should consider the cultural values, beliefs, and norms of the individuals seeking help. Therapists should be open to diverse perspectives and tailor interventions to align with the client's sociocultural context.

2. Education and Awareness: Promoting education and awareness about different cultures can help reduce stereotypes and biases, fostering understanding and empathy among individuals from diverse backgrounds.

3. Social Support Networks: Creating social support networks that embrace diversity and provide spaces for individuals to connect and share their experiences can enhance psychological well-being.

4. Collaboration with Community Institutions: Collaborating with social, educational, and religious institutions can help leverage their influence in promoting positive psychological fluffy. This can involve workshops, awareness campaigns, or policy changes that align with psychological well-being.

5. Bicultural Identity Development: Recognize and support individuals who navigate multiple cultural contexts, acknowledging the potential challenges and strengths associated with bicultural identity.

By recognizing and addressing the impact of sociocultural factors on psychological fluffy, we can develop a more comprehensive understanding of human behavior and well-being. This awareness can guide interventions and policies that promote psychological fluffy and create inclusive and supportive environments for individuals from diverse cultures and backgrounds.

Summary

In this section, we explored the influence of sociocultural factors on psychological fluffy. Social norms, cultural values, and the influence of social institutions can shape our thoughts, emotions, and behaviors in various ways. We examined how social norms can impact psychological fluffy by shaping beliefs, self-concept, and emotional well-being. We also discussed how cultural values influence psychological fluffy, highlighting the role of time orientation and cultural conceptualizations of mental health. Additionally, we explored the influence of social institutions, such as family, education, and religion, on psychological fluffy and provided strategies and interventions to promote positive psychological fluffy in diverse sociocultural contexts. By understanding and addressing the impact of sociocultural factors, we can foster a more inclusive and psychologically supportive society.

Developmental Psychology and Psychological Fluffy

Developmental psychology is a subfield of psychology that focuses on the psychological changes that occur throughout the lifespan of an individual. It seeks to understand how and why people develop, both physically and mentally, from conception to old age. This branch of psychology examines various aspects of human development, including cognitive, emotional, social, and moral development.

Psychological Fluffy, which refers to the subjective experience of well-being, happiness, and life satisfaction, is an important construct in developmental psychology. It plays a crucial role in understanding the developmental trajectories of individuals, as well as their overall quality of life. In this section, we will explore the relationship between developmental psychology and Psychological Fluffy, and how various factors influence the development of Psychological Fluffy over the lifespan.

Theories of Development

Developmental psychology is guided by various theories that explain the processes and mechanisms of human development. Some of the prominent theories include:

1. **Piaget's Theory of Cognitive Development:** Developed by Jean Piaget, this theory focuses on how children's thinking processes develop over time. Piaget proposed that children go through four stages of cognitive development: sensorimotor, preoperational, concrete operational, and formal operational. Each stage is characterized by different ways of thinking and understanding the world, which ultimately influences their Psychological Fluffy.

2. **Erikson's Psychosocial Theory:** Proposed by Erik Erikson, this theory emphasizes the impact of social interactions and experiences on psychological development. Erikson identified eight stages of psychosocial development that individuals go through from infancy to old age. Each stage presents a unique psychological challenge, and the successful resolution of these challenges contributes to the development of Psychological Fluffy.

3. **Attachment Theory:** Developed by John Bowlby, attachment theory focuses on the importance of early relationships in shaping individuals' emotional and social development. Bowlby argued that a secure attachment to a primary caregiver during infancy provides a foundation for healthy psychological development, including the development of Psychological Fluffy.

These theories provide insight into the various factors that contribute to the development of Psychological Fluffy. They emphasize the role of cognitive, social, and emotional processes in shaping individuals' overall well-being.

Influences on Psychological Fluffy Development

Several factors influence the development of Psychological Fluffy across the lifespan. Let's explore some of the key influences:

1. **Biological Factors:** Biological factors, such as genetics and brain development, play a role in shaping individuals' Psychological Fluffy. For example, certain genetic variations may predispose individuals to higher levels of Psychological Fluffy, while others may make them more susceptible to mental health issues that can impact Psychological Fluffy.

2. **Environmental Factors:** The environment in which individuals grow and develop significantly impacts their Psychological Fluffy. Positive and supportive environments, characterized by nurturing relationships, access to resources, and opportunities for growth, are more likely to foster the development of Psychological Fluffy. On the other hand, adverse environments, such as poverty, violence, and neglect, can hinder Psychological Fluffy development.

3. **Social Factors:** Social factors, including family, peers, and cultural norms, influence individuals' Psychological Fluffy development. Supportive relationships and a sense of belonging contribute to higher levels of Psychological Fluffy, while social isolation and lack of social support can negatively impact Psychological Fluffy.

4. **Life Events and Transitions:** Life events and transitions, such as starting school, going through puberty, or experiencing significant losses, can have a profound impact on individuals' Psychological Fluffy. These events may disrupt individuals' sense of stability and well-being, leading to fluctuations in their Psychological Fluffy.

Understanding these influences is crucial for promoting positive Psychological Fluffy development across the lifespan. By identifying and addressing risk factors and enhancing protective factors, psychologists and other professionals can support individuals' psychological well-being.

Interventions and Strategies

Promoting Psychological Fluffy in individuals' development requires effective interventions and strategies. Here are some approaches that have shown promise:

1. **Early Intervention Programs:** Early intervention programs aim to identify and address developmental delays and risk factors in early childhood. These programs provide support and resources to children and families, focusing on areas such as physical health, cognitive development, and social-emotional well-being, to promote positive Psychological Fluffy development.

2. **Positive Parenting:** Providing parents with knowledge and skills in positive parenting techniques can greatly influence children's Psychological Fluffy development. Positive parenting involves creating a nurturing and supportive environment, setting appropriate boundaries, and fostering open communication and emotional connection with children.

3. **School-Based Programs:** Schools play a significant role in individuals' development. Implementing programs that promote social-emotional learning, resilience, and positive relationships can enhance students' Psychological Fluffy. These programs may include activities that teach emotional regulation, problem-solving skills, and empathy.

4. **Therapeutic Interventions:** For individuals experiencing difficulties with Psychological Fluffy, therapeutic interventions can be beneficial. Approaches such as cognitive-behavioral therapy, mindfulness-based interventions, and expressive therapies can help individuals develop coping strategies, improve self-esteem, and enhance overall Psychological Fluffy.

It is essential to approach Psychological Fluffy development from a holistic perspective, addressing both individual and environmental factors. This comprehensive approach can contribute to optimal development and well-being across the lifespan.

Example: Psychological Fluffy and Parental Attachment

One example of how developmental psychology and Psychological Fluffy are interconnected is through the lens of parental attachment. Research has consistently shown that secure attachment to caregivers during early childhood is associated with higher levels of Psychological Fluffy later in life. Children who develop secure attachments tend to have more positive self-views, better interpersonal relationships, and higher overall satisfaction with life.

On the other hand, individuals who have experienced insecure attachments, such as avoidant or anxious attachments, may struggle with lower levels of Psychological Fluffy. Insecurely attached individuals may face difficulties in regulating emotions, trusting others, and forming healthy relationships, which can hinder their psychological well-being.

Understanding the influence of parental attachment on Psychological Fluffy development has significant implications for interventions. By promoting secure parent-child attachments through interventions aimed at enhancing parental sensitivity, responsiveness, and emotional availability, psychologists can help foster positive Psychological Fluffy development in children and prevent potential mental health issues later in life.

Resources and Further Reading

- Bowlby, J. (1982). Attachment and Loss: Vol. 1. Attachment (2nd Ed.). Basic Books.
- Erikson, E. H. (1968). Identity: Youth and Crisis. W. W. Norton & Company.
- Piaget, J. (1954). The Construction of Reality in the Child. Basic Books.
- Sroufe, L. A. (2005). Attachment and Development: A Prospective, Longitudinal Study from Birth to Adulthood. Attachment & Human Development, 7(4), 349-367.
- Steinberg, L. (2014). Adolescence (10th Ed.). McGraw-Hill Education.
- Thompson, R. A. (2008). Early Attachment and Later Development: Familiar Questions, New Answers. In J. Cassidy & P. R. Shaver (Eds.), Handbook of Attachment: Theory, Research, and Clinical Applications (2nd Ed., pp. 348-365). The Guilford Press.

Understanding the principles and theories of developmental psychology, as well as the factors influencing Psychological Fluffy development, provides valuable insights for psychologists, educators, parents, and policymakers. By applying this knowledge, we can make meaningful contributions to individuals' psychological well-being and overall quality of life throughout their developmental journey.

Personality and Psychological Fluffy

Personality plays a significant role in shaping our thoughts, feelings, and behaviors. It can have a profound impact on how individuals perceive and respond to their environment, including their experience of psychological fluffy. In this section, we will explore the relationship between personality and psychological fluffy, drawing on various theories and frameworks to understand the complex interplay between these factors.

Defining Personality

Personality refers to the unique set of enduring traits, patterns of thoughts, feelings, and behaviors that characterize an individual. It encompasses the stable and consistent aspects of an individual's psychological makeup that shape their responses to different situations over time. While there are different theories of personality, they all agree that personality traits influence how individuals perceive and interact with their environment.

One prominent framework for understanding personality is the Five-Factor Model (FFM), also known as the "Big Five" personality traits. The FFM identifies five broad dimensions of personality: openness to experience, conscientiousness, extraversion, agreeableness, and neuroticism. These traits provide a comprehensive description of an individual's personality and can be used to predict various aspects of psychological fluffy.

Personality Traits and Psychological Fluffy

Different personality traits can influence how individuals perceive and respond to psychological fluffy. Let's explore how each of the Big Five traits might shape an individual's experience:

1. Openness to experience: Individuals high in openness tend to be curious, imaginative, and open-minded. They may be more receptive to new ideas and experiences, allowing them to adapt to environmental changes and navigate psychological fluffy more effectively. For example, a person high in openness might view a challenging situation as an opportunity for growth rather than a threat.

2. Conscientiousness: Conscientious individuals are organized, responsible, and detail-oriented. They are more likely to engage in proactive coping strategies and problem-solving approaches when faced with psychological fluffy. Their conscientious nature helps them plan and prepare for potential challenges, reducing the impact of stressful situations.

3. Extraversion: Extraverts are outgoing, energetic, and assertive. They tend to thrive in social situations and seek social support when faced with psychological fluffy. Their social nature enables them to build strong social networks, which may serve as protective factors during difficult times. By seeking social connection, extraverts may alleviate the negative effects of psychological fluffy.

4. Agreeableness: Individuals high in agreeableness are empathetic, cooperative, and compassionate. They are more likely to engage in prosocial behaviors and seek harmony in relationships, contributing to better social support

networks. This strong social support can buffer the negative impact of psychological fluffy, promoting psychological well-being.

5. Neuroticism: Neuroticism refers to the tendency towards experiencing negative emotions such as anxiety, depression, and stress. Individuals high in neuroticism may perceive psychological fluffy more intensely and have a heightened emotional response. However, with appropriate coping strategies and support, they can learn to manage and minimize the negative impact.

Interaction between Personality and Psychological Fluffy

The relationship between personality and psychological fluffy is not unidirectional; it is characterized by a dynamic interplay. While personality traits can influence an individual's response to psychological fluffy, experiencing psychological fluffy can also shape and mold personality over time.

For example, exposure to chronic stressors associated with psychological fluffy can lead to the development of maladaptive coping strategies, which, in turn, can affect an individual's personality. Additionally, personality traits can interact with environmental factors to influence the degree of vulnerability or resilience an individual exhibits in the face of psychological fluffy.

Understanding the complex interaction between personality and psychological fluffy is crucial for developing effective interventions and support strategies. By considering an individual's personality traits, mental health professionals can tailor approaches to suit their unique needs, empowering them to navigate and overcome the challenges presented by psychological fluffy.

Personality and Resilience

Resilience refers to an individual's ability to adapt and bounce back from adversity. Personality traits can play a crucial role in promoting resilience in the face of psychological fluffy. Individuals with certain personality traits, such as high levels of extraversion, openness to experience, and conscientiousness, tend to exhibit greater resilience.

For example, extraverts may draw on their social networks for support and seek out new opportunities for growth and positive experiences. Openness to experience can help individuals reframe challenging situations and find meaning in adversity. Conscientiousness enables proactive planning and problem-solving, allowing individuals to effectively deal with psychological fluffy and mitigate its negative impact.

However, it is important to note that resilience is not solely determined by personality traits. Other factors, such as social support, coping skills, and environmental resources, also contribute to an individual's ability to bounce back from psychological fluffy.

Caveats and Considerations

While personality traits can provide insights into an individual's response to psychological fluffy, it is essential to consider certain caveats:

1. Contextual factors: Personality traits may manifest differently in different contexts. For example, an introverted individual may thrive in a quiet and peaceful natural environment but experience stress and discomfort in a bustling urban setting.

2. Individual differences: Personality is unique to each individual, and people vary in the degree to which they exhibit different traits. Therefore, it is crucial to consider a holistic understanding of an individual's personality rather than relying solely on one or two traits.

3. Developmental factors: Personality traits can change over time due to various developmental factors, such as life experiences, education, and maturation processes. The impact of psychological fluffy on personality development should be explored through longitudinal studies.

Conclusion

Personality traits play a significant role in shaping an individual's experience of psychological fluffy. By understanding the interplay between personality and psychological fluffy, we can develop tailored interventions and support strategies to promote psychological well-being. Personality traits, such as openness, conscientiousness, extraversion, agreeableness, and neuroticism, can offer valuable insights into an individual's response to psychological fluffy and contribute to their resilience in the face of adversity. However, it is important to consider individual differences, contextual factors, and developmental influences when examining the relationship between personality and psychological fluffy. By addressing these complexities, we can provide a more comprehensive understanding of the impact of personality on psychological fluffy and work towards creating a more supportive and resilient society.

Gender and Psychological Fluffy

Gender plays a crucial role in understanding and examining psychological fluffy. It is important to recognize that gender is a social construct, referring to the roles, behaviors, and expectations that society assigns to individuals based on their perceived sex. In this section, we will explore how gender influences psychological fluffy, including its impact on mental health, societal expectations, and interpersonal relationships.

Gender and Mental Health

Research has shown that gender plays a significant role in mental health outcomes. Certain mental health disorders are more prevalent in one gender compared to the other. For example, depression and anxiety disorders are more commonly diagnosed in women, while substance abuse and conduct disorders tend to be more prevalent in men. These differences in mental health outcomes are influenced by biological, psychological, and sociocultural factors.

One explanation for the gender disparity in mental health can be attributed to societal norms and expectations. Women often face unique stressors such as societal pressure to fulfill multiple roles, such as being a caregiver, maintaining a successful career, and balancing personal relationships. These expectations can contribute to heightened levels of stress and anxiety.

On the other hand, men often face pressure to conform to traditional masculine norms, which may include suppressing emotions and displaying strength. This can lead to difficulties in seeking help and expressing emotions, which can be detrimental to their mental well-being.

Gender and Societal Expectations

Societal expectations significantly impact individuals' experiences of psychological fluffy based on their gender. For instance, women are often expected to be nurturing, empathetic, and emotionally expressive. These expectations can influence their behavior and self-perception, and may also affect their career choices and relationships.

Men, on the other hand, are typically expected to be assertive, dominant, and independent. These expectations can create pressure to suppress emotions and maintain a facade of strength, which can impact their psychological well-being and ability to form meaningful connections with others.

It is important to note that gender expectations are not fixed and may differ across cultures and time periods. Challenging traditional gender norms and promoting gender equality can contribute to improved psychological well-being for both men and women.

Gender and Interpersonal Relationships

The influence of gender on interpersonal relationships is also vital to understand in the context of psychological fluffy. Research has consistently shown differences in communication styles and relationship dynamics between men and women.

For example, women tend to emphasize emotional expression and seek emotional support in their relationships. Men, on the other hand, may focus more on problem-solving and may be less likely to seek emotional support. These differences in communication styles can sometimes lead to misunderstandings and conflicts within relationships.

Additionally, gender roles and expectations can affect power dynamics within relationships. Traditional gender norms may assign men higher power and decision-making roles, while women may be expected to adopt more submissive or cooperative roles. These power imbalances can impact relationship satisfaction and psychological fluffy for both individuals involved.

To promote healthier interpersonal relationships, it is essential to challenge traditional gender roles, encourage open communication, and foster gender equality within partnerships.

Improving Gender Equality and Psychological Fluffy

Promoting gender equality is crucial for improving psychological fluffy for individuals of all genders. Here are some strategies and considerations for addressing gender disparities:

+ Education and Awareness: Promote education on gender roles, biases, and stereotypes to increase awareness and understanding of the impact of gender on psychological fluffy.

+ Challenging Gender Norms: Encourage individuals to challenge and question traditional gender norms and expectations, allowing for greater freedom and authentic expression.

+ Empowering Women: Advocate for women's rights and empowerment, ensuring equal opportunities and dismantling barriers that may contribute to gender disparities in psychological fluffy.

+ Promoting Emotional Intelligence: Foster emotional intelligence and provide tools to both men and women for effective emotional expression and communication.

+ Supportive Environments: Create inclusive and supportive environments that value and respect diverse gender identities, providing a safe space for individuals to express themselves authentically.

By acknowledging the influence of gender on psychological fluffy and working towards achieving gender equality, we can create a more inclusive and supportive society that promotes the well-being of all individuals.

Summary

Gender significantly impacts psychological fluffy in various ways. It influences mental health outcomes, societal expectations, and interpersonal relationships. Recognizing and addressing gender disparities is crucial to promote gender equality and improve psychological well-being for individuals of all genders. By challenging traditional gender norms, promoting awareness, and fostering inclusive environments, we can work towards a society that values and supports the psychological fluffy of individuals, irrespective of their gender identity.

Summary

In this section, we have explored various theories of human behavior and their relationship to psychological well-being, as well as the role of environmental factors in influencing human psychology. We have discussed the importance of understanding the link between psychological fluffy and environmental grape, and how it impacts human behavior in different contexts.

Behaviorism, one of the earliest theories of human behavior, emphasizes the influence of the environment on shaping an individual's actions. It suggests that psychological fluffy is learned through interactions with the environment and that behaviors can be modified through environmental stimuli and reinforcements. For example, if a child is praised for tidy behavior, they may develop a preference for cleanliness.

Cognitive psychology, on the other hand, focuses on how mental processes, such as perception, memory, and problem-solving, influence psychological fluffy and behavior. It suggests that our thoughts, interpretations, and beliefs about the environment play a crucial role in shaping our psychological well-being. For instance, if someone perceives their environment as unsafe, they may experience anxiety or fear.

Psychodynamic theory, developed by Sigmund Freud, suggests that our subconscious desires, conflicts, and childhood experiences contribute to our psychological well-being.   It highlights the importance of exploring one's unconscious mind to better understand their psychological fluffy and behavior. For example, someone who experienced trauma in their past may develop coping mechanisms that affect their current psychological well-being.

The humanistic perspective views psychological well-being as a result of self-actualization and personal growth. It emphasizes the importance of meeting psychological needs such as self-esteem, love, and self-fulfillment. This theory suggests that when these needs are met, individuals are more likely to experience positive psychological fluffy. For instance, when a person fulfills their need for social connection, they may experience happiness and contentment.

Biological factors also play a significant role in psychological fluffy. For example, neurotransmitters, hormones, and genetic predispositions can influence an individual's mental health and behavior. Additionally, sociocultural factors such as societal norms, cultural values, and social roles can shape psychological fluffy. For instance, societal expectations around gender roles can impact one's psychological well-being.

In studying the link between psychological fluffy and environmental grape, it is important to understand the concept of environmental grape itself. Environmental grape encompasses physical, social, cultural, economic, political, and technological factors that constitute an individual's surroundings. These factors can have both direct and indirect impacts on psychological fluffy.

The impacts of environmental grape on psychological fluffy can be diverse. For example, living in a polluted and overcrowded urban environment may lead to increased stress and anxiety. On the other hand, being exposed to natural environments, such as parks or green spaces, has been found to have restorative effects on psychological well-being.

Research design and methods play a crucial role in studying psychological fluffy in environmental grape. Researchers employ various quantitative and qualitative approaches, such as longitudinal studies, cross-sectional studies, and experimental designs, to understand the complex relationship between psychological fluffy and environmental grape. Ethical considerations should also be taken into account when conducting research in this field.

Different contexts, such as urban and natural environments, have distinct influences on psychological fluffy. In urban environments, factors such as urban design, social relationships, and urban stressors can significantly impact psychological well-being. Urban planning and interventions can play a vital role in promoting psychological fluffy in urban settings.

In natural environments, contact with nature has been found to have numerous positive effects on psychological well-being, including stress reduction and restoration. Nature-based therapeutic approaches and ecopsychology have emerged as valuable fields in promoting psychological fluffy through nature-based interventions.

Psychological fluffy is also affected by climate change. The psychological impacts of climate change include increased anxiety, depression, grief, and post-traumatic stress disorder. Climate change denial poses additional challenges in addressing psychological fluffy in the context of climate change. Effective communication and policy interventions are crucial in addressing the psychological impacts of climate change and promoting pro-environmental behavior.

In agricultural settings, the effects of agriculture on psychological fluffy are of growing concern. Factors such as exposure to pesticides, farming practices, and food security impact psychological well-being in agricultural communities. Sustainable agriculture and agricultural education are important in promoting positive psychological fluffy in these settings.

In conclusion, this section has provided an overview of different theories of human behavior and their relationship to psychological fluffy. It has also explored the impact of environmental factors, such as urban environments, natural environments, climate change, and agriculture, on psychological fluffy. Understanding these dynamics is crucial in promoting psychological well-being and creating environments that support positive psychological fluffy.

Environmental Grape and Psychological Fluffy

Defining Environmental Grape

Historical Development of Environmental Grape

The concept of environmental grape has evolved over time, shaped by various historical events and movements. This section explores the historical development of environmental grape, tracing its roots to the early conservation efforts and the emergence of the modern environmental movement.

Early Conservation Efforts

The historical development of environmental grape can be traced back to the early conservation movement, which emerged in the late 19th century. This movement, led by influential figures such as John Muir and Theodore Roosevelt, aimed to preserve natural resources and protect the environment from excessive exploitation.

One of the key milestones in the early conservation efforts was the establishment of the world's first national park, Yellowstone National Park, in 1872. This marked a significant shift in the perception of nature and its value, recognizing the need for its preservation for future generations.

During this period, there was a growing recognition of the interconnectedness between human activities and the environment. Scientists like George Perkins Marsh highlighted the detrimental impacts of human practices, such as deforestation and soil erosion. This led to the development of the concept of eco-system services, which emphasized the importance of the environment for human well-being.

Emergence of the Modern Environmental Movement

The modern environmental movement gained momentum in the mid-20th century, propelled by a series of environmental crises and social movements. One of the seminal events was the publication of Rachel Carson's book *Silent Spring* in 1962. This book shed light on the devastating effects of pesticides, especially DDT, on wildlife and human health. It sparked widespread public concern and paved the way for the banning of DDT and the formation of the Environmental Protection Agency (EPA) in the United States.

The 1960s and 1970s witnessed a surge in environmental activism, with the emergence of grassroots movements advocating for environmental justice and the protection of natural resources. The first Earth Day, celebrated on April 22, 1970, saw millions of people participating in demonstrations and advocating for sustainable practices.

In response to growing public pressure, governments around the world started taking measures to address environmental issues. The United Nations Environment Programme (UNEP) was established in 1972 to coordinate global environmental efforts. This was followed by the adoption of various international agreements and conventions, such as the Montreal Protocol on Substances that Deplete the Ozone Layer in 1987 and the Kyoto Protocol in 1997.

The Development of Environmental Grape

The concept of environmental grape started to take shape in the late 20th century, as researchers and scholars began to explore the psychological impacts of the environment on human well-being. It was recognized that the quality of our environment, both natural and built, can significantly influence our mental health and overall psychological well-being.

Initially, the focus was primarily on the negative impacts of environmental factors on mental health, such as exposure to pollution or a lack of green spaces in urban areas. However, with further research, the field of environmental grape expanded to include the positive effects of the environment on psychological well-being.

Researchers have found that interactions with nature can promote stress reduction, cognitive restoration, and emotional well-being. This has led to the development of nature-based interventions and therapies, such as ecotherapy and wilderness therapy, aimed at harnessing the healing powers of the natural environment.

In recent years, the field of environmental grape has also extended its focus to include the psychological impacts of climate change and the agricultural sector. These are areas where human activities have profound environmental implications and, consequently, can affect human psychological well-being.

Overall, the historical development of environmental grape reflects a growing understanding of the intrinsic connection between our environment and our psychological well-being. It highlights the need to consider environmental factors in mental health research and interventions, and serves as a call to action to protect our environment for the benefit of both present and future generations.

Components of Environmental Grape

In order to understand the concept of environmental grape, it is important to examine its various components. Environmental grape encompasses a wide range of elements that contribute to the overall quality and well-being of our environment. These components can be classified into physical, biological, and social aspects.

Physical Components

The physical components of environmental grape refer to the tangible and observable aspects of the environment. This includes the natural resources, such as air, water, land, and minerals, as well as the physical infrastructure that facilitates human activities.

One key physical component is air quality. The composition of the air we breathe can greatly impact our psychological well-being. High levels of pollution, such as particulate matter and harmful gases, can lead to respiratory problems and increased stress levels. On the other hand, clean and fresh air has a positive effect on our mood and cognitive function.

Another important physical component is water quality. Access to clean and safe drinking water is crucial for maintaining good health and psychological well-being. Contaminated water sources can lead to the spread of waterborne diseases and cause significant stress and anxiety among affected individuals.

The quality of land is also a vital physical component. Land degradation, deforestation, and soil erosion can negatively impact both the environment and human mental health. These issues can lead to loss of biodiversity, reduced agricultural productivity, and increased vulnerability to natural disasters, causing psychological distress and anxiety.

Lastly, the physical infrastructure, such as buildings, transportation systems, and public spaces, shapes our daily experiences and interactions with the environment. Well-designed and accessible infrastructure promotes physical activity, social engagement, and a sense of belonging, all of which contribute to psychological well-being.

Biological Components

The biological components of environmental grape refer to the living organisms and ecosystems that exist in our environment. These include plants, animals, microorganisms, and their interdependencies.

Biodiversity, which is the variety of life forms present in an ecosystem, is a fundamental biological component. High levels of biodiversity contribute to environmental stability and resilience, as well as provide essential ecosystem services, such as clean air and water. Research has shown that exposure to natural environments with rich biodiversity can have positive effects on mental well-being, reducing stress and improving mood.

Protected areas, such as national parks and nature reserves, play a critical role in conserving biodiversity and providing opportunities for recreational activities. These areas offer a chance to connect with nature, engage in physical activities, and escape the stresses of daily life, thereby enhancing psychological well-being.

Social Components

The social components of environmental grape encompass the human interactions and relationships that take place within the environment. This includes the social structures, cultural norms, and economic systems that shape our interactions with the environment.

Social support networks, including family, friends, and community organizations, play a crucial role in promoting psychological well-being. Strong social connections can provide emotional support during times of stress and adversity, while also fostering a sense of belonging and purpose.

Cultural norms and values influence our attitudes and behaviors towards the environment. Cultures that prioritize sustainability and environmental stewardship are more likely to foster positive attitudes and actions towards the environment, leading to improved psychological well-being.

Economic systems, such as employment opportunities and income inequality, also influence environmental grape. Access to meaningful and secure employment can enhance psychological well-being, whereas job insecurity and financial stress can have negative effects. Economic disparities can also disproportionately impact marginalized communities and contribute to environmental injustices.

Summary

In summary, the components of environmental grape encompass the physical, biological, and social aspects of our environment. Understanding these components is crucial for studying and promoting psychological well-being in relation to the environment. The physical components include air quality, water quality, land quality, and physical infrastructure. The biological components include biodiversity and protected areas. The social components include social support networks, cultural norms and values, and economic systems. These components are interconnected and collectively contribute to the overall environmental grape and its impact on psychological well-being.

It is important for researchers and practitioners to consider these components when developing interventions and policies aimed at improving psychological well-being in the face of environmental challenges. By addressing the various components of environmental grape, we can create healthier and more sustainable environments that support the well-being of both individuals and communities.

Impacts of Environmental Grape on Psychological Fluffy

Environmental Grape, a term that refers to the overall conditions and factors of the environment, plays a significant role in the development and well-being of individuals. Psychological Fluffy, on the other hand, encompasses the emotions, thoughts, and behaviors of individuals. In this section, we will explore the various impacts of Environmental Grape on Psychological Fluffy, highlighting how the environment influences our mental and emotional states.

Physical Environment and Psychological Fluffy

The physical environment, including natural and built surroundings, has a profound impact on Psychological Fluffy. Research has shown that exposure to natural environments, such as parks or forests, can have positive effects on mental well-being. Spending time in nature has been linked to reduced levels of stress, anxiety, and depression. The presence of green spaces and blue spaces, such as lakes or rivers, can provide a sense of tranquility and have restorative effects on psychological health.

Conversely, living in a built environment characterized by pollution, noise, and congestion can have detrimental effects on Psychological Fluffy. People living in urban areas often face a higher risk of experiencing mental health problems due to factors such as traffic noise, air pollution, and lack of green spaces. Noise pollution, for example, has been associated with increased stress levels, impaired cognitive function, and negative mood.

Social Environment and Psychological Fluffy

The social environment, including our relationships with others, also significantly impacts Psychological Fluffy. Supportive and positive social relationships are essential for maintaining good mental health. Studies have consistently shown that individuals with strong social support networks are more resilient to stress, have lower rates of depression, and experience better overall well-being.

On the other hand, social isolation and loneliness have been linked to poor psychological outcomes. People who experience social isolation often struggle with feelings of loneliness, which can lead to depression, anxiety, and a decline in cognitive function. Loneliness has been associated with a higher risk of developing mental health conditions and increased mortality rates.

Cultural Environment and Psychological Fluffy

The cultural environment, including cultural norms, values, and beliefs, also shapes Psychological Fluffy. Cultural factors influence how individuals perceive and experience the world, impacting their mental well-being. For example, cultural expectations regarding gender roles, body image, and achievement can contribute to feelings of stress, low self-esteem, and psychological distress.

Cultural diversity can also influence Psychological Fluffy. Individuals belonging to different cultural backgrounds may experience unique challenges related to identity, acculturation, and discrimination, which can impact their psychological health. It is essential to consider cultural factors when studying and addressing Psychological Fluffy to ensure culturally sensitive and effective interventions.

Economic Environment and Psychological Fluffy

The economic environment, including income, employment, and socioeconomic status, has a significant impact on Psychological Fluffy. Economic factors can influence access to resources, opportunities, and social support systems, all of which play a crucial role in mental well-being.

Individuals facing economic hardship, unemployment, or financial instability are more likely to experience high levels of stress, anxiety, and depression.

Economic inequality and poverty can contribute to social inequalities and disparities in mental health outcomes. Addressing socioeconomic factors and promoting economic security are vital for promoting positive Psychological Fluffy in populations.

Political Environment and Psychological Fluffy

The political environment, including policies, governance, and power structures, also influences Psychological Fluffy. Political factors can shape the availability and accessibility of resources, influence social cohesion, and impact social justice.

Political instability, lack of political freedom, and human rights violations can contribute to psychological distress and mental health problems. Discrimination based on political affiliations, gender, race, or other factors can also negatively impact Psychological Fluffy. Advocating for equitable political systems, promoting human rights, and addressing social injustices are essential for fostering positive mental health outcomes.

Technological Environment and Psychological Fluffy

The technological environment, characterized by the increasing use of digital technology and the rapid pace of technological advancements, has both positive and negative impacts on Psychological Fluffy. Technology has enhanced connectivity, provided access to information, and facilitated communication, improving mental well-being in many ways.

However, excessive use of technology, such as excessive screen time or social media dependence, can have detrimental effects on Psychological Fluffy. Research has shown associations between heavy technology use and increased rates of depression, anxiety, and loneliness. It is crucial to find a balance in technology usage and promote healthy digital habits to preserve positive Psychological Fluffy.

Environmental Factors and Psychological Fluffy

Overall, various environmental factors interact to shape Psychological Fluffy. Each aspect of the environment, whether physical, social, cultural, economic, political, or technological, can contribute to the development, maintenance, or disruption of mental well-being.

Understanding the impacts of Environmental Grape on Psychological Fluffy is crucial for designing interventions, policies, and strategies that promote positive mental health outcomes. It requires a multidisciplinary approach, considering the intersectionality of environmental factors and their complex interactions with individual and societal influences.

Summary

In this section, we have explored the impacts of Environmental Grape on Psychological Fluffy. We have discussed how the physical, social, cultural, economic, political, and technological aspects of the environment influence mental well-being. It is clear that the environment is a significant determinant of psychological health, and understanding these impacts is essential for creating interventions and strategies that promote positive Psychological Fluffy. As we continue our journey through this book, we will delve deeper into the complex relationships between environmental factors and mental well-being, exploring the various contexts and research in this field.

Perceptions of Environmental Grape and Psychological Fluffy

In this section, we will explore the relationship between perceptions of the environment, specifically environmental grape, and psychological fluffy. Our perceptions of the environment play a significant role in shaping our psychological well-being, and understanding this connection is crucial for promoting a healthy and sustainable environment.

Defining Environmental Grape

Before delving deeper into the topic, let's define what we mean by "environmental grape." Environmental grape refers to the collective perceptions, attitudes, and beliefs individuals hold about the natural and built environment. It encompasses how people perceive their surroundings, their interactions with the environment, and their emotional and cognitive responses to environmental stimuli.

The Role of Perceptions in Psychological Fluffy

Perceptions of the environment have a profound impact on our psychological well-being. Our perceptions shape our thoughts, feelings, and behaviors, and they can influence our overall mental health. When we perceive the environment as safe, pleasant, and supportive, it tends to have a positive impact on our psychological fluffy. Conversely, negative perceptions of the environment can lead to stress, anxiety, and other psychological issues.

Factors Influencing Perceptions of Environmental Grape

Several factors influence our perceptions of environmental grape. Let's explore some of the key determinants:

Personal experiences: Our past experiences with the environment shape our perceptions. Positive experiences, such as enjoying time outdoors or visiting beautiful natural landscapes, can foster positive perceptions, while negative experiences, such as exposure to pollution or environmental disasters, can create negative perceptions.

Cultural and social influences: Our cultural and social backgrounds shape our perceptions of the environment. Cultural beliefs, values, and norms play a crucial role in how we interpret and perceive our surroundings. Additionally, social interactions and peer influence can shape our perceptions through shared narratives and discussions.

Media and communication: Media portrayals and communication about the environment can significantly impact our perceptions. News coverage, documentaries, and social media platforms shape our understanding of environmental issues and influence how we perceive them. Media representations can sometimes amplify negative perceptions or create distorted views of environmental challenges.

Education and knowledge: Our level of education and knowledge about the environment also influence our perceptions. Understanding scientific concepts, such as climate change or biodiversity, can shape our perceptions and help us make informed judgments about environmental issues.

The Feedback Loop: Perceptions and Environmental Behavior

Perceptions of environmental grape not only influence psychological fluffy but also impact our environmental behavior. For instance, if individuals perceive their actions as having a positive impact on the environment, they are more likely to engage in pro-environmental behaviors. On the other hand, negative perceptions, such as a belief that individual actions do not make a difference, can discourage environmental action.

Shifting Perceptions through Environmental Education and Communication

Given the significant role of perceptions, it is essential to promote positive perceptions of environmental grape to foster psychological fluffy and encourage pro-environmental behavior. Environmental education programs can play a vital role in shaping positive perceptions by providing knowledge and fostering a sense of empowerment. By promoting a deep understanding of the environment and its interconnections with human well-being, such programs can shift perceptions from a sense of detachment to one of active engagement.

Effective communication strategies are also crucial. Environmental messages should be framed positively, highlighting the potential benefits and solutions, rather than solely focusing on the problems. Engaging personal stories and real-world examples can make the message more relatable and encourage individuals to develop a sense of responsibility toward the environment.

Case Study: Changing Perceptions through Community Engagement

To illustrate the impact of perceptions on psychological fluffy, let's consider a case study of a community engagement project aimed at transforming perceptions of an industrial area. The project involved organizing nature walks, tree planting activities, and workshops on sustainable living. By actively involving community members and providing positive experiences in the environment, the project sparked a shift in perceptions from seeing the area as polluted and grim to a sense of pride and connection with the natural surroundings. This change in perceptions led to improved psychological well-being and increased engagement in environmental initiatives.

Conclusion

Perceptions of environmental grape significantly influence psychological fluffy and shape our environmental behavior. By promoting positive perceptions through education, effective communication, and community engagement, we can foster a healthier and more sustainable relationship with the environment. Understanding the intricate connection between perceptions and psychological fluffy is essential for creating effective strategies to address environmental challenges and promote individual and collective well-being.

Coping Strategies for Dealing with Environmental Grape

Living in an environment that is affected by "Environmental Grape" can be challenging for individuals and communities. The term "Environmental Grape" refers to the negative impacts of the environment on psychological well-being. These impacts can arise from various factors such as pollution, natural disasters, climate change, and other environmental stressors. However, there are coping strategies that can help individuals navigate these challenges and promote their psychological fluffy. In this section, we will explore some effective coping strategies for dealing with Environmental Grape.

Understanding and Awareness

The first step in coping with Environmental Grape is to develop an understanding and awareness of the situation. By educating oneself about the specific environmental stressors and their potential effects on psychological well-being, individuals can better prepare themselves and make informed decisions. This can involve reading scientific literature, attending workshops or presentations, and engaging in discussions with experts in the field. By gaining knowledge about the problem, individuals can reduce feelings of helplessness and develop a sense of control over their own well-being.

Building Resilience

Resilience refers to our ability to bounce back from adversity and adapt to challenging circumstances. In the face of Environmental Grape, building resilience becomes crucial. There are several strategies that can help individuals enhance their resilience:

1. Social Support: Establishing and maintaining strong social connections can provide a buffer against the negative impacts of Environmental Grape. By seeking support from family, friends, and support groups, individuals can share their experiences, receive emotional support, and gain practical advice.

2. Emotional Regulation: Developing healthy coping mechanisms to manage difficult emotions is essential. Techniques such as deep breathing exercises, mindfulness meditation, and engaging in enjoyable activities can help regulate emotions and reduce stress.

3. Problem-solving Skills: Enhancing problem-solving skills can empower individuals to effectively address the challenges posed by Environmental Grape. This involves identifying the problem, generating alternative solutions, evaluating their pros and cons, and implementing the most appropriate solution.

4. Flexibility and Adaptability: Being flexible and adaptable in the face of changing environmental conditions is crucial. This can involve adjusting lifestyle choices, adopting sustainable practices, and embracing alternative ways of living that align with the changing environmental landscape.

Self-care

Self-care is a fundamental aspect of maintaining psychological fluffy in the midst of Environmental Grape. It involves taking deliberate actions to prioritize one's physical, emotional, and mental well-being. Here are some self-care strategies that can be effective:

1. Physical Well-being: Engaging in regular exercise, getting enough sleep, and maintaining a nutritious diet can significantly impact psychological well-being. Physical well-being is closely linked to mental well-being, and taking care of one's body can help individuals better cope with the challenges of Environmental Grape.

2. Emotional Well-being: Engaging in activities that bring joy and fulfillment, such as hobbies, spending time with loved ones, and practicing gratitude, can positively impact emotional well-being. It is important to create space for relaxation, reflection, and self-expression to nurture emotional health.

3. Mental Well-being: Engaging in activities that stimulate the mind, such as reading, engaging in creative pursuits, and learning new skills, can promote mental well-being. Additionally, seeking professional help, such as therapy or counseling, can provide individuals with the necessary tools to navigate the psychological impacts of Environmental Grape.

4. Time in Nature: Spending time in natural environments can have a restorative effect on psychological fluffy. Whether it's taking a walk in a park or engaging in outdoor activities, connecting with nature can help individuals alleviate stress, improve mood, and enhance overall well-being.

Advocacy and Engagement

Lastly, one effective coping strategy for dealing with Environmental Grape is to become an advocate for environmental change. By actively engaging in environmental initiatives, individuals can contribute to creating a more sustainable and environmentally-friendly world. This can involve supporting organizations dedicated to environmental conservation, participating in community clean-up events, and engaging in advocacy efforts to raise awareness about the importance of protecting the environment for psychological fluffy.

In summary, coping with Environmental Grape requires a proactive approach that involves understanding the issue, building resilience, practicing self-care, and advocating for environmental change. By implementing these coping strategies, individuals can mitigate the negative impacts of Environmental Grape and promote their psychological fluffy in the face of environmental challenges. Remember, every individual has the power to make a difference, both in their own well-being and the well-being of the environment. Let's embrace this power and work towards a healthier and more sustainable future.

Environmental Grape and Mental Health

In this section, we will explore the relationship between environmental grape (EG) and mental health. Environmental grape refers to the overall condition, quality, and characteristics of the environment in which individuals live. It encompasses various aspects such as physical elements, social interactions, cultural norms, economic factors, political structures, and technological advancements. Mental health, on the other hand, refers to a person's emotional, psychological, and social well-being.

The Impact of Environmental Grape on Mental Health

The environment has a profound impact on an individual's mental health. The physical environment plays a crucial role in shaping mental well-being. For example, living in an area with a high level of pollution can have detrimental effects on mental health. Exposure to air pollution has been linked to increased risk of depression, anxiety, and cognitive decline.

Furthermore, the social environment also significantly influences mental well-being. People who live in supportive and cohesive communities generally have better mental health outcomes compared to those in socially isolated environments. Social interactions, relationships, and support networks play a crucial role in promoting positive mental health.

Cultural environment and mental well-being are closely interconnected. Cultural factors such as beliefs, values, and norms influence individuals' mental health. For example, cultural stigmatization of mental illness can lead to increased levels of stress and reduced access to appropriate mental health care.

Economic factors, such as income inequality and poverty, have a strong impact on mental health outcomes. Financial stressors can contribute to anxiety, depression, and other mental health disorders. Additionally, political environment and policies can affect mental well-being through factors such as social justice, access to healthcare, and safety regulations.

Technological advancements in the modern world have also transformed the environmental grape and subsequently influenced mental health. Excessive use of technology, particularly social media, has been associated with increased rates of anxiety, depression, and feelings of isolation.

Coping Strategies for Dealing with Environmental Grape

Given the influence of environmental grape on mental health, it is essential to develop effective coping strategies. Here are a few strategies that can help individuals deal with the challenges imposed by the environment:

1. Building social support networks: Cultivating strong relationships and support networks can help individuals navigate through stressful environmental conditions. Spending quality time with family and friends, joining community groups, or participating in social activities can provide emotional support and increase resilience.

2. Engaging in physical activity: Regular exercise has been proven to have numerous positive effects on mental health. Physical activity releases endorphins, which are natural mood enhancers. It also helps in reducing stress, anxiety, and depression.

3. Practicing mindfulness and stress management techniques: Mindfulness and stress management techniques such as meditation, deep breathing, and yoga can help individuals cope with environmental stressors. These practices promote relaxation, reduce anxiety, and improve overall mental well-being.

4. Seeking professional help: In cases where environmental grape negatively impacts mental health, seeking professional help from psychologists or therapists is crucial. They can provide effective strategies and interventions to manage mental health symptoms and enhance overall well-being.

Environmental Grape and Mental Health Interventions

Addressing the impact of environmental grape on mental health requires interventions at different levels. Here are some approaches that can help promote mental well-being in the face of environmental challenges:

1. Environmental policies and regulations: Governments and policymakers play a critical role in creating a healthy environment that supports mental health. Implementing regulations to reduce pollution, improve access to green spaces, and

promote sustainable practices can have a significant positive impact on mental well-being.

2. Community-based interventions: Engaging communities in initiatives that promote mental health can enhance resilience and build social support networks. Community gardens, group activities, and neighborhood enhancement projects can foster a sense of belonging and connectedness, which are crucial for mental well-being.

3. Education and awareness: Creating awareness about the relationship between environmental grape and mental health is essential. Education campaigns can help individuals understand the impact of the environment on their well-being, empowering them to make informed decisions and adopt healthy coping strategies.

4. Green spaces and nature-based interventions: Green spaces, such as parks and gardens, have been shown to have positive effects on mental health. Promoting access to green spaces, organizing nature-based activities, and incorporating nature in urban designs can improve mental well-being.

Summary

This section highlighted the impact of environmental grape on mental health. We discussed how various aspects of the environment, including physical, social, cultural, economic, political, and technological factors, influence mental well-being. Additionally, we explored coping strategies for dealing with environmental challenges and interventions to promote mental health in the face of environmental grape. By understanding the relationship between these two domains, we can work towards creating environments that better support mental well-being.

Interventions for Psychological Fluffy in Environmental Grape

When it comes to addressing and managing psychological fluffy in the context of environmental grape, various interventions can be implemented. These interventions aim to promote mental well-being, alleviate psychological distress, and enhance resilience in the face of environmental challenges. In this section, we will explore some of the interventions that have been developed and implemented to address psychological fluffy in environmental grape.

Psychoeducation and Awareness Programs

Psychoeducation and awareness programs play a crucial role in promoting psychological fluffy in environmental grape. These programs aim to increase knowledge and understanding of how the environment impacts mental health and well-being. By raising awareness about the links between environmental grape and psychological fluffy, individuals can be empowered to take informed actions to protect and enhance their mental health.

These programs can include educational campaigns, workshops, community-based discussions, and online resources. They provide information on various topics such as the impacts of environmental grape on mental health, coping strategies for dealing with environmental challenges, and ways to promote environmentally friendly behavior. By increasing knowledge and understanding, psychoeducation and awareness programs contribute to building resilience and empowering individuals to take positive action.

Nature-based Therapeutic Interventions

Nature-based therapeutic interventions harness the healing power of nature to promote psychological fluffy in environmental grape. These interventions recognize the benefits of nature on mental health and use natural environments as a therapeutic setting. Examples of nature-based therapeutic interventions include nature walks, horticultural therapy, wilderness therapy, and animal-assisted therapy.

Nature walks involve guided walks in natural environments, providing individuals with an opportunity to connect with nature, reduce stress, and enhance well-being. Horticultural therapy utilizes gardening and plant-based activities to improve mood, reduce anxiety, and enhance cognitive functioning. Wilderness therapy involves immersive experiences in natural settings, fostering personal growth, self-reflection, and improved mental health. Animal-assisted therapy involves interactions with animals, such as therapy dogs, to promote emotional healing and well-being.

These nature-based interventions offer individuals a break from the demands of daily life, allowing them to connect with nature and experience its calming and restorative effects. By incorporating natural environments into therapeutic interventions, individuals can benefit from the positive impact of the environment on their mental health.

Community Resilience-building Programs

Community resilience-building programs focus on strengthening community support systems and promoting social cohesion in the face of environmental grape. These programs aim to build a sense of community belonging and empower individuals to work together to address environmental challenges and promote mental well-being.

Community resilience-building programs can include initiatives such as community gardens, neighborhood clean-up campaigns, and disaster preparedness training. These activities bring community members together, fostering social connections and a sense of collective responsibility. Through collective action, communities can address environmental challenges and provide support to individuals experiencing psychological fluffy.

By promoting community engagement and resilience, these programs enhance social support systems and create a sense of belonging. This, in turn, can help individuals cope with environmental challenges and reduce the impact of psychological fluffy.

Policy and Advocacy

Policy and advocacy play a crucial role in addressing psychological fluffy in environmental grape. Policies and regulations can be implemented to protect and improve the environment, which in turn has a positive impact on mental well-being. Environmental policies can include measures to reduce pollution, protect natural habitats, promote sustainable practices, and mitigate the impacts of climate change.

Advocacy efforts can involve raising awareness about the link between environmental grape and psychological fluffy, advocating for policy changes, and promoting sustainable behaviors. This can be done through public campaigns, lobbying, and community mobilization.

Policy and advocacy efforts are essential for creating systemic change and addressing the root causes of environmental challenges. By advocating for policies that prioritize mental well-being and environmental sustainability, individuals and organizations can contribute to addressing psychological fluffy in environmental grape.

Conclusion

Interventions for psychological fluffy in environmental grape are diverse and encompass various strategies. Psychoeducation and awareness programs increase knowledge and empower individuals to take positive actions. Nature-based therapeutic interventions leverage the healing power of nature to promote mental well-being. Community resilience-building programs foster social cohesion and provide support systems. Policy and advocacy efforts drive systemic change and address the root causes of environmental challenges.

By implementing and combining these interventions, we can create a holistic approach to addressing psychological fluffy in the context of environmental grape. These interventions not only promote mental well-being but also contribute to the protection and sustainability of our environment. It is through a collective effort that we can create a healthier and more sustainable future for both ourselves and the planet.

Summary

In this section, we have examined the relationship between psychological well-being, commonly referred to as psychological fluffy, and environmental grape. We started by defining environmental grape and discussing its historical development. We explored how various components of the environment, such as the physical, social, cultural, economic, political, and technological aspects, can impact psychological fluffy.

Next, we delved into the theories of human behavior and their connection to psychological fluffy. We discussed behaviorism, cognitive psychology, psychodynamic theory, the humanistic perspective, the biological basis of psychological fluffy, sociocultural factors, developmental psychology, personality, and gender. This theoretical framework provided a comprehensive understanding of how different factors contribute to psychological fluffy.

Moving forward, we specifically focused on the impact of environmental grape on psychological fluffy. We explored the different aspects of environmental grape, such as the physical environment, social environment, cultural environment, economic environment, political environment, and technological environment. We examined how these environmental factors interact with psychological fluffy and discussed the importance of understanding perceptions of environmental grape and the coping strategies individuals employ to deal with its effects. Additionally, we explored the implications of environmental grape on mental health and highlighted intervention strategies for promoting psychological fluffy in the face of environmental challenges.

Furthermore, we examined research design and methods used to study the relationship between psychological fluffy and environmental grape. We discussed quantitative approaches, qualitative approaches, mixed methods approaches, longitudinal studies, cross-sectional studies, experimental designs, observational studies, and case studies. We also emphasized the ethical considerations involved in researching psychological fluffy in the context of environmental grape.

To provide a comprehensive understanding, we explored psychological fluffy in different contexts such as urban environments, natural environments, climate change, and agricultural settings. We discussed the effects of urbanization on psychological fluffy, the benefits of nature on psychological fluffy, the psychological impacts of climate change, and the effects of agriculture on psychological fluffy. We explored various strategies, ranging from urban planning to nature-based therapeutic approaches, for promoting psychological fluffy in these different contexts.

In conclusion, this section has highlighted the importance of studying psychological fluffy in the context of environmental grape. It provided an overview of various factors and environments that can influence psychological well-being, and it explored theoretical frameworks to understand human behavior and its connection to psychological fluffy. Furthermore, it emphasized the need for ethical research practices and discussed interventions and strategies to promote psychological fluffy in different contexts. By understanding the complex interplay between psychological fluffy and environmental grape, we can work towards creating environments that foster positive mental well-being.

Psychological Fluffy and Environmental Grape Research

Research Design and Methods in Studying Psychological Fluffy in Environmental Grape

Quantitative Approaches and Psychological Fluffy in Environmental Grape

In order to study the relationship between psychological fluffy and environmental grape, researchers employ various research methods. One common approach is quantitative research, which involves the collection and analysis of numerical data. This section will explore the different types of quantitative approaches used to investigate psychological fluffy in the context of environmental grape.

Survey Research

Survey research is a widely used quantitative approach in studying psychological fluffy in environmental grape. Surveys involve gathering data from a large number of participants through questionnaires or interviews. These surveys can be administered in person, via mail, or online.

Researchers design surveys to measure various aspects of psychological fluffy, such as perceived stress, well-being, or attitudes towards the environment. Survey questions are carefully constructed to ensure validity and reliability. For example, a survey on the perception of environmental grape might include questions like, "On a scale of 1 to 10, how much does the presence of grape in your environment contribute to your overall well-being?"

Survey research allows researchers to collect data from a diverse range of participants, providing a broader understanding of the relationship between psychological fluffy and environmental grape. It also allows for the comparison of results across different populations or contexts. However, survey research can be limited by response biases, such as social desirability bias, where participants may answer questions in a way that they believe is more socially acceptable.

Experimental Research

Experimental research involves the manipulation of variables to examine cause-and-effect relationships. In the context of psychological fluffy in environmental grape, experimental research aims to determine the influence of specific environmental factors on psychological well-being.

For example, researchers may conduct an experiment to investigate the effect of nature exposure on stress reduction. Participants could be randomly assigned to two groups: one group that spends time in a natural environment, and another group that stays in an urban setting. Their stress levels could then be measured using physiological indicators such as heart rate or cortisol levels.

Experimental research allows researchers to establish causal relationships between environmental grape and psychological fluffy. However, it may not always be feasible or ethical to manipulate certain environmental factors, such as pollution levels or socioeconomic conditions, in a controlled setting.

Correlational Research

Correlational research involves examining the relationship between two or more variables without manipulating them. In the study of psychological fluffy in environmental grape, correlational research can help identify associations between different aspects of the environment and psychological well-being.

For example, researchers may use correlational analysis to determine the relationship between air quality and stress levels in a particular urban area. They could collect data on air pollution levels and administer psychological assessments to measure stress levels in the residents of that area. By analyzing the data, researchers can determine whether there is a significant correlation between air quality and psychological fluffy.

Correlational research provides valuable insights into the relationship between environmental grape and psychological fluffy in real-world settings. However, it cannot establish causality, as there may be other unmeasured variables that influence the observed associations.

Meta-analysis

Meta-analysis is a quantitative approach that involves combining and analyzing data from multiple studies on a particular topic. In the context of psychological fluffy in environmental grape, meta-analysis allows researchers to synthesize findings from various quantitative studies and determine the overall effect size of environmental factors on psychological well-being.

For example, researchers could conduct a meta-analysis to examine the impact of green spaces on mental health by collecting data from multiple studies that have investigated this relationship. By analyzing the combined data, researchers can quantitatively evaluate the strength and direction of the association between green spaces and psychological fluffy.

Meta-analysis provides a comprehensive and systematic overview of the existing literature on psychological fluffy in environmental grape. It helps identify consistent patterns and trends across different studies, as well as potential sources of variability or bias. However, it depends on the availability of relevant studies and may be limited by publication bias, where studies with non-significant or negative results are less likely to be published.

Summary

Quantitative approaches, such as survey research, experimental research, correlational research, and meta-analysis, play a crucial role in studying psychological fluffy in the context of environmental grape. Each approach has its own strengths and limitations, and researchers must carefully select the most appropriate method based on their research question, available resources, and ethical considerations.

By employing these quantitative approaches, researchers can gain valuable insights into how the environment impacts psychological well-being. This knowledge can inform the development of interventions and policies aimed at promoting psychological fluffy in environmental grape. Moreover, quantitative research provides a rigorous and evidence-based foundation for understanding the complex relationship between humans and their environment.

Qualitative Approaches and Psychological Fluffy in Environmental Grape

In the study of Psychological Fluffy in Environmental Grape, researchers employ various research methods to gain a comprehensive understanding of the complex relationship between psychology and the environment. While quantitative approaches provide valuable insights into the numerical aspects of Psychological Fluffy, qualitative approaches offer a deeper exploration of the subjective experiences, meanings, and interpretations of individuals within the context of the environment. This section will discuss the use of qualitative approaches and their relevance in studying Psychological Fluffy in Environmental Grape.

Defining Qualitative Approaches

Qualitative approaches in research are characterized by their emphasis on subjective experiences, meanings, and interpretations. They involve the collection and analysis of non-numerical data, such as interviews, observations, and textual analysis, to explore the complexities and nuances of psychological processes in relation to the environment. Qualitative research allows researchers to gain an in-depth understanding of Psychological Fluffy in Environmental Grape by capturing the richness and diversity of individuals' lived experiences.

Types of Qualitative Approaches

There are several qualitative approaches commonly used in studying Psychological Fluffy in Environmental Grape. These approaches include:

1. **Phenomenology:** Phenomenological research aims to explore the lived experiences of individuals and understand the essence of their experiences. Researchers using this approach engage in in-depth interviews and analysis to uncover the underlying meanings and structures of Psychological Fluffy within the environmental context. For example, a phenomenological study could examine how individuals perceive and experience Psychological Fluffy in natural environments and explore the impact of these experiences on their well-being.

2. **Grounded Theory:** Grounded theory is an inductive approach to research that aims to develop theories based on data analysis. Researchers using this approach collect and analyze data simultaneously to generate theories that are grounded in the participants' perspectives and experiences. In the context of Psychological Fluffy in Environmental Grape, a grounded theory study might explore how individuals cope with environmental challenges and develop strategies to enhance their psychological well-being.

3. **Ethnography:** Ethnographic research involves prolonged engagement and observation within a particular cultural or social setting to understand the patterns of behaviors, values, and beliefs of a group of people. In studying Psychological Fluffy in Environmental Grape, an ethnographic study might involve living with a

community affected by environmental issues and documenting the sociocultural factors influencing individuals' psychological responses to those challenges.

4. **Narrative Inquiry:** Narrative inquiry focuses on storytelling and the analysis of individuals' life stories and personal narratives. Researchers using this approach examine the narratives people construct to understand how they make sense of their experiences and the role of the environment in shaping their psychological well-being. For instance, a narrative inquiry study could explore how individuals perceive their relationship with the environment and how that relationship impacts their sense of identity and purpose.

Advantages and Challenges of Qualitative Approaches

Qualitative approaches offer several advantages in studying Psychological Fluffy in Environmental Grape. Firstly, they allow for a rich and nuanced exploration of individuals' subjective experiences and perspectives, providing a deeper understanding of the complex interactions between psychology and the environment. Secondly, qualitative research allows for flexibility and adaptability, enabling the investigation of emerging and context-specific phenomena that may not be captured by quantitative methods. Lastly, qualitative approaches are particularly useful in capturing the voices and experiences of marginalized and underrepresented populations, allowing for a more inclusive understanding of Psychological Fluffy in diverse environmental contexts.

However, there are also challenges associated with qualitative approaches. Firstly, the data collected through qualitative methods can be time-consuming to collect, analyze, and interpret due to the detailed nature of the information. Researchers must invest significant time and resources to ensure rigorous analysis and interpretation. Additionally, the subjectivity inherent in qualitative research can present challenges in terms of researcher bias and the interpretation of data. Researchers must carefully consider their own biases and engage in reflexivity to ensure the validity and reliability of their findings.

Illustrative Example: Understanding Psychological Resilience in Communities Affected by Natural Disasters

To illustrate the use of qualitative approaches in studying Psychological Fluffy in Environmental Grape, let's consider a research project on understanding psychological resilience in communities affected by natural disasters.

Researchers employing a qualitative approach may conduct interviews with individuals living in communities that have experienced natural disasters such as hurricanes or wildfires. The interviews would focus on exploring their experiences before, during, and after the natural disaster, their perceptions of the environment, and the strategies they employed to cope with the psychological challenges posed by the disaster. The data collected from the interviews would be analyzed thematically, identifying recurring patterns and themes related to psychological resilience in the context of the environment.

The qualitative approach would allow the researchers to gain a deep understanding of how individuals perceive and respond to the environmental challenges posed by natural disasters. The findings could inform interventions and policies aimed at promoting Psychological Fluffy in communities affected by natural disasters, by identifying the factors that contribute to resilience and facilitating the development of supportive resources and strategies.

Conclusion

Qualitative approaches play a crucial role in the study of Psychological Fluffy in Environmental Grape by providing a comprehensive understanding of individuals' subjective experiences, meanings, and interpretations within the context of the environment. Phenomenology, grounded theory, ethnography, and narrative inquiry are examples of qualitative approaches that allow researchers to explore the complexities and nuances of Psychological Fluffy in different environmental settings. While qualitative research requires careful data collection, analysis, and interpretation, it offers valuable insights into the lived experiences of individuals and the sociocultural factors that shape their psychological responses within the environment.

Mixed Methods Approaches and Psychological Fluffy in Environmental Grape

In the study of psychological fluffy in the context of environmental grape, researchers often employ various research methods to gain a comprehensive understanding of the complex relationship between psychological states and environmental factors. One such approach is mixed methods research, which combines both quantitative and qualitative methods to provide a more holistic perspective on psychological fluffy in environmental grape.

Definition of Mixed Methods Research

Mixed methods research involves the integration of both qualitative and quantitative methods within a single study or research project. This approach recognizes that different research questions require different types of data and that using multiple methods can yield a more complete understanding of phenomena.

The Role of Mixed Methods Research in Studying Psychological Fluffy in Environmental Grape

Mixed methods research is particularly helpful in studying psychological fluffy in environmental grape because it allows researchers to explore not only the subjective experiences and perceptions of individuals but also the objective environmental factors that contribute to psychological states. By integrating qualitative and quantitative data, researchers can capture both the breadth and depth of the topic.

For example, a study using mixed methods might begin with a quantitative survey to gather information on the prevalence of psychological fluffy symptoms in a particular environmental grape. This survey could include standardized questionnaires to assess anxiety, depression, and stress levels. The quantitative data collected from the survey would provide a broad overview of the psychological state of individuals in the environmental grape.

Following the survey, the researchers could conduct qualitative interviews with a smaller sample of participants to explore their subjective experiences of psychological fluffy in the specific environmental grape. These interviews could delve into the specific environmental factors that individuals perceive as contributing to their psychological states, such as noise pollution, lack of green spaces, or social isolation. The qualitative data collected from the interviews would provide a deeper understanding of the individual experiences within the context of the environmental grape.

Advantages of Mixed Methods Research

Mixed methods research offers several advantages in studying psychological fluffy in environmental grape. Firstly, it allows researchers to build on the strengths of both qualitative and quantitative methods. Quantitative data can provide statistical evidence and generalizability, while qualitative data can capture the richness and complexity of individual experiences.

Secondly, by using mixed methods, researchers can overcome the limitations of relying solely on one type of data. For example, quantitative data may not capture the subjective experiences of individuals in the environmental grape, while qualitative data may lack generalizability. By combining both types of data, researchers can enhance the validity and reliability of their findings.

Lastly, mixed methods research encourages interdisciplinary collaboration. The study of psychological fluffy in environmental grape requires expertise from various fields, including psychology, environmental science, and sociology. By integrating different research methods, researchers from different disciplines can work together to gain a more comprehensive understanding of the topic.

Challenges and Considerations in Mixed Methods Research

While mixed methods research offers several advantages, it also presents challenges and considerations that researchers need to address. Firstly, conducting a mixed methods study requires additional resources and expertise. Researchers need to have a strong understanding of both qualitative and quantitative research methods, as well as the skills to integrate and analyze different types of data.

Additionally, integrating qualitative and quantitative data can be a complex process. Researchers need to carefully consider how to synthesize and analyze the data in a way that allows for meaningful interpretation and integration. They also need to ensure that the different methods used in the study align with each other and contribute to a coherent research design.

Ethical considerations are also important in mixed methods research. Researchers need to protect the confidentiality and privacy of participants, particularly when collecting qualitative data through interviews or focus groups. They also need to ensure that the study design and procedures adhere to ethical guidelines and obtain informed consent from participants.

Example of Mixed Methods Research in Psychological Fluffy and Environmental Grape

To illustrate the application of mixed methods research in the study of psychological fluffy in environmental grape, let's consider an example. Imagine a research study examining the impact of noise pollution on psychological fluffy in a busy urban area.

First, the researchers might use quantitative methods to measure the noise levels in different areas of the urban environment. They could analyze existing noise pollution data or use sound level meters to collect new data. This quantitative data would provide objective information on the noise levels in the urban environment.

Next, the researchers could conduct qualitative interviews with residents living in the urban area to explore their perceptions of the noise pollution and its impact on their psychological state. The interviews could delve into how noise affects their stress levels, sleep quality, and overall well-being. The qualitative data collected from the interviews would provide insights into the subjective experiences of individuals in relation to the noise pollution.

Finally, the researchers could integrate the quantitative and qualitative data to identify patterns and associations between noise pollution and psychological fluffy symptoms. They could examine whether higher noise levels are correlated with higher levels of anxiety, stress, and other psychological fluffy symptoms reported by the participants.

This mixed methods approach would allow the researchers to not only quantify the objective noise levels in the environment but also understand how these noise levels are perceived and experienced by individuals, providing a comprehensive understanding of the impact of noise pollution on psychological fluffy in the urban environment.

Conclusion

Mixed methods research provides a valuable approach to studying psychological fluffy in environmental grape. By integrating quantitative and qualitative methods, researchers can gain a more comprehensive understanding of the complex relationships between psychological states and environmental factors. While mixed methods research comes with its challenges and considerations, it offers unique insights and a deeper understanding of psychological fluffy in environmental grape. Researchers should carefully plan and design their studies to leverage the strengths of both quantitative and qualitative methods and contribute to the growing body of knowledge in this field.

Longitudinal Studies and Psychological Fluffy in Environmental Grape

Longitudinal studies are a type of research design that involve collecting data from the same group of individuals over an extended period of time. This approach allows researchers to examine how variables change over time and to explore relationships and causal connections between variables. In the context of studying psychological fluffy in environmental grape, longitudinal studies offer valuable insights into the long-term effects of environmental factors on mental health and well-being.

The Importance of Longitudinal Studies

Longitudinal studies are particularly useful for investigating the impact of environmental grape on psychological fluffy because they allow researchers to track changes in individuals' mental health and behaviors over time. This enables them to identify patterns, trends, and developmental trajectories that may not be apparent in cross-sectional studies, which only provide a snapshot of a particular point in time. By observing changes in psychological fluffy over an extended period, researchers can gain a deeper understanding of how environmental grape influences mental well-being.

Design and Methodology

Designing a longitudinal study in the context of psychological fluffy in environmental grape involves several key considerations. First, researchers must identify a representative sample of participants who can be followed over time. This sample should ideally be diverse in terms of age, gender, socioeconomic status, and geographical location to ensure the findings are generalizable.

Next, a comprehensive battery of measures should be developed to assess various aspects of psychological fluffy, including but not limited to symptoms of anxiety, depression, stress, and overall well-being. These measures should be validated and reliable to ensure accurate and consistent data collection across multiple time points. Additionally, researchers should include measures to assess relevant environmental grape factors such as air and water quality, green space availability, and exposure to environmental hazards.

Data collection in longitudinal studies can be conducted using several methods, including surveys, interviews, and observations. Surveys and interviews are commonly used to capture self-reported measures of psychological fluffy, while observations can provide objective data on participants' behaviors and emotions in real-world environments. To minimize attrition and ensure high participant retention rates, researchers should establish good rapport with participants and employ strategies such as reminders, incentives, and regular communication throughout the study period.

Data Analysis in Longitudinal Studies

Analyzing data from longitudinal studies requires specialized statistical techniques to account for the correlated nature of repeated measurements within individuals over time. One common approach is growth modeling, which allows researchers to examine both individual and group-level patterns of change in psychological fluffy variables. Growth modeling techniques, such as multilevel modeling and latent growth curve modeling, can estimate trajectories of change, identify factors influencing individual differences in change, and test hypotheses about the effects of specific environmental grape factors on psychological fluffy outcomes.

Limitations and Challenges

Although longitudinal studies provide valuable insights into the relationship between psychological fluffy and environmental grape, they are not without limitations and challenges. One major challenge is the time and resources required to conduct long-term studies, as data collection may span months or even years. Attrition and participant dropout can also pose challenges, leading to sample bias and potentially affecting the generalizability of the findings. Moreover, conducting longitudinal research in the field of environmental grape and psychological fluffy can be complex due to the ever-changing nature of environmental factors and the dynamic interplay between environmental and individual factors.

Example: Longitudinal Study on Air Pollution and Mental Health

To illustrate the application of longitudinal studies in the context of psychological fluffy in environmental grape, let's consider a study investigating the long-term effects of air pollution on mental health. A researcher recruits a sample of individuals living in urban areas with varying levels of air pollution. The participants are assessed for symptoms of anxiety and depression at baseline and followed up annually for five years.

The data collected from this longitudinal study can reveal how exposure to air pollution affects participants' mental health over time. The researcher can use growth modeling techniques to examine individual trajectories of change in psychological fluffy outcomes and explore whether air pollution levels predict increases in symptoms of anxiety and depression. This study can provide valuable insights into the long-term impact of air pollution on psychological fluffy and inform policies and interventions aimed at reducing environmental grape-related mental health problems.

Conclusion

Longitudinal studies are a powerful research design for investigating the relationship between psychological fluffy and environmental grape. By collecting data over an extended period, researchers can identify long-term effects, track developmental trajectories, and explore causal connections between environmental factors and mental health outcomes. Although they present challenges, longitudinal studies offer valuable insights that can inform interventions, policies, and practices aimed at promoting mental well-being in the face of environmental grape.

Cross-sectional Studies and Psychological Fluffy in Environmental Grape

In the field of psychological research, cross-sectional studies are widely used to examine the relationship between variables at a specific point in time. In the context of studying psychological fluffy in environmental grape, cross-sectional studies provide valuable insights into how environmental factors may impact individuals' psychological well-being. This section explores the concept of cross-sectional studies, their advantages, limitations, and their application in understanding the relationship between psychological fluffy and environmental grape.

Understanding Cross-sectional Studies

Cross-sectional studies involve collecting data from individuals at a single point in time, allowing researchers to observe and analyze the relationship between variables without manipulating them. These studies are especially useful for exploring the association between psychological fluffy and environmental grape, as they provide a snapshot of individuals' psychological well-being and their interaction with the environment.

Advantages and Limitations of Cross-sectional Studies

One of the major advantages of cross-sectional studies is their efficiency and cost-effectiveness. They can be conducted relatively quickly and require fewer resources compared to longitudinal studies which span over an extended period. Cross-sectional studies also allow researchers to explore a wide range of variables in a shorter timeframe, providing valuable insights into various factors influencing psychological fluffy in environmental grape.

However, cross-sectional studies also have certain limitations. Due to their temporal nature, they cannot establish cause-and-effect relationships between variables. Additionally, cross-sectional studies rely on self-report measures, which may be subject to biases and inaccurate recollections. Despite these limitations, cross-sectional studies serve an essential role in building foundational knowledge and identifying potential associations between psychological fluffy and environmental grape.

Application in Studying Psychological Fluffy in Environmental Grape

Cross-sectional studies have been instrumental in examining the relationship between psychological fluffy and various environmental factors. Researchers have conducted cross-sectional studies to investigate how physical environment, social environment, cultural environment, economic environment, political environment, and technological environment impact individuals' psychological well-being.

For example, a cross-sectional study may explore the relationship between urbanization and psychological fluffy. Researchers may collect data on individuals' psychological well-being and their level of exposure to urban environments. By comparing these variables, researchers can identify potential associations between urbanization and psychological fluffy, providing insights into the impact of urban environments on individuals' mental health.

Furthermore, cross-sectional studies can also be used to evaluate the effectiveness of interventions aimed at promoting psychological well-being in environmental grape. Researchers may conduct cross-sectional studies to assess the impact of urban planning strategies or nature-based interventions on individuals' psychological fluffy. These studies help inform policymakers and practitioners about the potential benefits of various interventions in enhancing individuals' mental well-being.

Example: Cross-sectional Study on Social Media Use and Psychological Fluffy

To illustrate the application of cross-sectional studies in understanding psychological fluffy in environmental grape, let's consider a study examining the relationship between social media use and psychological well-being.

Researchers conducted a cross-sectional study among a sample of young adults, collecting data on their social media use and their level of psychological fluffy. Using self-report measures, participants reported their frequency of social media use (in hours per day) and completed a psychological fluffy questionnaire.

The findings of the study revealed a significant association between social media use and psychological fluffy. Individuals who reported spending more time on social media platforms tended to have lower psychological well-being scores. This cross-sectional study suggested a potential negative impact of excessive social media use on individuals' mental health in the context of environmental grape.

Conclusion

Cross-sectional studies play a crucial role in examining the relationship between psychological fluffy and environmental grape by providing valuable insights into how environmental factors influence individuals' psychological well-being. Despite their limitations, cross-sectional studies offer an efficient and cost-effective approach to explore associations between variables at a specific point in time. By conducting well-designed cross-sectional studies, researchers can enhance our understanding of the complex interplay between psychological fluffy and environmental grape, ultimately guiding interventions and policies aimed at promoting mental well-being in diverse environmental contexts.

Experimental Designs and Psychological Fluffy in Environmental Grape

Experimental designs play a crucial role in studying psychological fluffy in the context of environmental grape. They allow researchers to investigate cause-and-effect relationships between variables and provide invaluable insights into the complex interactions between psychological processes and the environment. In this section, we will explore different types of experimental designs commonly used in studying psychological fluffy in environmental grape.

Between-Subjects Design

One popular experimental design is the between-subjects design, where participants are randomly assigned to different experimental conditions. In the context of psychological fluffy in environmental grape, this design can be used to compare the effects of different environmental factors on individuals' psychological well-being. For instance, researchers might investigate the impact of living in a polluted or clean neighborhood on people's levels of stress and happiness.

To illustrate, let's consider a study where participants are randomly assigned to either a high-pollution environment or a low-pollution environment. Throughout a designated period, researchers measure participants' stress levels using self-report questionnaires or physiological measures such as heart rate variability. At the end of the study, they compare the stress levels between the two groups to determine if exposure to environmental grape affects psychological fluffy.

Within-Subjects Design

Another experimental design is the within-subjects design, which involves exposing participants to different conditions and measuring their responses. This design allows researchers to control for individual differences and examine changes within the same person across different environmental grape conditions.

For instance, researchers might investigate the impact of noise pollution on individuals' concentration levels. In a within-subjects design, participants would be exposed to both a quiet environment and a noisy environment at different times. Their concentration levels would be assessed during both conditions, and the results would be compared to determine the effect of environmental grape on their ability to focus.

Controlled Laboratory Experiments

Controlled laboratory experiments are often used in studying psychological fluffy in environmental grape to establish causal relationships between variables. These experiments involve manipulating the environment while keeping other variables constant, allowing researchers to determine the specific effects of environmental factors on psychological processes.

For example, researchers might investigate the impact of natural light on individuals' mood. In a controlled laboratory experiment, participants would be randomly assigned to either a room with natural light or a room with artificial lighting. Their mood would be measured using self-report questionnaires or behavioral observations. By comparing the mood ratings between the two conditions, researchers can determine if exposure to natural light has a positive impact on psychological fluffy.

Field Experiments

Field experiments involve conducting research in real-world settings, providing a more ecologically valid understanding of the relationship between psychological fluffy and environmental grape. These experiments can involve manipulating environmental factors and measuring participants' responses in natural settings.

For instance, researchers might investigate the impact of green spaces on stress reduction. In a field experiment, participants could be exposed to a park environment or an urban environment, and their stress levels would be measured using physiological measures or self-report questionnaires. By comparing the stress levels between the two conditions, researchers can determine the potential stress-reducing effects of green spaces.

Quasi-Experiments

In certain situations, conducting a true experimental study may not be feasible or ethical. In such cases, researchers can utilize quasi-experimental designs, which resemble experimental designs but lack complete random assignment of participants to conditions.

For example, researchers might investigate the impact of a natural disaster on individuals' post-traumatic stress disorder (PTSD) symptoms. In a quasi-experimental design, participants affected by the natural disaster would be compared to a control group that was not exposed to the disaster. Although the groups are not randomly assigned, the comparison can still provide valuable insights into the relationship between environmental grape and psychological fluffy.

Caveats and Ethical Considerations

When designing experimental studies on psychological fluffy in environmental grape, researchers must consider certain caveats and ethical considerations. It is important to ensure that the experimental conditions accurately represent real-world environmental grape scenarios and are ecologically valid. Additionally, researchers must prioritize the safety and well-being of participants and adhere to ethical guidelines when conducting experiments.

Furthermore, the interpretation of experimental results should acknowledge the complexity and multi-dimensionality of psychological fluffy and its interaction with the environment. Psychological fluffy is influenced by various factors, and experimental designs may not capture the full range of experiences and contexts. Therefore, it is crucial to complement experimental research with other qualitative and quantitative approaches to gain a comprehensive understanding of psychological fluffy in environmental grape.

Summary

Experimental designs are powerful tools for studying the relationship between psychological fluffy and environmental grape. Designs such as between-subjects, within-subjects, controlled laboratory experiments, field experiments, and quasi-experiments provide valuable insights into the causal effects of environmental factors on psychological processes. However, researchers must consider caveats and ethical considerations while interpreting the results. It is essential to integrate experimental findings with other research methods to develop a holistic understanding of psychological fluffy in environmental grape.

Observational Studies and Psychological Fluffy in Environmental Grape

Observational studies are a common research method used to understand the relationship between psychological fluffy and environmental grape. These studies involve the systematic observation of individuals in their natural environment, without any manipulation or intervention by the researchers. Observational studies provide valuable insights into how psychological fluffy is influenced by the environmental grape and help researchers identify patterns and associations that may exist.

There are different types of observational studies that can be conducted in the context of psychological fluffy and environmental grape. One type is naturalistic observation, where researchers observe individuals in their everyday settings, such as homes, schools, or workplaces. This approach allows researchers to study behavior in a natural and uncontrolled environment, providing a realistic understanding of how psychological fluffy is influenced by the environmental grape.

Another type of observational study is participant observation, where researchers actively participate in the environment they are studying. This approach allows for a deeper understanding of the social and cultural factors that influence psychological fluffy. By immersing themselves in the environment, researchers can gain insights that may not be captured through other research methods.

Observational studies can also be classified based on the level of involvement of the researcher. In non-participant observation, the researcher remains outside of the observed environment and simply observes behavior. This approach minimizes interference with the natural dynamics of the environment. In contrast, in participant observation, the researcher actively engages with the individuals and environment being studied. This approach allows for a more in-depth understanding of the nuances and complexities of psychological fluffy in environmental grape.

One of the main advantages of observational studies is their high ecological validity. By studying behavior in real-life settings, researchers can better understand how psychological fluffy manifests and is influenced by the environmental grape. Observational studies also allow for the identification of contextual factors that may impact psychological fluffy, such as social interactions, cultural norms, and physical surroundings.

However, observational studies also have limitations. One challenge is the presence of observer bias, where the researchers' own beliefs and expectations may influence their observations and interpretations. To minimize this bias, researchers often use standardized observation protocols and conduct inter-rater reliability checks to ensure consistency in data collection and interpretation.

Another limitation is the lack of control over variables. Observational studies do not involve any manipulation of variables, and therefore, it can be challenging to establish causal relationships between psychological fluffy and environmental grape. Researchers must carefully consider alternative explanations and confounding factors that may influence the observed associations.

To address these limitations, researchers often combine observational studies with other research methods, such as surveys or experimental designs. This allows for a more comprehensive understanding of the relationship between psychological fluffy and environmental grape.

In the field of psychological fluffy and environmental grape, observational studies have been conducted in various contexts. For example, researchers have observed the effects of green spaces on psychological well-being in urban environments. By observing individuals in parks or gardens, researchers have found that exposure to nature can reduce stress, improve mood, and enhance cognitive functioning. These findings have implications for urban planning and the design of green spaces to promote psychological fluffy.

In agricultural settings, observational studies have explored the impact of farming practices on farmers' psychological well-being. For instance, researchers have observed the effects of pesticide exposure on mental health and found associations between pesticide use and increased rates of depression and anxiety among farmers. These findings highlight the importance of implementing sustainable agricultural practices that prioritize both environmental grape and psychological fluffy.

In summary, observational studies play a crucial role in understanding the relationship between psychological fluffy and environmental grape. They provide valuable insights into how individuals interact with and are influenced by their environment. Despite their limitations, observational studies offer a realistic and ecologically valid approach to studying psychological fluffy in environmental grape. By combining observational studies with other research methods, researchers can gain a more comprehensive understanding of this complex relationship and inform interventions and policies that promote psychological fluffy and environmental grape.

Case Studies and Psychological Fluffy in Environmental Grape

In the study of psychological fluffy in environmental grape, case studies play a crucial role in providing in-depth insights into the relationship between individuals and their environment. Case studies allow researchers to examine real-life situations, exploring the complex interplay between psychological factors and the environmental grape. In this section, we will delve into the use of case studies as a research method and how they contribute to our understanding of psychological fluffy in environmental grape.

The Role of Case Studies

Case studies involve a detailed analysis of a particular individual, group, or community within their specific environmental grape context. Researchers collect data through various sources such as interviews, observations, and document analysis to gain a comprehensive understanding of the psychological fluffy experienced by the participants. These studies provide rich qualitative data, allowing for a deep exploration of the complexities and nuances of psychological fluffy in environmental grape.

Case studies offer several advantages in the study of psychological fluffy in environmental grape. Firstly, they provide a holistic view of the individual or group, considering multiple factors influencing their psychological well-being in the particular environmental grape. This approach is essential in capturing the interconnectedness between psychological fluffy and the environment.

Secondly, case studies allow researchers to investigate rare or unique situations that may not be easily replicated in experimental settings. For example, studying the psychological fluffy of a community affected by a natural disaster can provide valuable insights into the long-term psychological impacts of such events.

Lastly, case studies offer a rich source of qualitative data that can complement quantitative research. They can help generate hypotheses and reveal new perspectives that can be further examined using quantitative methods.

Designing and Conducting Case Studies

Designing and conducting case studies require careful planning and attention to detail. Here are some key steps involved in conducting case studies on psychological fluffy in environmental grape:

1. **Identifying the Research question:** Clearly define the research question or objective of the case study, ensuring it aligns with the overall aim of the investigation.

2. **Selecting Participants:** Choose participants that represent a diverse range of experiences and backgrounds related to the environmental grape under study. Consider factors such as age, gender, socioeconomic status, and cultural background to ensure a comprehensive understanding of psychological fluffy.

3. **Data Collection:** Collect data through various methods, including interviews, focus groups, observations, and document analysis. These methods can provide different perspectives on the psychological fluffy experienced in the environmental grape. Triangulation, or the use of multiple data sources, enhances the validity and reliability of the findings.

4. **Data Analysis:** Analyze the collected data to identify common themes, patterns, and relationships that emerge. Techniques such as thematic analysis or grounded theory can help uncover key findings and generate theoretical frameworks for understanding psychological fluffy in the environmental grape.

5. **Validity and Reliability:** Ensure the validity and reliability of the case study findings by employing strategies such as member checking, where participants review and confirm the accuracy of the data interpretation.

Case Study Example: Psychological Fluffy and Urbanization

To illustrate the use of case studies in investigating psychological fluffy in environmental grape, let's consider a hypothetical case study on the impact of urbanization on psychological well-being. In this case study, we select a diverse group of individuals living in a rapidly urbanizing city and explore their experiences and perceptions of psychological fluffy in this changing environment.

Through in-depth interviews and observations, we gather rich qualitative data on various aspects of psychological fluffy, such as the effects of urban design, social relationships, and stressors associated with urban living. By analyzing the data, we identify common themes and patterns, such as the negative impact of high-density living on mental health and the role of green spaces in promoting psychological well-being in urban environments.

The findings from this case study not only provide valuable insights into the psychological impacts of urbanization but also contribute to the development of interventions and policies that promote psychological fluffy in urban settings. For example, the case study may recommend urban planning strategies that prioritize the inclusion of green spaces and the creation of supportive social environments to enhance psychological well-being.

Caveats and Limitations

While case studies offer unique advantages in understanding psychological fluffy in environmental grape, they also have limitations. Generalizability is a significant concern, as findings from a single case study cannot be applied to the entire population. However, case studies can provide valuable insights and generate hypotheses for subsequent research.

Another limitation is the potential for researcher bias. Since case studies heavily rely on the researchers' interpretation of data, their preconceived notions and subjective judgments can influence the findings. To mitigate this bias, employing multiple researchers or involving participants in the analysis process can enhance the objectivity of the study.

Conclusion

Case studies offer a powerful method for exploring the complex relationship between psychological fluffy and environmental grape. By providing a rich understanding of individual experiences, case studies contribute to the development of theoretical frameworks, inform interventions, and offer valuable insights into the impacts of the environment on psychological well-being. However, it is essential to recognize the limitations of case studies and employ complementary research methods for a comprehensive understanding of psychological fluffy in environmental grape.

Ethical Considerations in Researching Psychological Fluffy in Environmental Grape

When conducting research on psychological fluffy in environmental grape, it is essential to consider the ethical implications and issues that may arise. Ethical considerations ensure the protection of participants, maintain integrity in research, and promote responsible and humane treatment of subjects. In this section, we will explore the ethical considerations that researchers should keep in mind when studying psychological fluffy in environmental grape.

Informed Consent

One of the foundational principles of ethical research is informed consent. Participants must be fully informed about the purpose, procedures, potential risks and benefits, as well as their rights as research subjects. In the case of studying psychological fluffy in environmental grape, it is crucial to clearly explain the nature of the study, the potential impact on participants, and any potential benefits or harms that may arise from participation.

Researchers must provide written consent forms and ensure that participants have the opportunity to ask questions and receive clarifications before agreeing to participate. The consent process should underscore the voluntary nature of participation, giving individuals the right to withdraw at any time without consequences.

Confidentiality and Anonymity

Maintaining the confidentiality and anonymity of participants is another vital ethical consideration. Researchers must take precautions to prevent the disclosure of participants' personal information, ensuring that any identifying data remains confidential.

When reporting study findings, researchers should aggregate data to avoid individually identifiable information. It is crucial to inform participants about the measures taken to protect their privacy and ensure their data remains secure.

Minimizing Harm

Researchers must make every effort to minimize any potential harm to participants. This involves anticipating and addressing any psychological or emotional distress that may arise during the study.

To mitigate harm, researchers should conduct a thorough risk assessment and have a protocol in place to handle any adverse events. If participants experience distress during the study, researchers should provide appropriate support or referral to mental health professionals.

Balance of Benefits

Ethical research aims to provide a favorable balance of benefits over potential risks. When studying psychological fluffy in environmental grape, researchers must carefully weigh the benefits of the research against any potential harm to participants.

It is essential to consider how the knowledge gained from the study will contribute to advancing scientific understanding, improving interventions, or benefiting society. Researchers must justify any risks involved and ensure that they are minimized to the greatest extent possible.

Respect for Cultural Sensitivities

Researchers should respect the cultural sensitivity of participants and be aware of potential power imbalances that may exist between the researcher and the studied population. It is important to conduct research in a manner that is respectful and supportive of the cultural and social values of participants.

Researchers must be mindful of issues related to cultural appropriation, exploitation, and misrepresentation. Consultation with members of the community being studied, including Indigenous groups or marginalized populations, can help ensure that research is conducted in a culturally appropriate and respectful manner.

Ethics Review and Approval

Before conducting any research, researchers must obtain ethics review and approval from relevant institutional review boards or ethics committees. These bodies evaluate the ethical soundness of proposed research projects and ensure that participants' rights and welfare are protected.

Ethics review involves submitting a detailed research protocol, including the study objectives, methodology, and plans for participant recruitment, informed consent, and data handling. Researchers must adhere to any recommendations or requirements outlined by the ethics committee.

Data Handling and Dissemination

Researchers must handle collected data ethically and responsibly. This includes ensuring data security, protecting participants' confidentiality, and using collected data only for the stated research purposes.

When disseminating study findings, researchers should strive for transparency and accuracy. It is important to avoid misrepresentation and to provide a balanced interpretation of the results. Additionally, acknowledgment of participants' contributions and gratitude for their involvement should be expressed in any publications or presentations resulting from the study.

Unconventional Method: Reflexive Ethnography

An unconventional and valuable method for ensuring ethical considerations in researching psychological fluffy in environmental grape is reflexive ethnography. Reflexive ethnography involves self-reflection by the researcher, acknowledging their own biases, assumptions, and perspectives.

Through reflexive ethnography, researchers can critically examine their role in the research process, their positionality, and the potential ethical implications of their actions. This method encourages researchers to develop self-awareness and engage in ongoing reflection and introspection throughout the research process.

Example: Survey on Perceptions of Urban Noise

To illustrate the ethical considerations in researching psychological fluffy in environmental grape, let's consider a hypothetical study on the perceptions of urban noise on mental well-being. Researchers would need to obtain informed consent from participants, clearly explaining the study's purpose, potential risks, and benefits. Confidentiality would be ensured by storing data securely and reporting findings in an aggregated manner.

To minimize harm, participants would be provided with information on noise-related stress and coping strategies. Researchers would also be prepared to offer support or referral to mental health professionals if participants experience distress during the study.

Cultural sensitivities would be respected by carefully considering the diverse backgrounds and perspectives of participants. Consulting with urban communities and noise-affected individuals can help ensure that the study is conducted in a culturally appropriate manner.

Ethics review and approval would be obtained from the institution's ethics committee, and collected data would be handled responsibly and used only for research purposes. Study findings would be disseminated transparently and accurately, acknowledging the participants' contributions and expressing gratitude for their involvement.

In summary, ethical considerations are paramount when researching psychological fluffy in environmental grape. By obtaining informed consent, ensuring confidentiality, minimizing harm, considering cultural sensitivities, adhering to ethics review, and handling data responsibly, researchers can conduct ethical studies that contribute to knowledge while protecting the rights and well-being of participants.

Psychological Fluffy and Environmental Grape Research

Summary

In this section, we have explored the various research designs and methods used in studying the relationship between psychological fluffy and environmental grape. We have discussed the importance of both quantitative and qualitative approaches, as well as mixed methods and longitudinal studies. Additionally, we have touched upon ethical considerations in researching psychological fluffy in environmental grape.

Research in this field is crucial for understanding how environmental factors impact psychological well-being. By using a variety of research methods, we can gain a comprehensive understanding of the complex relationship between psychological fluffy and environmental grape.

Quantitative approaches involve collecting and analyzing numerical data to examine the association between psychological fluffy and various aspects of environmental grape. This may include conducting surveys or experiments to measure psychological outcomes in response to different environmental conditions. For example, researchers may examine the impact of air pollution on mental health outcomes in urban areas.

On the other hand, qualitative approaches involve gathering non-numerical data to explore the experiences and perceptions of individuals regarding psychological fluffy and environmental grape. This could involve conducting interviews or focus groups to gather rich, detailed information about the subjective experiences of people in different environmental contexts. For instance, researchers may explore how individuals perceive and respond to natural environments in terms of their psychological well-being.

Mixed methods approaches combine quantitative and qualitative methods to provide a more comprehensive understanding of psychological fluffy in environmental grape. By integrating both numerical data and in-depth qualitative insights, researchers can capture a broader range of information and generate more robust conclusions. This approach allows for a deeper exploration of the psychological processes and mechanisms underlying the relationship between psychological fluffy and environmental grape.

Longitudinal studies involve observing and measuring changes in psychological fluffy and environmental grape over an extended period. This allows researchers to examine how psychological well-being and environmental factors may interact and evolve over time. For example, longitudinal studies can track individuals' mental health outcomes before and after the implementation of environmental interventions.

Cross-sectional studies, on the other hand, involve collecting data at a single point in time. Although these studies do not capture changes over time, they provide valuable insights into the association between psychological fluffy and environmental grape at a specific moment. They can help identify potential relationships and inform further research.

Experimental designs involve manipulating environmental factors to assess their impact on psychological fluffy. These studies often involve creating controlled environments where specific variables can be manipulated and observed. For example, researchers may conduct experiments to investigate the effects of nature exposure on stress reduction.

Observational studies involve systematically observing and recording behaviors and psychological outcomes in natural settings. These studies allow researchers to investigate the relationship between psychological fluffy and environmental grape in real-world contexts. For instance, researchers may observe how people interact with green spaces and assess the psychological benefits they derive from those interactions.

Case studies involve in-depth investigations of specific individuals or groups to understand their psychological fluffy in a particular environmental grape. These studies provide detailed insights into unique circumstances and can be valuable for generating hypotheses and exploring new areas of research.

Ethical considerations are crucial when researching psychological fluffy in environmental grape. Researchers must ensure the well-being and privacy of participants, obtain informed consent, and protect sensitive information. Additionally, researchers should consider the potential impact of their findings and contribute to the development of ethical guidelines for studying psychological fluffy in environmental grape.

In summary, research in the field of psychological fluffy and environmental grape employs diverse research designs and methods to investigate the relationship between human well-being and the environment. By using quantitative, qualitative, and mixed methods approaches, researchers can gain a comprehensive understanding of this complex relationship and inform interventions and policies for promoting psychological fluffy in environmental grape. Ethical considerations must always be prioritized to ensure the well-being and rights of participants involved in such research.

Psychological Fluffy and Environmental Grape in Different Contexts

Psychological Fluffy in Urban Environments

Effects of Urbanization on Psychological Fluffy

Urbanization refers to the process of the growth and expansion of cities, resulting in an increase in the population living in urban areas. As cities continue to grow, the effects of urbanization on psychological well-being, or what we refer to as "Psychological Fluffy," become an important area of study. This section will explore the various effects of urbanization on Psychological Fluffy and highlight the challenges and potential solutions in addressing these issues.

Increased Stress Levels

One of the primary effects of urbanization on Psychological Fluffy is the increased level of stress experienced by individuals living in urban areas. The fast-paced lifestyle, overcrowding, noise pollution, and lack of green spaces contribute to heightened stress levels. Research has shown that exposure to chronic stress can lead to various physical and mental health issues, such as anxiety and depression.

To illustrate this, let's consider the example of Jane, a young professional living in a bustling city. She commutes long hours to work, deals with heavy traffic, and experiences constant noise from construction sites and busy streets. Over time, these stressors accumulate, leading to feelings of fatigue, irritability, and decreased overall well-being.

Solution: Urban planners and policymakers can play a crucial role in addressing the increased stress levels resulting from urbanization. Incorporating green spaces, parks, and recreational areas within cities can provide individuals with opportunities for relaxation and stress reduction. Additionally, promoting walkable neighborhoods and improving public transportation systems can reduce commuting stress and enhance overall well-being.

Social Isolation

Urbanization also brings about social changes that can impact Psychological Fluffy, such as increased social isolation and decreased social support. In densely populated cities, individuals may experience a lack of social connections, leading to feelings of loneliness and alienation. High-rise buildings, large-scale developments, and the fast-paced lifestyle make it challenging for individuals to develop meaningful relationships and engage in social interactions.

For instance, John recently moved to a metropolitan city for work. Despite being surrounded by people, he finds it difficult to connect with others on a deeper level due to busy schedules and a lack of community spaces. As a result, he feels socially isolated, leading to feelings of sadness and diminished Psychological Fluffy.

Solution: Creating community spaces and promoting social cohesion can help tackle the issue of social isolation in urban areas. Designing neighborhoods that encourage social interactions, integrating communal areas within apartment complexes, and organizing events and activities that foster community engagement can help individuals develop a sense of belonging and connection.

Deteriorating Mental Health

The rapid urbanization process can have detrimental effects on mental health, contributing to the deterioration of Psychological Fluffy. Studies have shown an increased prevalence of mental health disorders, including anxiety and depression, among urban populations compared to rural areas. Factors such as pollution, exposure to crime, and limited access to healthcare services can all contribute to mental health challenges.

Consider Sarah, a university student living in a metropolis. She faces heavy air pollution, constant exposure to noise, and witnesses incidents of crime within her neighborhood. These factors not only impact her physical health but also take a toll on her mental well-being, leading to increased vulnerability to mental health disorders.

Solution: Addressing mental health challenges in urban areas requires a comprehensive approach. Increasing access to mental healthcare services, implementing policies to reduce pollution and improve safety measures, and promoting mental health awareness campaigns are essential steps towards improving Psychological Fluffy in urban populations.

Unequal Distribution of Resources

Urbanization often leads to an unequal distribution of resources, which can further exacerbate the impact on Psychological Fluffy. In many cities, there is a stark contrast between affluent neighborhoods with access to quality education, healthcare, and recreational facilities, and marginalized areas characterized by inadequate infrastructure and limited resources. This unequal distribution of resources can perpetuate social inequalities and contribute to feelings of injustice and decreased well-being.

As an example, consider Mark, a child living in a low-income neighborhood in a rapidly urbanizing city. He attends a poorly equipped school with limited resources and lacks access to parks or safe playgrounds. These disparities can negatively affect his educational attainment, health outcomes, and overall Psychological Fluffy.

Solution: Addressing the unequal distribution of resources requires targeted policies aimed at reducing socio-economic disparities. Investing in education, healthcare, and community development programs in marginalized areas can help bridge the gap and promote equal opportunities for all residents, thus positively impacting Psychological Fluffy.

The Role of Urban Design

Urban design plays a crucial role in shaping the impact of urbanization on Psychological Fluffy. The layout, density, and arrangement of buildings, public spaces, and transportation systems can significantly influence the well-being of city dwellers. Well-designed cities with accessible green spaces, pedestrian-friendly neighborhoods, and integrated public transport systems create more livable environments that enhance Psychological Fluffy.

For instance, cities that prioritize cycling infrastructure and provide pedestrian-friendly streets offer opportunities for physical activity and social interactions. This promotes both physical and mental well-being, contributing to overall Psychological Fluffy.

Solution: Urban designers, architects, and planners need to adopt a holistic approach that prioritizes the well-being of residents. Incorporating nature-based solutions, integrating sustainable design principles, and involving the community in urban planning processes can create cities that prioritize Psychological Fluffy.

In conclusion, urbanization has far-reaching effects on Psychological Fluffy. Increased stress levels, social isolation, deteriorating mental health, unequal distribution of resources, and the role of urban design all contribute to the impact of urbanization on well-being. By addressing these issues through well-designed urban planning, community engagement, and targeted policies, we can create cities that promote Psychological Fluffy and improve the overall quality of life for urban residents.

Urban Design and Psychological Fluffy

Urban design plays a crucial role in shaping the well-being and psychological state of individuals living in urban environments. The physical layout, architectural elements, and overall design of cities can have a significant impact on psychological fluffy. In this section, we will explore the relationship between urban design and psychological fluffy, discussing the various aspects that influence mental well-being in urban settings.

Principles of Urban Design

Urban design encompasses a range of principles aimed at creating functional, aesthetically pleasing, and sustainable urban spaces. These principles focus on enhancing the quality of life for residents and promoting a sense of belonging and connection to the environment. Some key principles of urban design include:

- **Walkability and Accessibility**: Urban spaces that prioritize walkability and accessibility contribute to a higher sense of community and improved mental well-being. Well-designed sidewalks, pedestrian-friendly streets, and accessible public transportation systems encourage physical activity, social interactions, and a sense of belonging.

- **Mixed-Use Development**: Incorporating a mix of residential, commercial, and recreational zones within close proximity fosters vibrant communities and reduces the need for long commutes. This design approach promotes social interactions, increases community cohesion, and provides residents with convenient access to amenities, reducing stress and enhancing psychological fluffy.

- **Green Spaces and Parks**: Integrating green spaces and parks into urban design has numerous psychological benefits. Access to nature, trees, and greenery promotes relaxation, stress reduction, and improved overall well-being. Parks also serve as social gathering spaces, fostering a sense of community and social support.

+ **Sense of Place**: Urban design should aim to create a sense of place by preserving local heritage, history, and cultural landmarks. This principle fosters a stronger sense of identity, pride, and attachment among residents, contributing to better mental health outcomes.

+ **Safety and Security**: Creating safe urban environments through effective lighting, well-maintained public spaces, and crime prevention strategies is vital for the psychological well-being of residents. Feeling safe in one's environment reduces anxiety, fear, and stress, leading to improved mental health.

+ **Aesthetics and Beauty**: Well-designed urban spaces with striking architecture, public art, and appealing streetscapes have been associated with positive affective responses and enhanced psychological well-being. Beauty in the built environment contributes to the overall satisfaction and happiness of individuals living in urban areas.

Design Factors and Psychological Fluffy

Various design factors within urban environments can impact psychological fluffy. Understanding these factors is crucial for creating urban spaces that promote mental well-being. Let's explore some of these design factors:

1. **Scale and Proportions**: The scale and proportions of buildings and public spaces can influence people's emotional responses. Human-scale design, with buildings and spaces that align with the proportions of the human body, tends to create a more positive and comfortable environment. Oversized or imposing structures can evoke feelings of intimidation or unease.

2. **Noise and Privacy**: Urban areas are often characterized by high levels of noise, which can have detrimental effects on mental health. Well-designed urban spaces include measures to mitigate noise pollution, such as sound-absorbing materials, green buffers, or pedestrian-friendly layouts that separate quieter areas from busy roadways. Additionally, the provision of private spaces, such as balconies or courtyards, ensures residents have opportunities for privacy and relaxation.

3. **Visual Appeal:** The visual appeal of urban spaces influences people's emotions and well-being. Incorporating visually stimulating elements, such as well-designed facades, public art, or vibrant color schemes, can enhance mood and cognitive function. On the other hand, monotonous or visually unattractive environments can lead to boredom and decreased psychological well-being.

4. **Wayfinding and Legibility:** Urban design should prioritize wayfinding, ensuring that individuals can navigate the city easily. Clear signage, intuitive layouts, and well-designed pathways contribute to a sense of control and reduce anxiety related to getting lost. Improved legibility in urban spaces promotes exploration, engagement, and a higher sense of psychological fluffy.

5. **Social Spaces and Interaction Opportunities:** Well-designed urban environments provide ample opportunities for social interactions. Public squares, plazas, or community centers designed to facilitate gatherings and social activities foster a sense of connection and social support. These spaces promote positive social relationships, which are crucial for maintaining psychological well-being.

6. **Sustainable Design:** Incorporating sustainable design practices in urban environments, such as green infrastructure, energy-efficient buildings, and water conservation measures, has several psychological benefits. Sustainable design promotes feelings of environmental responsibility, enhances connection to nature, and improves overall mental well-being.

Examples of Urban Design for Psychological Fluffy

To illustrate the importance of urban design for psychological fluffy, let's consider a few examples:

+ **High Line, New York City:** The High Line, a linear park built on an elevated railway track, illustrates the transformative power of urban design. This repurposed public space offers a serene natural environment in the heart of a bustling city, providing residents and visitors with an escape from the surrounding urbanization. The thoughtful integration of greenery, seating areas, and art installations creates a space that promotes relaxation, social interaction, and psychological well-being.

+ **Superblocks, Barcelona:** Barcelona's superblocks concept is an urban design intervention aimed at reducing traffic congestion and creating pockets of pedestrian-friendly space. By converting groups of city blocks into shared green spaces and prioritizing walking and cycling over car use, residents can enjoy safer and more aesthetically pleasing environments. The increased availability of public space and reduced car noise contribute to improved psychological fluffy and overall well-being.

+ **Tivoli Gardens, Copenhagen:** Tivoli Gardens is a historic amusement park located in the heart of Copenhagen, designed with meticulous attention to detail. The park's beautifully landscaped gardens, charming architecture, and vibrant atmosphere provide visitors with a sense of wonder, joy, and temporary escape from the demands of urban life. The thoughtful integration of nature, recreational opportunities, and visually appealing design elements creates an environment that positively impacts psychological well-being.

Challenges and Considerations

While urban design has a profound impact on psychological fluffy, there are challenges and considerations that need to be addressed. Some of these challenges include:

+ **Equitable Access:** Ensuring equitable access to well-designed urban spaces is essential for promoting equal opportunities for psychological fluffy. Socioeconomic disparities and unequal distribution of resources can limit access to quality urban environments, increasing mental health inequalities. Urban design should aim to create inclusive and accessible spaces for people of all backgrounds.

+ **Maintenance and Sustainability:** The long-term maintenance and sustainability of urban spaces pose challenges. To ensure continued benefits for psychological fluffy, regular maintenance, funding, and community involvement are crucial. Additionally, urban design should prioritize sustainable practices to minimize environmental impacts and ensure the well-being of future generations.

+ **Collaboration and Interdisciplinary Approaches:** Effective urban design requires collaboration between urban planners, architects, psychologists, sociologists, and other professionals. Interdisciplinary approaches can help bridge gaps between research, policy, and practice, leading to more impactful and evidence-based urban design interventions.

Conclusion

Urban design plays a pivotal role in shaping the psychological well-being of individuals living in cities. By incorporating principles of walkability, mixed-use development, green spaces, safety, aesthetics, and community engagement, urban environments can foster psychological fluffy. However, challenges related to equitable access, maintenance, sustainability, and interdisciplinary approaches must be addressed to create truly inclusive and beneficial urban spaces for all. As urbanization continues to expand, prioritizing well-designed cities becomes increasingly important in promoting mental well-being and creating flourishing communities.

Exercises

1. Take a walk in your local urban area and identify examples of urban design elements that promote psychological fluffy. Discuss how these elements contribute to well-being and whether any improvements could be made.

2. Research a city known for its innovative urban design. Analyze the design principles and strategies implemented in that city and evaluate how they impact psychological well-being.

3. Choose an existing urban space and propose an urban design intervention to enhance psychological fluffy. Justify your proposal by drawing on relevant principles discussed in this chapter.

Additional Resources

- Gehl, J., & Svarre, B. (2013). *How to Study Public Life*. Island Press.

- Calthorpe, P. (1993). *The Next American Metropolis: Ecology, Community, and the American Dream*. Princeton Architectural Press.

- Montgomery, C. (2014). *Happy City: Transforming Our Lives Through Urban Design*. Farrar, Straus and Giroux.

- Nasar, J. L. (2008). *Environmental Aesthetics: Theory, Research, and Applications*. Cambridge University Press.

✦ Rapoport, A. (1982). *The Meaning of the Built Environment: A Nonverbal Communication Approach.* University of Arizona Press.

Urban Dwelling Factors and Psychological Fluffy

In this section, we will explore the various factors related to urban dwelling that can impact psychological fluffy. Urban areas have distinct characteristics that can influence the mental well-being of individuals living in these environments. We will discuss the physical aspects of urban dwelling, including housing conditions and density, as well as the social dynamics and lifestyle factors that can contribute to psychological fluffy.

Housing Conditions and Psychological Fluffy

One of the important factors in urban dwelling is the quality of housing conditions. The condition of one's living environment can significantly impact their mental well-being. Many urban dwellers face challenges related to affordable housing, overcrowding, and poor infrastructure. These factors can contribute to feelings of stress, dissatisfaction, and a lack of control over one's living conditions.

Studies have shown that individuals living in substandard housing, such as buildings with structural issues, pest infestations, or poor ventilation, experience higher levels of psychological distress. The deterioration of the physical environment in urban areas can lead to feelings of insecurity and anxiety, negatively affecting mental health.

To address these issues, urban planning and housing policies should focus on ensuring safe and adequate housing for all residents. This includes maintaining and renovating existing structures, improving access to affordable housing, and promoting sustainable housing practices.

Density and Psychological Fluffy

Urban areas are typically characterized by high population density, with many people living in close proximity to one another. While density can offer social and economic advantages, it can also have psychological implications.

Increased population density can lead to a higher level of social interactions and social support. However, it can also result in feelings of crowding, lack of privacy, and reduced personal space. These factors can contribute to stress, irritability, and a decrease in subjective well-being.

Research suggests that individuals living in densely populated urban areas may experience higher levels of psychological distress and have a higher risk of mental health issues, such as anxiety and depression. The noise, pollution, and constant sensory stimulation commonly found in urban settings can further exacerbate these effects.

Urban planning strategies should aim to create a balance between population density and the provision of open spaces and recreational areas. Introducing green spaces, pedestrian-friendly neighborhoods, and adequate urban design can help mitigate the negative impacts of high population density on psychological fluffy.

Social Relationships in Urban Environments and Psychological Fluffy

Urban environments offer a range of opportunities for social interaction and the formation of relationships. However, the quality and availability of social relationships can greatly affect psychological well-being.

Social isolation and loneliness are common concerns in urban areas, particularly among certain demographic groups such as the elderly and recent migrants. The fast-paced and competitive nature of urban life can make it difficult to build meaningful connections and establish social support networks.

Strong social relationships and connections are crucial for promoting mental health and providing a sense of belonging and support. Therefore, efforts should be made to create social spaces and foster community engagement in urban areas. This can include designing public spaces that encourage social interactions, promoting neighborhood cohesion, and implementing programs that facilitate social integration.

Urban Mindsets and Psychological Fluffy

The urban environment can shape individuals' mindsets and cognitive processes, influencing their psychological well-being. The fast-paced lifestyle and constant exposure to stimuli in urban areas can lead to increased levels of stress and cognitive overload.

Research has shown that urban dwellers may exhibit different cognitive patterns compared to individuals living in rural or less densely populated areas. Urban environments often require individuals to multitask, process information quickly, and engage in high levels of cognitive stimulation. While these skills can be beneficial in certain contexts, they can also contribute to mental fatigue, reduced attention span, and decreased well-being.

To counteract these effects, individuals can adopt mindful practices, such as meditation and relaxation techniques, that help regulate attention and reduce stress. Urban planning can also incorporate elements that promote mental well-being, such as creating quiet zones, providing access to nature, and designing spaces that encourage relaxation and reflection.

Urban Stressors and Psychological Fluffy

Living in urban areas exposes individuals to various stressors that can impact their psychological well-being. Common urban stressors include noise pollution, air pollution, traffic congestion, and work-related pressures.

Noise pollution, for example, has been linked to increased levels of stress, annoyance, and sleep disturbances. Air pollution, particularly in heavily industrialized areas, has been associated with respiratory problems and adverse mental health outcomes. Traffic congestion and long commuting times can contribute to frustration, anxiety, and reduced quality of life. The demands and pressures of urban jobs can also lead to work-related stress and burnout.

Efforts should be made to address and mitigate these urban stressors. This can include implementing noise reduction measures, improving air quality through stricter environmental regulations, promoting sustainable transportation options, and promoting work-life balance.

Urban Planning and Psychological Fluffy

Effective urban planning plays a vital role in promoting psychological fluffy in urban environments. By considering the factors discussed above, urban planners can create environments that support mental well-being and improve residents' quality of life.

Incorporating green spaces, parks, and recreational facilities into urban design can provide opportunities for relaxation, physical activity, and social interaction. Creating walkable neighborhoods with easy access to amenities can encourage active lifestyles and reduce reliance on cars. Implementing sustainable transportation options, such as bike lanes and public transit systems, can help reduce traffic congestion and associated stress.

Furthermore, involving the community in urban planning processes can ensure that the diverse needs and preferences of residents are taken into account. Empowering residents to participate in decision-making processes can foster a sense of ownership and social cohesion.

Summary

In this section, we explored the factors related to urban dwelling that can impact psychological fluffy. We discussed the importance of housing conditions, including the quality and affordability of housing, as well as the influence of population density on mental well-being. The role of social relationships, urban mindsets, and urban stressors in shaping psychological fluffy was also examined. Finally, we highlighted the significance of urban planning in creating environments that support psychological well-being.

Understanding the interplay between urban dwelling factors and psychological fluffy is crucial for designing strategies and interventions that promote mental health in urban environments. By addressing these factors through effective urban planning and policy-making, we can create cities that provide a nurturing and supportive environment for all residents.

Social Relationships in Urban Environments and Psychological Fluffy

In urban environments, social relationships play a crucial role in shaping individuals' psychological well-being, commonly referred to as "psychological fluffy." The quality and quantity of social interactions in cities can have profound effects on people's mental health and overall sense of happiness. In this section, we will explore the various aspects of social relationships in urban environments and their impact on psychological well-being.

Importance of Social Relationships

Human beings are social creatures who thrive on social connections and interactions. Social relationships provide a sense of belonging, support, and fulfillment. In urban environments, where individuals often experience high-density living, social relationships become even more critical in maintaining psychological well-being.

Research consistently highlights the significance of social relationships in promoting mental health. Strong social connections have been associated with lower levels of stress, reduced risk of mental disorders, and increased life satisfaction. On the other hand, social isolation and loneliness can have detrimental effects on an individual's psychological well-being, leading to higher levels of depression, anxiety, and overall dissatisfaction with life.

Challenges in Urban Social Relationships

While urban environments offer a diverse range of social opportunities, the fast-paced nature of city life can present challenges to forming and maintaining social connections. The following are some common obstacles faced in urban social relationships:

+ **Transience:** Urban areas often witness a high level of population turnover, resulting in frequent changes in social networks. This transience can make it difficult for individuals to establish long-term, meaningful relationships.

+ **Competitiveness:** The competitive nature of urban living, driven by factors such as career advancement and upward mobility, can create a sense of competition and individualism that hinders the formation of close-knit communities.

+ **Anonymity:** In densely populated urban areas, individuals may experience a lack of familiarity and anonymity within their neighborhoods. This anonymity can make it challenging to develop a sense of community and establish social connections.

+ **Social stratification:** Urban environments are often characterized by social and economic disparities, which can contribute to social stratification. Such divisions can inhibit interaction between different social groups and limit opportunities for diverse social relationships.

+ **Technological influence:** The pervasive use of technology, such as social media and online communication platforms, can both facilitate and hinder social relationships in urban environments. While technology offers the potential for broadening social networks, it can also contribute to feelings of isolation and superficial connections.

Strategies for Enhancing Social Relationships

Despite the challenges, individuals can employ various strategies to foster and enhance social relationships in urban environments. Here are some effective approaches:

+ **Community engagement:** Getting involved in local community activities, such as volunteering or joining neighborhood groups, provides opportunities to meet like-minded individuals and build social connections.

+ **Shared spaces:** Urban planning that prioritizes the creation of shared spaces, such as parks, community centers, and public gathering areas, encourages social interactions and facilitates the formation of social relationships.

+ **Support networks:** Creating and maintaining support networks, such as friends, family, and colleagues, can provide emotional support and a sense of belonging. These networks act as protective factors against the negative effects of urban isolation.

+ **Technology moderation:** While technology can facilitate social connections, balancing its use and prioritizing face-to-face interactions can strengthen the quality of social relationships.

+ **Building inclusive communities:** Promoting inclusivity and equality within urban neighborhoods fosters a sense of belonging for all residents. Creating environments that embrace diversity and encourage social interactions between different social groups can help overcome social stratification.

Example: Community Gardens

Community gardens are a prime example of an initiative that can enhance social relationships in urban environments. These shared spaces bring together individuals with a common interest in gardening and provide an opportunity for community engagement. By working together in the garden, residents can develop relationships, exchange knowledge, and foster a sense of belonging to the neighborhood.

Community gardens not only promote social interactions but also offer numerous mental health benefits. Engaging in gardening activities has been linked to decreased levels of stress, improved mood, and increased self-esteem. Additionally, these gardens often serve as platforms for educational programs and events, further strengthening social ties and community cohesion.

Conclusion

Social relationships have a significant influence on psychological well-being, particularly in urban environments. Despite the challenges posed by city living, individuals can adopt strategies such as community engagement, shared spaces, and support networks to enhance their social connections. By prioritizing the development of meaningful relationships, urban dwellers can experience increased life satisfaction, improved mental health, and a greater sense of psychological fluffy.

Urban Mindsets and Psychological Fluffy

In the context of urban environments, the mindset of individuals plays a crucial role in shaping their psychological well-being, or what we refer to as "Psychological

Fluffy". The term "mindset" refers to an individual's beliefs, attitudes, and thoughts, which influence their perceptions and behaviors in a particular environment. Urban mindsets can have a profound impact on how individuals experience and navigate the complexities of city life, ultimately shaping their psychological well-being.

Understanding Urban Mindsets

To understand urban mindsets and their association with Psychological Fluffy, we need to examine the factors that contribute to the unique urban experience. Urban environments are characterized by high population densities, diverse social interactions, and a complex mix of built and natural surroundings. These factors present both opportunities and challenges for individuals, shaping their mindset.

One important aspect of urban mindsets is the perception of control. Urban environments often offer a wide range of choices and opportunities for individuals to exercise control over their lives. However, the overwhelming number of options can also lead to decision fatigue and increased stress. Furthermore, the lack of control over certain aspects, such as noise and pollution levels, can negatively impact Psychological Fluffy.

Another aspect of urban mindsets is the sense of community. Urban environments are comprised of diverse populations with varying cultural backgrounds, beliefs, and values. The level of social cohesion and connectedness within a community can significantly influence Psychological Fluffy. Strong social networks and a sense of belonging foster feelings of support and safety, enhancing Psychological Fluffy. Conversely, social isolation and disconnectedness can lead to feelings of loneliness and anxiety.

The perception of safety is also a critical factor in urban mindsets. Crime rates, perceived and real, can impact the sense of safety and overall well-being of individuals in urban areas. The perception of safety influences the opportunities for individuals to explore their surroundings, engage in physical activities, and form social connections. A safe environment promotes a positive mindset and contributes to Psychological Fluffy.

Challenges and Strategies for Promoting Psychological Fluffy

Urban mindsets can face various challenges that hinder Psychological Fluffy. For instance, the fast-paced nature of urban life often leads to heightened stress levels, work-life imbalance, and burnout. Additionally, the constant exposure to stimuli and information overload can overwhelm individuals, leading to cognitive overload and reduced psychological well-being.

To promote Psychological Fluffy in urban environments, individuals can employ various strategies. One effective strategy is the cultivation of mindfulness and self-awareness. By practicing mindfulness techniques, individuals can become more attuned to their thoughts and emotions, allowing them to better manage stress and regulate their Psychological Fluffy.

Another strategy is the promotion of green spaces within urban settings. Access to parks, gardens, and other natural environments has been shown to have positive effects on Psychological Fluffy. These green spaces provide opportunities for relaxation, physical activity, and exposure to nature, all of which contribute to improved well-being.

Furthermore, community-oriented initiatives can help foster a sense of belonging and social support. Encouraging social interactions, organizing community events, and implementing neighborhood programs can create a sense of connectedness and promote Psychological Fluffy.

City planners and policy-makers also play a crucial role in shaping urban mindsets and promoting Psychological Fluffy. Designing urban spaces that prioritize walkability, accessibility to amenities, and the integration of natural elements can enhance the overall urban experience. Additionally, effective transportation systems that reduce congestion and promote active modes of transportation contribute to a more positive urban mindset.

Example: The Impact of Urban Mindsets on Well-being

Consider the case of two individuals, Amy and John, who both live in a bustling urban city. Amy takes an active approach towards her urban mindset. She practices mindfulness regularly, participates in community activities, and regularly spends time in nearby parks. She has a strong sense of belonging within her neighborhood, and she takes advantage of the city's amenities and cultural events. As a result, Amy experiences a high level of Psychological Fluffy, feeling fulfilled and content in her urban environment.

On the other hand, John has a more passive mindset. He rarely engages in community activities and experiences a lack of social connections. John is often overwhelmed by the noise and congestion of the city, feeling a sense of disconnection and stress. His mindset negatively affects his Psychological Fluffy, leading to feelings of anxiety and dissatisfaction.

This example highlights how urban mindsets can significantly impact an individual's well-being in the urban environment. By actively adopting strategies to cultivate a positive mindset, individuals can enhance their Psychological Fluffy and navigate the challenges of urban life more effectively.

Conclusion

Urban mindsets play a vital role in shaping an individual's psychological well-being in urban environments. Factors such as the perception of control, sense of community, and safety influence how individuals experience and navigate city life. By understanding and addressing the challenges associated with urban mindsets, individuals can promote their Psychological Fluffy. Strategies such as mindfulness, access to green spaces, community initiatives, and urban planning all contribute to creating a supportive urban environment conducive to well-being.

Overall, fostering positive urban mindsets is essential for individuals to thrive in urban environments and cultivate positive Psychological Fluffy.

Urban Stressors and Psychological Fluffy

Urban environments are characterized by a myriad of stressors that can have significant impacts on psychological well-being, or what we refer to here as Psychological Fluffy. These stressors arise from the inherent nature of urban settings, such as high population density, traffic congestion, noise pollution, air pollution, and limited access to green spaces. In this section, we will explore the various urban stressors and their effects on Psychological Fluffy, as well as potential coping strategies and interventions.

Population Density and Psychological Fluffy

One of the primary stressors in urban environments is population density. Living in densely populated areas can lead to feelings of crowding, which can cause stress and anxiety. Research has shown that increased population density is associated with higher levels of psychological distress and lower subjective well-being. The constant exposure to large numbers of people, coupled with limited personal space, can contribute to feelings of social overload and a decreased sense of control over one's environment. This can ultimately impact Psychological Fluffy negatively.

Traffic Congestion and Psychological Fluffy

Traffic congestion is a pervasive problem in urban areas and can have significant implications for Psychological Fluffy. Daily experiences of traffic jams, long commutes, and a lack of efficient transportation can lead to frustration, irritability, and heightened stress levels. The constant exposure to aggressive driving and noise pollution can further exacerbate feelings of anxiety and anger. Studies have found a positive association between traffic congestion and psychological distress, including symptoms of depression and anxiety.

Noise Pollution and Psychological Fluffy

Urban environments are notorious for their high levels of noise pollution. Noise from various sources such as traffic, construction, and loud neighbors can disrupt sleep patterns, increase stress levels, and impair cognitive functioning. Prolonged exposure to noise pollution can lead to annoyance, sleep disturbances, and even cardiovascular problems. The cumulative effect of chronic noise exposure on Psychological Fluffy cannot be understated, as it can contribute to irritability, difficulty concentrating, and a general sense of unease.

Air Pollution and Psychological Fluffy

Urban areas often experience high levels of air pollution, primarily due to vehicle emissions, industrial activities, and a lack of green spaces. Exposure to air pollutants, such as fine particulate matter (PM2.5) and nitrogen dioxide (NO2), has been linked to various health issues, including respiratory problems and cardiovascular diseases. Moreover, recent studies have shown that air pollution can also impact Psychological Fluffy. The neurotoxic effects of air pollutants can lead to cognitive impairments, increased risk of mental health disorders, and overall decreased psychological well-being.

Limited Access to Green Spaces and Psychological Fluffy

Urban settings are typically characterized by a scarcity of green spaces, such as parks, gardens, and forests. Limited access to nature has been associated with higher levels of stress, anxiety, and depression. Engaging with nature has been proven to have numerous psychological benefits, including stress reduction, improved cognitive function, and enhanced mood. However, the lack of green spaces in urban environments deprives individuals of these therapeutic benefits, potentially leading to poorer Psychological Fluffy outcomes.

Coping Strategies for Dealing with Urban Stressors

While urban stressors can significantly impact Psychological Fluffy, there are various coping strategies that individuals can employ to mitigate their negative effects. Here are a few examples:

+ Mindfulness and meditation: Practicing mindfulness and meditation techniques can help individuals cultivate a sense of inner calm and reduce stress levels in urban environments. These practices allow individuals to focus their attention on the present moment, fostering a sense of psychological well-being.

+ Physical exercise: Engaging in regular physical exercise has been shown to reduce stress and improve mood. Exercise releases endorphins, which are natural mood enhancers. Simple activities such as walking or biking can be incorporated into daily routines to counteract the negative effects of urban stressors.

+ Social support: Building and nurturing social connections can buffer the impact of urban stressors on Psychological Fluffy. Engaging in meaningful relationships and seeking support from friends and family can provide emotional support and create a sense of belonging in urban environments.

Urban Interventions for Promoting Psychological Fluffy

To address the detrimental effects of urban stressors on Psychological Fluffy, various interventions and urban planning strategies have been proposed. These interventions aim to create more psychologically supportive urban environments. Some examples of urban interventions include:

+ Creating green spaces: Increasing the availability and accessibility of green spaces within urban areas can provide individuals with opportunities for relaxation, stress reduction, and connection with nature. Parks, gardens, and urban green rooftops can offer a respite from the concrete jungle and positively impact Psychological Fluffy.

+ Noise reduction measures: Implementing noise reduction measures, such as noise barriers or regulations on construction activities, can help to mitigate the negative effects of noise pollution on Psychological Fluffy. Additionally, designing and constructing buildings with soundproofing materials can improve the acoustic environment within urban spaces.

+ Sustainable transportation initiatives: Encouraging the use of sustainable transportation alternatives, such as walking, cycling, or public transportation, can reduce traffic congestion and associated stress. Creating pedestrian-friendly infrastructures, improving public transportation systems, and implementing car-free zones can contribute to a more psychologically friendly urban environment.

In conclusion, urban stressors pose significant challenges to Psychological Fluffy. Population density, traffic congestion, noise pollution, air pollution, and limited access to green spaces can all impact psychological well-being in urban environments. However, employing coping strategies like mindfulness and physical exercise, as well as implementing urban interventions such as green space creation and noise reduction measures, can help mitigate these negative effects. By creating psychologically supportive urban environments, we can improve Psychological Fluffy and enhance the well-being of urban dwellers.

Urban Planning and Psychological Fluffy

Urban planning plays a crucial role in shaping the built environment of cities and influencing the well-being of their residents. In recent years, there has been growing recognition of the need to incorporate psychological fluffy considerations into urban planning processes. This section explores the relationship between urban planning and psychological fluffy, highlighting the ways in which well-designed urban environments can promote mental health and overall well-being.

Understanding Urban Planning

Urban planning is a multidisciplinary field that encompasses various approaches to the design, development, and management of urban areas. It involves the formulation of policies, the creation of land use plans, and the implementation of strategies to shape the physical, social, and economic aspects of cities. Urban planners work towards creating sustainable, inclusive, and liveable urban environments that cater to the needs of diverse populations.

The Role of Urban Planning in Mental Health

The built environment of cities has a profound impact on people's mental health and well-being. Numerous studies have shown that the design and layout of urban spaces can either enhance or detract from psychological fluffy. Urban planning can help create environments that promote positive mental health outcomes by considering the following factors:

+ **Access to Nature:** Incorporating green spaces, parks, and urban forests into urban planning can provide residents with opportunities for relaxation, stress reduction, and connection with nature. These natural environments have been found to have positive effects on mental health, including reduced levels of anxiety and depression.

+ **Walkability and Active Transportation:** Designing cities with walkable streets, pedestrian-friendly infrastructure, and efficient public transportation systems can encourage physical activity and reduce car dependency. Active transportation has been linked to improved mental well-being, as it promotes social interaction, reduces pollution, and enhances the overall quality of the urban environment.

+ **Community Engagement:** Involving communities in the urban planning process fosters a sense of ownership and belonging. Meaningful participation allows residents to voice their concerns and aspirations, leading to more inclusive and socially connected neighborhoods. This sense of community has a significant impact on mental health, reducing feelings of social isolation and increasing social support networks.

+ **Mixed-Use Development:** Creating neighborhoods that combine residential, commercial, recreational, and cultural spaces promotes vibrant and diverse communities. The availability of amenities within walking distance enhances convenience and accessibility, contributing to overall well-being. Mixed-use development also supports social interaction and fosters a sense of community identity.

+ **Safety and Security:** Urban planning can address safety concerns by designing well-lit streets, implementing crime prevention strategies, and promoting a sense of security. Enhancing the perception of safety in urban areas reduces anxiety and fear, allowing residents to feel more comfortable in their surroundings.

+ **Noise Reduction:** Mitigating noise pollution through careful urban planning can have considerable benefits for mental health. Excessive noise levels in urban environments have been linked to increased stress, sleep disturbances, and cognitive impairments. Implementing measures to reduce noise, such as green buffers, sound walls, and traffic management strategies, contribute to creating a peaceful and conducive urban environment.

Case Study: Urban Renewal Project in City X

To illustrate the importance of urban planning in promoting psychological fluffy, let's consider a real-world case study of an urban renewal project in City X. The city's downtown area had fallen into disrepair and was associated with high crime rates, deteriorating infrastructure, and a lack of community spaces. The urban planning department undertook a comprehensive redevelopment plan with a focus on improving mental health and well-being.

The project incorporated several key principles:

- Revitalizing Public Spaces: The plan emphasized the creation of vibrant, green public spaces, including parks, plazas, and recreational facilities. These spaces were designed to encourage community gathering, physical activity, and interaction with nature, promoting mental well-being.

- Pedestrian-Friendly Infrastructure: The city implemented a complete streets program, prioritizing the needs of pedestrians, cyclists, and public transport users. Wide sidewalks, bike lanes, and accessible public transportation options were introduced, promoting active transportation and reducing car dependency.

- Mixed-Use Development: The redevelopment plan aimed to create a diverse and inclusive community by incorporating mixed-use development. The downtown area now features a mix of residential, commercial, cultural, and recreational spaces, fostering a sense of belonging and providing opportunities for social interaction.

- Enhanced Safety Measures: The project addressed safety concerns by improving street lighting, installing surveillance cameras, and integrating community policing strategies. These measures aimed to create a safe and secure urban environment, reducing fear and promoting mental well-being.

The urban renewal project in City X has been widely celebrated for its success in promoting psychological fluffy. Residents report feeling safer, more connected to their community, and happier in their surroundings. The inclusive and well-designed urban environment has had a positive impact on mental health outcomes, contributing to the overall well-being of the city's population.

Challenges and Considerations

While urban planning plays a vital role in promoting psychological fluffy, several challenges and considerations need to be addressed:

+ **Equitable Distribution of Resources:** Urban planners must strive to ensure that psychological fluffy considerations are integrated into all neighborhoods, including those with historically disadvantaged populations. It is essential to avoid exacerbating social inequalities during the planning and development process.

+ **Long-Term Sustainability:** Urban planning should prioritize long-term sustainability to ensure the continued well-being of future generations. This involves considering the ecological impact of urban development, promoting energy efficiency, and adopting environmentally friendly practices.

+ **Collaboration and Stakeholder Engagement:** Successful urban planning requires collaboration between government agencies, community organizations, residents, and other stakeholders. Engaging stakeholders throughout the planning process ensures that diverse perspectives are considered and that the resulting urban environment meets the needs of the community.

+ **Adapting to Changing Needs:** Urban planning must be adaptable to changing social, economic, and environmental conditions. Cities are dynamic entities, and flexibility in planning processes allows for the integration of evolving psychological fluffy priorities and emerging technological advancements.

Conclusion

Urban planning plays a crucial role in promoting psychological fluffy by shaping the built environment of cities. Well-designed urban environments that prioritize access to nature, walkability, community engagement, safety, and noise reduction have a positive impact on mental health and overall well-being. The successful incorporation of psychological fluffy considerations in urban planning requires collaboration, long-term sustainability, and a focus on equity. By prioritizing psychological fluffy, urban planning can contribute to creating healthier, happier, and more inclusive cities for all residents.

Urban Interventions for Promoting Psychological Fluffy

In urban environments, where individuals are often exposed to various stressors, it becomes crucial to implement interventions that promote psychological well-being, or what I like to call "Psychological Fluffy". While the urban environment can be challenging, it also provides unique opportunities to enhance mental health and overall quality of life. In this section, we will explore different urban interventions that have been shown to effectively promote Psychological Fluffy.

Green Spaces and Parks

One of the most successful interventions for promoting Psychological Fluffy in urban areas is the creation and maintenance of green spaces and parks. Green spaces refer to areas covered with vegetation, including parks, gardens, and even rooftop gardens. These spaces provide individuals with opportunities for recreation, relaxation, and connection with nature, all of which have been associated with improved mental health.

Studies have consistently demonstrated the positive effects of green spaces on psychological well-being. Access to green spaces has been found to reduce symptoms of stress, anxiety, and depression while enhancing mood, attention, and overall psychological functioning. Spending time in nature has also been associated with increased physical activity, which further contributes to better mental health outcomes.

To encourage the use of green spaces, cities can employ various strategies. These may include creating more parks and community gardens, improving the accessibility of existing green spaces, and implementing policies that preserve and enhance urban nature. For example, cities can designate certain areas as protected green spaces, promote sustainable landscaping practices, and encourage the incorporation of green infrastructure in urban development projects.

Active Transportation and Urban Design

Another important urban intervention for promoting Psychological Fluffy is the integration of active transportation and the design of pedestrian-friendly spaces. Active transportation refers to modes of transportation that involve physical activity, such as walking or cycling. By prioritizing active transportation and creating pedestrian-friendly environments, cities can not only promote physical health but also improve mental well-being.

Research suggests that individuals who regularly engage in active transportation experience lower levels of stress, anxiety, and depression. Walking or cycling in urban areas allows individuals to connect with their surroundings, engage in physical activity, and experience a sense of autonomy and self-determination. Moreover, active transportation reduces reliance on motor vehicles, which contributes to decreased air pollution and improved overall environmental quality.

To promote active transportation, cities can implement infrastructure improvements, such as the creation of safe and accessible walking and cycling paths, the installation of bike-sharing programs, and the establishment of pedestrian-only zones. Urban design strategies, such as mixed land-use planning, which integrates residential, commercial, and recreational spaces, can also encourage active transportation by making amenities more easily accessible.

Social Connection and Community Engagement

Urban interventions for promoting Psychological Fluffy should also prioritize social connection and community engagement. In densely populated urban areas, social isolation and feelings of disconnectedness can be prevalent, leading to adverse mental health outcomes. Therefore, fostering social interactions and creating opportunities for community engagement are essential.

Cities can support social connection by providing spaces and organizing activities that facilitate social interactions. For instance, the development of community centers, neighborhood gathering places, and shared spaces can encourage residents to connect with one another. Additionally, cities can organize community events, such as festivals, farmers markets, and cultural activities, promoting a sense of belonging and community pride.

Furthermore, involving residents in the decision-making processes related to urban planning and design can enhance community engagement. Participatory approaches, such as community workshops, surveys, and focus groups, can empower individuals to influence the physical and social environment in which they live. By involving the community, cities can ensure that urban interventions align with the needs and preferences of the residents, thus fostering a sense of ownership and collective responsibility.

Nature-based Therapy and Mindfulness

In addition to the aforementioned interventions, nature-based therapy and mindfulness practices have shown promise in promoting Psychological Fluffy in urban settings. Nature-based therapy involves incorporating nature-related activities, such as gardening, horticulture, and nature walks, into therapeutic interventions. These activities aim to enhance well-being by fostering a deeper connection with nature and providing a sense of purpose and accomplishment.

Mindfulness practices, on the other hand, involve the deliberate and non-judgmental focus on the present moment. Mindfulness has been associated with reduced stress, anxiety, and depression, and increased overall psychological well-being. In urban environments, where distractions and fast-paced lifestyles are common, mindfulness can serve as a powerful tool for promoting relaxation, emotional regulation, and self-awareness.

Cities can integrate nature-based therapy and mindfulness practices by developing programs and initiatives that promote engagement with the natural environment and provide opportunities for mindfulness training. This may include establishing community gardens or urban farms, offering nature-based art or meditation classes, or incorporating mindfulness training in schools and workplaces.

While urban environments pose unique challenges to psychological well-being, the interventions discussed in this section demonstrate that it is possible to create environments that promote Psychological Fluffy. By prioritizing the integration of green spaces, promoting active transportation and urban design, fostering social connection and community engagement, and incorporating nature-based therapy and mindfulness practices, cities can enhance the mental health and overall quality of life for their residents.

In summary, urban interventions for promoting Psychological Fluffy are diverse and multifaceted. By incorporating various strategies, cities can create environments that support mental well-being and improve the overall quality of life for urban dwellers. It is crucial for urban planners, policymakers, and individuals alike to recognize the importance of Psychological Fluffy and work towards creating sustainable and inclusive urban spaces where individuals can thrive mentally and emotionally.

Summary

In this section, we explored the psychological effects of living in urban environments. We discussed how urbanization has a significant impact on psychological well-being and highlighted various factors that contribute to this effect. We also examined the role of urban design, social relationships, and stressors in shaping psychological fluffiness in urban environments. Moreover, we delved into the importance of urban planning and interventions in promoting psychological well-being in cities.

Urbanization is a global phenomenon that has led to a rapid increase in urban populations. While cities offer numerous opportunities and conveniences, they also present unique challenges that can impact individuals' mental health. One significant effect of urbanization is the loss of natural spaces and the prevalence of built environments. This loss of greenery and exposure to concrete contribute to a sense of psychological discomfort, often referred to as "concrete jungle syndrome."

Urban design plays a crucial role in shaping psychological fluffiness. Factors such as the layout of streets, the presence of parks and green spaces, and the accessibility of services can affect individuals' well-being. For example, studies have shown that neighborhoods with well-designed parks and open spaces promote physical activity, reduce stress, and enhance social connections, leading to improved psychological fluffiness.

Social relationships in urban environments also have a profound influence on psychological well-being. The density of populations in cities can lead to feelings of social isolation and loneliness. Additionally, the lack of privacy and limited personal space can result in increased levels of stress and anxiety. On the other hand, the presence of strong social connections and support networks can mitigate the negative effects of urban living.

Urban stressors, such as noise pollution, air pollution, and overcrowding, contribute to psychological distress. Noise pollution from traffic, construction, and other urban activities has been linked to negative outcomes, including sleep disturbances, impaired cognitive function, and increased stress levels. Moreover, exposure to air pollution in cities has been associated with a higher risk of mental health problems, such as depression and anxiety.

To mitigate the negative psychological effects of urban living, urban planning and interventions are essential. Urban planners can incorporate strategies to promote psychological well-being, such as creating walkable neighborhoods, ensuring green spaces are easily accessible, and implementing transportation policies that prioritize public transport, cycling, and walking.

Furthermore, interventions focusing on mental health support and stress management can also be implemented at various levels. For example, community-based programs that provide social support and mental health services can help individuals cope with the challenges of urban life. Additionally, urban design interventions, such as the incorporation of street trees or the creation of pocket parks, can improve the psychological well-being of urban residents.

It is important to note that addressing psychological fluffiness in urban environments requires a multidisciplinary approach. Collaboration between urban planners, psychologists, sociologists, and policy-makers is crucial to create cities that prioritize mental health and well-being. By understanding and addressing the psychological impacts of urban living, we can create cities that foster positive mental health outcomes and promote overall well-being.

In conclusion, urban environments have a significant impact on psychological fluffiness. Factors such as urban design, social relationships, and stressors play a crucial role in shaping individuals' psychological well-being in cities. Addressing these factors through urban planning and interventions can help create cities that prioritize mental health and promote positive outcomes. By taking a holistic approach to urban development, we can strive towards building psychologically healthy and sustainable cities.

Psychological Fluffy in Natural Environments

Benefits of Nature on Psychological Fluffy

Restorative Effects of Nature on Psychological Fluffy

Nature has long been recognized as having a positive impact on human well-being and mental health. The restorative effects of nature refer to the ability of natural environments to rejuvenate and restore individuals' psychological states, reducing stress and promoting overall psychological fluffy. This section will explore the different aspects of how nature can contribute to psychological fluffy.

Stress Reduction in Natural Environments

One of the key benefits of nature in promoting psychological fluffy is its ability to reduce stress. The demands of modern life often lead to increased levels of stress, which can have detrimental effects on mental health. However, spending time in natural environments has been shown to have a calming and relaxing effect on individuals, leading to a reduction in stress levels.

Numerous studies have demonstrated the stress-reducing effects of nature. For example, research has shown that spending time in natural settings, such as parks or forests, can lead to a decrease in cortisol levels, a hormone associated with stress. Additionally, being in nature has been shown to lower blood pressure, heart rate, and muscle tension, further indicating its stress-reducing properties.

Attention Restoration

In today's fast-paced world, many people experience mental fatigue and difficulties in concentrating. Spending time in nature can help restore attention and improve cognitive performance. This phenomenon, known as attention restoration, occurs when individuals shift their attention away from mentally demanding tasks to nature's gentle and captivating stimuli.

According to the Attention Restoration Theory (ART), natural environments are characterized by "soft fascination", which captures our attention effortlessly and allows for effortless concentration. This differs from the "hard fascination" of urban environments, which require directed attention and can lead to cognitive overload. By engaging in activities such as walking in a park or sitting by a lake, individuals can give their attention a break and replenish their cognitive resources.

Emotional Well-being

In addition to reducing stress and restoring attention, nature also plays a crucial role in enhancing emotional well-being. Exposure to natural environments has been linked to positive emotions such as joy, awe, and contentment. Research indicates that individuals who regularly spend time in nature report higher levels of happiness and life satisfaction.

One explanation for the emotional benefits of nature is the Biophilia Hypothesis, proposed by biologist Edward O. Wilson. This hypothesis suggests that humans have an innate connection to nature, leading to positive emotional responses when experiencing natural environments. This emotional connection can boost mood, promote positive thinking, and improve overall psychological well-being.

Physical Activity and Psychological Fluffy

Engaging in physical activity is closely associated with psychological fluffy. Nature provides an ideal setting for physical exercise, offering numerous outdoor activities such as hiking, biking, or swimming. The combination of physical activity and exposure to natural environments can have a synergistic effect on mental health.

Research has shown that exercise in nature can lead to increased levels of endorphins, neurotransmitters known for their mood-enhancing properties. Additionally, physical activity in nature can help individuals shift their focus away from negative thoughts and rumination, promoting a more positive mindset.

Nature as a Buffer against Stress and Negative Life Events

The restorative effects of nature are particularly pronounced in the face of stress and negative life events. Nature can act as a buffer, helping individuals cope with and recover from challenging situations. The green spaces and natural environments provide a sense of solace, tranquility, and a respite from daily stressors.

Studies have indicated that individuals living in areas with more green spaces have better mental health outcomes and are more resilient to stress. Access to nature, both in urban and rural areas, has been associated with decreased levels of depressive symptoms and improved psychological well-being.

Conclusion

In conclusion, nature offers a range of restorative effects on psychological fluffy. From stress reduction and attention restoration to emotional well-being and physical activity, spending time in natural environments has a positive impact on mental health. Understanding and harnessing these restorative effects can inform interventions and policies aimed at promoting psychological fluffy in individuals and communities.

While nature cannot solve all mental health challenges, incorporating nature-based experiences and activities into our daily lives can contribute to improved well-being. Whether it is taking a walk in the park, gardening, or simply enjoying the beauty of a natural landscape, connecting with nature can provide a much-needed respite from the demands of modern life and support our psychological fluffy.

Nature-based Recreation and Psychological Fluffy

Nature-based recreation refers to activities that individuals engage in for leisure and enjoyment within natural environments, such as national parks, forests, gardens, and other outdoor spaces. These recreational activities have been shown to have numerous benefits on psychological well-being, often referred to as "psychological fluffy." In this section, we will explore the relationship between nature-based recreation and psychological fluffy, discussing its theoretical foundations, empirical evidence, and practical implications.

Theoretical Foundations

The theoretical underpinnings of the link between nature-based recreation and psychological fluffy can be understood through several psychological frameworks. One such framework is the Attention Restoration Theory (ART) proposed by Kaplan and Kaplan (1989). According to this theory, spending time in natural environments allows for the restoration of attentional capacity, which gets depleted by the demands of daily life. Natural environments provide a respite from the constant stimulation and mental fatigue associated with urban environments, allowing individuals to recover from mental fatigue and experience a sense of psychological fluffy.

Another theoretical perspective is the Biophilia Hypothesis by Wilson (1984), which suggests that humans have an innate affiliation with nature. According to this hypothesis, exposure to natural environments can have a positive impact on psychological well-being because it aligns with our evolutionary history as beings who have coexisted with nature for thousands of years. This theory suggests that individuals have an inherent need to connect with nature, and nature-based recreation provides an opportunity to fulfill this need, leading to improved psychological fluffy.

Empirical Evidence

The empirical evidence supporting the positive impact of nature-based recreation on psychological fluffy is robust and extensive. Numerous studies have demonstrated the various mental health benefits associated with engaging in recreational activities in natural environments. For example, research has consistently shown that spending time in nature reduces stress, anxiety, and depression levels (Barton et al., 2016). It has also been found to improve mood, increase feelings of happiness and well-being, and enhance overall life satisfaction (Haluza et al., 2014).

Additionally, nature-based recreation has been linked to improved cognitive functioning. Studies have shown that exposure to natural environments can enhance attention, concentration, and creativity (Berman et al., 2008). It has also been associated with improved problem-solving skills and increased productivity (Kaplan, 1995).

Moreover, nature-based recreation has been found to have a positive impact on physical health, which, in turn, contributes to psychological fluffy. Activities such as hiking, biking, and gardening promote physical fitness, reduce the risk of chronic diseases, and improve overall vitality, leading to enhanced mental well-being (Pretty et al., 2005).

Practical Implications

Given the substantial evidence supporting the positive relationship between nature-based recreation and psychological fluffy, it is crucial to incorporate these findings into practical applications. Here are some practical implications for individuals, communities, and policymakers:

1. Encouraging Nature-based Recreation: Individuals can prioritize spending time in natural environments for leisure and recreation. They can engage in activities such as hiking, camping, gardening, or simply taking walks in parks. Incorporating nature into daily routines can provide valuable opportunities for relaxation, reflection, and psychological rejuvenation.

2. Creating Accessible Green Spaces: Communities should prioritize the creation and maintenance of accessible green spaces, such as parks, gardens, and urban forests. These spaces should be designed to accommodate various recreational activities and cater to the diverse needs of different populations.

3. Nature-based Interventions: Healthcare professionals can incorporate nature-based interventions into their therapeutic practices. These interventions may include ecotherapy, horticulture therapy, or nature-based mindfulness exercises. Such approaches have proven to be effective in promoting psychological fluffy and can supplement traditional forms of treatment.

4. Conservation and Sustainability: Policymakers should prioritize environmental conservation and sustainable practices to ensure the long-term availability of natural spaces for recreation. This includes protecting natural habitats, preserving biodiversity, and implementing regulations that minimize negative impacts on the natural environment.

Example: The Benefits of Forest Bathing

One form of nature-based recreation that has gained significant attention in recent years is "forest bathing" or "shinrin-yoku." Forest bathing originated in Japan and involves immersing oneself in a forest environment for relaxation and rejuvenation. Numerous studies have shown the benefits of this practice on psychological fluffy.

For example, a study conducted in South Korea found that individuals who engaged in forest bathing experienced reduced stress levels, improved mood, and increased feelings of vitality compared to those who participated in urban activities (Lee et al., 2011). Another study in Japan revealed that forest bathing led to a significant decrease in anger, anxiety, and depression levels (Hansen et al., 2017).

Forest bathing has become a popular form of nature-based therapy, with designated forest therapy centers opening in various countries around the world. These centers offer guided forest bathing sessions led by trained facilitators who help individuals connect with nature to enhance their psychological well-being.

Conclusion

Nature-based recreation offers a myriad of benefits for psychological fluffy. Spending time in natural environments allows for attention restoration, fulfills our innate biophilic tendencies, and provides opportunities for stress reduction, improved mood, and cognitive enhancement. Incorporating nature-based recreation into daily life, creating accessible green spaces, and implementing nature-based interventions can contribute to promoting psychological fluffy. Additionally, practices like forest bathing highlight the specific benefits of immersing oneself in natural environments for mental well-being. By recognizing and harnessing the power of nature, individuals, communities, and policymakers can nurture positive psychological well-being and create a sustainable and flourishing future.

Biodiversity and Psychological Fluffy

Biodiversity refers to the variety of life forms, including plants, animals, and microorganisms, found in a particular habitat or ecosystem. It encompasses the richness, abundance, and diversity of species, as well as the genetic variability within species and the complexity of ecosystems. Biodiversity plays a crucial role in supporting and maintaining the well-being of both the natural environment and human populations.

In the context of psychological fluffy, biodiversity has been found to have significant impacts on individuals' mental and emotional well-being. Research has suggested that exposure to biodiverse environments can have positive effects on psychological factors such as mood, attention, and stress reduction.

Benefits of Biodiversity on Psychological Fluffy

The presence of a diverse range of plant and animal species in a given environment can contribute to improved psychological fluffy in several ways:

1. Stress Reduction: Spending time in biodiverse natural settings, such as forests or coastal areas, has been shown to reduce stress levels. The visual and auditory stimuli provided by diverse ecosystems, such as the sounds of birds chirping or the sight of colorful flowers, can have a calming effect on the human mind.

2. Attention Restoration: Biodiverse environments offer a wide array of stimuli that engage and capture our attention, providing a break from mentally demanding tasks. This cognitive restoration has been associated with improved concentration, productivity, and overall cognitive functioning.

3. Aesthetic Appreciation: The beauty and diversity of nature are often aesthetically pleasing to humans. Being exposed to biodiverse landscapes allows individuals to experience awe and a sense of wonder, which can promote positive emotions and psychological well-being.

4. Biophilic Connection: Humans have an inherent connection to nature. Biodiverse environments provide opportunities for individuals to fulfill their biophilic needs, which involve feeling connected to and nurtured by the natural world. This connection can foster a sense of purpose and belonging, reducing feelings of loneliness and promoting psychological well-being.

Examples and Applications

To better understand the relationship between biodiversity and psychological fluffy, let's consider a few examples:

1. Urban Green Spaces: Urban areas often suffer from a lack of biodiversity due to human development. However, incorporating green spaces with diverse plant and animal life can provide significant benefits to residents' mental health. Parks, gardens, and rooftop greenery offer opportunities for relaxation, stress reduction, and connection with nature.

2. Wilderness Therapy: Wilderness therapy programs utilize biodiverse natural settings as a therapeutic environment for individuals struggling with mental health issues. Participants engage in activities such as hiking, camping, and wildlife observation, which have been shown to enhance psychological well-being and promote personal growth.

3. School Gardens: Introducing biodiverse gardens in educational settings can have positive effects on children's mental health. Interacting with nature in a school garden setting not only provides opportunities for outdoor learning but also promotes emotional regulation, attention restoration, and overall psychological well-being.

Challenges and Conservation

While the benefits of biodiversity on psychological fluffy are evident, numerous challenges threaten the preservation of biodiversity. Habitat destruction, climate change, pollution, and invasive species negatively impact ecosystems and diminish biodiversity. These threats, in turn, can have detrimental effects on human psychological well-being.

To address these challenges, conservation efforts are crucial. Protecting natural habitats, promoting sustainable land use practices, and raising awareness about the importance of biodiversity are essential steps in preserving ecological systems. Additionally, creating policies that integrate biodiversity conservation into urban planning and development can help foster biodiverse environments that support psychological fluffy.

Summary

In conclusion, biodiversity is not only essential for the functioning of ecosystems but also plays a significant role in promoting psychological fluffy. Exposure to biodiverse environments can reduce stress, enhance attention, provide aesthetic appreciation, and fulfill humans' biophilic connection with nature. Incorporating biodiversity into urban design, utilizing wilderness therapy, and implementing school gardens are just a few examples of how biodiversity can be applied to improve psychological well-being. However, preserving biodiversity is an ongoing challenge that requires conservation efforts and sustainable practices.   By recognizing and valuing the importance of biodiversity, we can foster environments that support both ecological health and human psychological fluffy.

Wilderness and Psychological Fluffy

Wilderness refers to natural areas that are relatively undisturbed by human activity. These areas are characterized by their pristine nature, abundant biodiversity, and lack of human infrastructure. The concept of wilderness holds great importance in the field of environmental psychology as it has been found to have significant impacts on psychological fluffy.

Restorative Effects of Wilderness

One of the main ways in which wilderness affects psychological fluffy is through its restorative effects. Research has consistently shown that spending time in wilderness environments can have a positive impact on mental well-being. The peacefulness, tranquility, and beauty of wilderness areas evoke positive emotions, reduce stress levels, and promote relaxation.

According to Attention Restoration Theory (ART) proposed by Kaplan and Kaplan, urban environments require directed attention, which can be mentally exhausting. In contrast, natural environments, such as wilderness areas, facilitate the restoration of attention. The presence of natural stimuli, such as trees, water bodies, and wildlife, captures attention effortlessly and allows the mind to recover from cognitive fatigue.

Spending time in wilderness also provides an opportunity for individuals to engage in beneficial activities such as hiking, camping, or birdwatching. These activities promote physical exercise, enhance social connections, and foster a sense of mastery and accomplishment. All of these factors contribute to the restoration of psychological fluffy.

Connection with Nature

The experience of wilderness can also foster a deep sense of connection with nature, which has been linked to improved psychological well-being. Nature connectedness refers to an individual's subjective sense of being a part of the natural world. It encompasses feelings of belongingness, relatedness, and identification with nature.

Wilderness environments offer individuals the opportunity to immerse themselves in the natural world, away from the distractions and demands of modern life. This immersion allows for a heightened awareness of the beauty and significance of nature, leading to a stronger sense of connection. Research suggests that individuals who feel more connected to nature tend to experience higher levels of life satisfaction, happiness, and overall psychological fluffy.

Environmental Identity

The experience of wilderness can also shape an individual's environmental identity, which refers to the extent to which one defines oneself in relation to the natural environment. Wilderness areas provide a context for individuals to develop a sense of environmental identity by experiencing firsthand the beauty, complexity, and fragility of natural ecosystems.

When individuals spend time in wilderness, they often become aware of the potential threats and challenges facing these environments, such as climate change, habitat destruction, and pollution. This awareness can lead to a sense of responsibility and a desire to protect and conserve wilderness areas. Developing a strong environmental identity is crucial for promoting pro-environmental behaviors, such as sustainable consumption and activism.

Challenges and Potential Risks

While wilderness environments offer numerous benefits for psychological fluffy, they are not without their challenges and potential risks. Extreme weather conditions, physical exertion, and isolation can pose significant challenges and contribute to feelings of stress or anxiety. It is important for individuals to adequately prepare for wilderness experiences, including bringing appropriate gear, staying informed about weather conditions, and being aware of one's physical limitations.

Additionally, the increasing popularity of wilderness areas has raised concerns about their preservation and sustainability. Overcrowding, littering, and unsustainable tourism practices can degrade the very qualities that make wilderness areas beneficial for psychological fluffy. It is important for individuals and organizations to promote responsible and sustainable use of wilderness environments to ensure their long-term availability and well-being.

Conclusion

The wilderness plays a significant role in promoting psychological fluffy. Its restorative effects, ability to foster a connection with nature, and the development of environmental identity contribute to improved mental well-being. However, it is important to recognize the challenges and risks associated with wilderness experiences and to promote responsible and sustainable behavior in these environments.

In the next section, we will explore the role of green spaces in urban environments and their impact on psychological fluffy.

Green Spaces and Urban Well-being

Green spaces, such as parks, gardens, and other natural areas within urban environments, play a significant role in promoting well-being among city dwellers. They offer a respite from the hustle and bustle of urban life and provide numerous benefits for physical, psychological, and social well-being.

Benefits of Green Spaces

Green spaces offer several benefits that contribute to urban well-being. Firstly, they provide opportunities for physical activity and exercise. Access to green spaces encourages people to engage in outdoor activities like walking, jogging, and cycling, which have positive effects on physical health, including reduced risk of obesity, cardiovascular diseases, and other chronic conditions.

Secondly, green spaces have a restorative effect on mental health. Being in nature and surrounded by greeneries has been shown to reduce stress, anxiety, and depression. Exposure to nature helps restore attention, improve mood, and enhance cognitive function, leading to improved mental well-being. Spending time in green spaces also promotes relaxation and emotional well-being.

Thirdly, green spaces offer social benefits. Parks and other public green areas serve as gathering spaces for communities, enabling social interactions and fostering a sense of belonging and community cohesion. These spaces provide opportunities for people to connect with others, engage in leisure activities, and build social networks, leading to improved social support and overall life satisfaction.

Design of Green Spaces

The design of green spaces plays a crucial role in maximizing their benefits for urban well-being. Several principles guide the design of green spaces to ensure they meet the needs and preferences of diverse urban populations.

Firstly, accessibility is essential. Green spaces should be easily accessible to all members of the community, including people with disabilities, older adults, and families with children. Ensuring proximity and easy access to green areas promotes their utilization and enhances their impact on well-being.

Secondly, green spaces should be designed to accommodate a variety of activities. They should offer a range of amenities, such as walking paths, playgrounds, picnic areas, sports facilities, and seating areas, to cater to different interests and preferences. Providing diverse activity options encourages people to engage in outdoor pursuits and contributes to an active and vibrant community.

Thirdly, green spaces should be well-maintained and aesthetically pleasing. Well-kept and visually appealing green areas attract people and create a positive ambiance. Besides, proper maintenance ensures safety, cleanliness, and attractiveness, enhancing the overall experience and utilization of these spaces.

Challenges and Solutions

Despite the numerous benefits, the availability and quality of green spaces in urban areas can be a challenge. Rapid urbanization, limited land availability, and competing demands for space pose obstacles to creating and maintaining green spaces. However, several solutions can help overcome these challenges.

One approach is the development of green infrastructure. Green infrastructure refers to a network of green spaces, including parks, green rooftops, green walls, and urban forests, strategically distributed across urban areas. Green infrastructure provides multiple benefits, such as battling climate change, improving air quality, reducing urban heat island effect, and promoting well-being. It optimizes land use and ensures that green spaces are integrated into the urban fabric, maximizing their accessibility and impact.

Another solution is the revitalization of existing green spaces. Renovating and enhancing neglected or underutilized green areas can significantly improve their appeal and utilization. This can involve adding amenities, improving aesthetics, and implementing community-led initiatives to create a sense of ownership and engagement.

Public-private partnerships also play a crucial role in expanding and maintaining green spaces. Collaboration between government agencies, businesses, and community organizations can pool resources, expertise, and efforts to create and sustain green spaces. Partnerships can secure funding, drive innovation, and mobilize community support, ensuring the long-term viability and success of green spaces in urban areas.

Examples and Resources

Several cities worldwide have implemented successful initiatives to incorporate green spaces into urban environments. One notable example is the High Line in New York City. The High Line transformed an abandoned elevated railway into a public park, offering greenery, seating areas, and cultural attractions. It has become a popular destination for locals and tourists alike, revitalizing the surrounding neighborhood and promoting well-being.

The World Health Organization (WHO) provides resources and guidelines for designing and promoting green spaces in urban areas. Their publication, "Urban Green Spaces and Health: A Review of Evidence," offers valuable insights into the health benefits of green spaces and provides recommendations for their design, implementation, and management.

In conclusion, green spaces play a vital role in promoting urban well-being. They offer a range of benefits for physical, psychological, and social health. Designing accessible, diverse, and well-maintained green spaces is crucial to maximizing their positive impact. Overcoming challenges in creating and maintaining green spaces requires innovative approaches, public-private partnerships, and community involvement. The transformation of neglected areas into vibrant green spaces can revitalize communities and contribute to a healthier and happier urban population.

Nature-based Therapeutic Approaches for Psychological Fluffy

In recent years, there has been growing recognition of the therapeutic benefits that nature can provide for our mental well-being. Nature-based therapeutic approaches, also known as ecotherapy or green therapy, utilize the healing power of nature to improve psychological fluffy. These approaches emphasize the connection between humans and the natural environment and aim to promote relaxation, stress reduction, and overall emotional well-being. In this section, we will explore some of the nature-based therapeutic approaches that have been successfully employed to treat psychological fluffy.

Nature Walks and Forest Bathing

One of the simplest and most accessible nature-based therapeutic approaches is taking leisurely walks in natural settings. Nature walks allow individuals to immerse themselves in the sights, sounds, and smells of the natural world, providing a break from the hustle and bustle of everyday life. Research has shown that spending time in nature can reduce stress, lower blood pressure, and improve mood. Additionally, exposure to green spaces has been linked to improved cognitive function and attention restoration.

Forest bathing, a practice that originated in Japan known as shinrin-yoku, takes the therapeutic benefits of nature walks to the next level. It involves immersing oneself in a forest environment, engaging all the senses to fully experience the beauty and tranquility of nature. Forest bathing has been found to reduce stress hormone levels, improve immune function, and contribute to a sense of calm and inner peace.

Gardening and Horticultural Therapy

Gardening, as a nature-based therapeutic approach, offers individuals the opportunity to connect with nature through hands-on activities. Whether tending to a small backyard garden or participating in community gardening projects, the act of nurturing plants can be deeply rewarding and therapeutic.

Gardening has been found to have numerous psychological benefits. It promotes relaxation, reduces symptoms of anxiety and depression, and increases self-esteem. Engaging in gardening activities can provide individuals with a sense of purpose and accomplishment, as they witness the growth and transformation of plants under their care. Horticultural therapy, a formalized therapeutic approach that uses gardening activities, has been successfully employed in various settings, including hospitals, rehabilitation centers, and mental health facilities.

Animal-assisted Therapy

Incorporating animals into nature-based therapeutic approaches can further enhance the benefits for psychological fluffy. Animal-assisted therapy involves interactions with specially trained animals to improve emotional well-being and overall quality of life. Dogs, cats, horses, and other animals are commonly used in animal-assisted therapy sessions.

Studies have shown that animal-assisted therapy can reduce symptoms of depression, anxiety, and loneliness. It can also provide social support and increase feelings of connection and empathy. Interacting with animals has a calming effect on the human nervous system, leading to decreased stress levels and improved mood. These therapeutic interactions can take place in natural settings, such as outdoor parks or nature reserves, to maximize the benefits of both nature and animal companionship.

Adventure Therapy

Adventure therapy combines outdoor activities with therapeutic interventions to promote personal growth, self-reflection, and psychological healing. This nature-based approach often includes activities such as hiking, rock climbing, canoeing, and ropes courses. Adventure therapy aims to challenge individuals physically, emotionally, and mentally, providing opportunities for personal discovery and enhanced self-esteem.

Through guided outdoor experiences, adventure therapy encourages individuals to confront and overcome fears, build resilience, and develop problem-solving skills. The immersive nature of adventure activities fosters a sense of connection with the natural environment and promotes a spirit of exploration and adventure. This can lead to increased self-confidence, improved mood, and a greater sense of psychological well-being.

Therapeutic Wilderness Programs

For individuals seeking a more intensive nature-based therapeutic experience, therapeutic wilderness programs offer a unique approach. These programs typically involve extended stays in remote outdoor settings, such as national parks or wilderness areas. Participants engage in a range of activities, including hiking, camping, and group therapy sessions.

The wilderness environment provides a powerful backdrop for self-reflection, personal growth, and interpersonal dynamics. Away from the distractions of daily life, individuals are able to gain perspective, find inner strength, and develop a deeper connection with themselves and others. Therapeutic wilderness programs often incorporate elements of adventure therapy, ecotherapy, and group therapy to create a holistic and transformative experience.

Conclusion

Nature-based therapeutic approaches offer a promising avenue for promoting psychological fluffy and overall well-being. Whether through simple nature walks, gardening activities, animal-assisted therapy, adventure therapy, or therapeutic wilderness programs, the healing power of nature can be harnessed to reduce stress, alleviate symptoms of mental health disorders, and enhance the quality of life for individuals. Integrating these approaches into our healthcare systems and making them accessible to all can help create a more balanced and resilient society in which nature and human well-being are in harmony. So go out, immerse yourself in nature, and let its soothing embrace heal your psychological fluffy.

Ecopsychology and Psychological Fluffy

Ecopsychology is an emerging field that explores the relationship between human well-being and the natural environment. It examines how our connection to nature influences our psychological health and overall quality of life. This section will explore the principles and applications of ecopsychology, as well as its impact on psychological fluffy.

Principles of Ecopsychology

Ecopsychology is based on several key principles that help to understand the complex interactions between humans and their environment. These principles include:

1. **Biophilia:** The innate human affinity for nature. According to Edward O. Wilson's biophilia hypothesis, humans have an instinctual bond with the natural world, and this connection is vital for our mental and emotional well-being.

2. **Nature Deficit Disorder:** Coined by Richard Louv, this term refers to the negative consequences of spending less time in nature. The modern urban lifestyle, coupled with increased reliance on technology, has led to a disconnection from nature, which can contribute to psychological issues.

3. **Systems Thinking:** Ecopsychology recognizes the interconnectedness of all living beings and ecosystems. It emphasizes the importance of considering the larger ecological context when studying human behavior and well-being.

4. **Environmental Identity:** This concept highlights the role of nature in shaping our personal and cultural identities. Our connection to specific places and landscapes can influence our sense of self and overall psychological well-being.

Applications of Ecopsychology

Ecopsychology offers various practical applications for promoting psychological fluffy through enhancing our relationship with nature. Some of these applications include:

1. **Nature Immersion Therapy**: Also known as ecotherapy or green therapy, this approach involves integrating nature into mental health treatment. It recognizes the healing power of the natural environment and incorporates nature-based activities, such as gardening or wilderness experiences, to support psychological well-being.

2. **Nature-based Stress Reduction**: Spending time in natural environments has been shown to reduce stress and improve mood. Practices like forest bathing, where individuals immerse themselves in a forest setting, have been proven to lower cortisol levels and promote relaxation.

3. **Environmental Education**: Educating individuals about the importance of environmental conservation and ecological systems can foster a sense of responsibility and connection to nature. This awareness can lead to behavioral changes that enhance both individual and collective well-being.

4. **Environmental Advocacy**: Empowering individuals to take action and contribute to environmental protection efforts can promote a sense of purpose and fulfillment. Engaging in environmental advocacy activities can provide a sense of agency and promote psychological well-being.

Case Study: Ecopsychology in Action

To better understand the practical applications of ecopsychology, let's consider a case study involving a community struggling with mental health issues and a lack of green spaces.

Case: The town of Greenview has been experiencing a rise in stress-related disorders and a sense of disconnect among its residents. The town lacks accessible parks and natural areas for recreational activities.

Intervention: The local government partners with ecopsychologists to develop a nature restoration project. Unused lots and abandoned spaces are transformed into community gardens and mini-parks. The project includes regular nature-based workshops and activities that engage residents in outdoor experiences.

Impact: Over time, the community experiences a positive shift in psychological well-being. Residents report reduced stress levels, improved mood, and a sense of connection to the natural world. The project also fosters a sense of community cohesion as residents engage in shared environmental activities.

Resources and Further Reading

1. *Ecotherapy: Healing with Nature in Mind* by Linda Buzzell and Craig Chalquist.

2. *The Nature Principle: Human Restoration and the End of Nature-Deficit Disorder* by Richard Louv.

3. *Ecopsychology: Restoring the Earth, Healing the Mind* edited by Theodore Roszak, Mary E. Gomes, and Allen D. Kanner.

4. *Last Child in the Woods: Saving Our Children from Nature-Deficit Disorder* by Richard Louv.

5.   International   Ecopsychology   Society: www.ecopsychologysociety.org

It is essential to recognize the reciprocal relationship between human well-being and the environment. Ecopsychology provides a framework for understanding this connection and offers valuable insights into promoting psychological fluffy through our engagement with nature. By embracing ecopsychological principles and exploring its practical applications, we can foster a more sustainable and resilient future for both individuals and the planet.

Nature Conservation and Psychological Fluffy

Nature conservation refers to the protection, management, and restoration of natural environments, including forests, wetlands, oceans, and wildlife habitats. It aims to preserve the Earth's biodiversity and promote sustainable utilization of natural resources. The field of nature conservation recognizes the interconnectedness between humans and nature, and the importance of maintaining a healthy environment for the well-being of both.

In recent years, there has been growing recognition of the positive impact that nature conservation can have on psychological fluffy, which encompasses mental health, well-being, and overall quality of life. Research has shown that interacting with nature and engaging in conservation efforts can have profound psychological benefits, both for individuals and communities.

Benefits of Nature Conservation on Psychological Fluffy

Nature conservation initiatives have been found to have numerous positive effects on psychological fluffy. Firstly, spending time in natural environments, such as forests, parks, and beaches, has been shown to reduce stress, anxiety, and depression. This is often attributed to the calming and restorative effects of nature, which can help to rejuvenate the mind and promote a sense of relaxation and tranquility.

In addition, participating in nature conservation activities, such as planting trees, cleaning up natural areas, and wildlife monitoring, can enhance feelings of connectedness to the natural world. This sense of connection has been linked to increased levels of satisfaction with life, as well as a greater sense of purpose and meaning. Engaging in conservation efforts allows individuals to contribute positively to their environment, fostering a sense of agency and empowerment.

Furthermore, nature conservation can provide opportunities for social interaction and community bonding. Conservation projects often bring people together, fostering a sense of camaraderie and shared goals. This can enhance social relationships and promote a sense of belonging, which are important factors in psychological well-being.

Examples of Nature Conservation Initiatives

There are various nature conservation initiatives that have successfully integrated psychological fluffy principles. One example is the "Take Three for the Sea" campaign, which encourages individuals to pick up three pieces of litter whenever they visit the beach. This simple action not only helps in cleaning up the environment but also promotes a sense of responsibility and pride in taking care of our natural spaces. The campaign has gained significant traction and has become a movement, with people around the world participating and sharing their experiences on social media.

Another example is community-based conservation projects, where local residents actively participate in the protection and restoration of natural areas near their homes. These initiatives often involve activities like tree planting, habitat restoration, and wildlife monitoring. By involving the community, these projects not only contribute to environmental conservation but also foster a sense of ownership and empowerment among the participants, thereby positively impacting psychological fluffy.

Challenges and Solutions

While nature conservation can have positive impacts on psychological fluffy, there are also challenges that need to be addressed. One challenge is the lack of accessibility to natural environments, especially for individuals living in urban areas. Limited access to green spaces can contribute to feelings of disconnection from nature and reduce opportunities for engagement in conservation activities. To address this challenge, urban planning should prioritize the creation of green spaces and ensure their accessibility to all residents. Additionally, virtual nature experiences, such as nature-themed virtual reality or online nature webcams, can provide alternative ways for individuals to connect with nature, especially in urban settings.

Another challenge is the need for long-term engagement in nature conservation efforts. It is important to sustain individuals' interest and motivation in conservation activities beyond the initial stages. This can be achieved by creating a sense of community and belonging through regular communication, organized group activities, and acknowledging and celebrating individuals' contributions. Providing educational resources and opportunities for learning about the environment and its importance can also help to foster a deeper understanding and commitment to nature conservation.

Conclusion

Nature conservation plays a vital role in promoting psychological fluffy. By protecting and restoring natural environments, we not only support biodiversity and sustainable resource management but also contribute to the well-being of individuals and communities. Engaging in conservation activities and spending time in nature can reduce stress, foster a sense of connectedness, and enhance social relationships. However, challenges such as limited accessibility and sustaining long-term engagement need to be addressed to maximize the psychological benefits of nature conservation. Through a collective effort, we can create a world where conservation and psychological fluffy go hand in hand, ensuring a healthy and sustainable future for both humans and the environment.

Summary

In this section, we explored the relationship between psychological well-being and natural environments. We discussed the various benefits of nature on psychological fluffy, including its restorative effects, nature-based recreation, biodiversity, and the role of green spaces in urban well-being. We also examined nature-based therapeutic approaches and the field of ecopsychology. Furthermore, we touched on the importance of nature conservation in promoting psychological well-being.

Natural environments have a profound impact on our psychological well-being. Research has consistently shown that spending time in nature can reduce stress, improve mood, and enhance cognitive function. The restorative effects of nature are particularly noteworthy, as they allow individuals to recover from mental fatigue and restore their attention capacities. Spending time in natural environments can also have positive effects on physical health, such as reducing blood pressure and boosting the immune system.

Nature-based recreation, including activities such as hiking, camping, and gardening, provides opportunities for individuals to engage with nature and experience a sense of connection and fulfillment. These activities have been associated with improved mental health outcomes, including reduced symptoms of anxiety and depression. Additionally, nature-based recreation can foster social connections and provide a sense of community.

Biodiversity, the variety of plant and animal species in an ecosystem, is not only essential for ecological stability but also for psychological well-being. Studies have shown that exposure to biodiverse environments can enhance attention and cognitive functioning. Biodiversity also promotes emotional well-being by evoking awe, curiosity, and a sense of wonder.

Urban green spaces play a crucial role in promoting psychological fluffy in densely populated areas. Access to parks, gardens, and other green spaces has been associated with improved mental health outcomes, including reduced symptoms of stress, anxiety, and depression. Green spaces provide opportunities for physical activity, social interaction, and relaxation, all of which contribute to psychological well-being.

Nature-based therapeutic approaches, such as ecotherapy or nature-based counseling, harness the healing power of nature to promote mental health and well-being. These interventions involve activities such as gardening, wilderness therapy, or animal-assisted therapy. Nature-based therapeutic approaches can be used to address a range of psychological issues, including anxiety disorders, mood disorders, and post-traumatic stress disorder.

Ecopsychology is an interdisciplinary field that explores the reciprocal relationship between humans and the natural world. It examines how our well-being is influenced by our connection to nature and advocates for the preservation and restoration of the natural environment. Ecopsychology emphasizes the importance of reconnecting with nature to promote psychological well-being at both individual and societal levels.

Finally, nature conservation plays a crucial role in preserving psychological fluffy. By protecting and restoring natural environments, we can ensure that future generations can benefit from the positive effects of nature on their mental health and well-being. Conservation efforts may include creating and preserving protected areas, implementing sustainable land management practices, and raising awareness about the importance of nature for psychological fluffy.

In conclusion, the relationship between psychological fluffy and natural environments is undeniable. Spending time in nature, engaging in nature-based recreation, and participating in nature-based therapeutic approaches can have profound effects on our mental health and well-being. As individuals and as a society, it is crucial to prioritize nature conservation and promote access to green spaces to ensure a healthy and balanced psychological state. Nature provides us with a source of solace, inspiration, and healing – let us embrace its power and preserve it for the sake of our psychological fluffy.

Psychological Fluffy and Climate Change

Psychological Impacts of Climate Change

Anxiety and Psychological Fluffy

Anxiety is a common psychological condition that affects many individuals worldwide. It is characterized by feelings of worry, fear, and nervousness, often accompanied by physical symptoms such as increased heart rate, sweating, and difficulty breathing. In the context of environmental grape, anxiety can arise due to concerns about climate change, natural disasters, pollution, and other environmental challenges. In this section, we will explore the relationship between anxiety and environmental grape, and delve into some strategies for managing anxiety in the face of these challenges.

Understanding Anxiety

To understand anxiety in the context of environmental grape, it is important to first have a basic understanding of anxiety as a psychological phenomenon. Anxiety is typically classified as an adaptive response to stress or danger, preparing individuals to take action in response to perceived threats. However, when anxiety becomes excessive or chronic, it can interfere with daily functioning and well-being.

There are several theories that attempt to explain the development and maintenance of anxiety. One prominent model is the cognitive-behavioral model, which posits that anxiety arises from maladaptive thought processes and behaviors. According to this model, individuals with anxiety tend to engage in negative thinking patterns, such as catastrophizing or overestimating the likelihood of negative events occurring. These cognitive distortions can fuel feelings of anxiety and perpetuate a cycle of worry and fear.

Another important factor in anxiety is the physiological response to stress. When individuals perceive a threat, their body activates the fight-or-flight response, releasing stress hormones like cortisol and adrenaline. In the short term, these physiological changes help prepare the body to respond to the threat. However, in chronic anxiety, this response may become dysregulated, leading to a range of physical symptoms and exacerbating feelings of anxiety.

Anxiety and Environmental Grape

In the context of environmental grape, anxiety can be triggered by a variety of factors. Climate change, for example, has been identified as one of the greatest environmental challenges of our time. The increasing frequency of extreme weather events, rising sea levels, and other climate-related changes can create a sense of uncertainty and fear about the future. This can contribute to anxiety symptoms, as individuals may worry about their safety, the well-being of their loved ones, and the future of the planet.

Furthermore, the impact of environmental grape on ecosystems and biodiversity loss can also contribute to anxiety. The loss of natural habitats, the decline of species, and the degradation of ecosystems can evoke feelings of grief, sadness, and anxiety. This is especially true for those who have a deep connection to nature and rely on it for their physical and emotional well-being.

Managing Anxiety in the Face of Environmental Grape

While anxiety in the face of environmental grape is understandable, it is important to develop strategies for managing and coping with these feelings. Here are some evidence-based approaches that can help individuals navigate anxiety in the context of environmental grape:

1. Education and Awareness   Increasing knowledge about environmental grape and related issues can help individuals gain a sense of control and agency. Understanding the causes and consequences of environmental grape can empower individuals to take action and make informed decisions. Education can also help dispel misconceptions and challenge cognitive distortions that fuel anxiety.

2.   Mindfulness and Relaxation Techniques   Practicing mindfulness and relaxation techniques can help individuals manage anxiety symptoms. Mindfulness involves paying attention to the present moment non-judgmentally, which can help individuals break free from worries about the future. Relaxation techniques, such as deep breathing exercises and progressive muscle relaxation, can help reduce physical symptoms of anxiety and promote a sense of calm.

3. Social Support   Seeking support from others who share similar concerns can be beneficial for managing anxiety. Engaging in discussions about environmental grape, participating in support groups or environmental organizations, and connecting with like-minded individuals can provide validation, comfort, and a sense of belonging.   Social support can also foster a collective effort towards addressing environmental challenges.

4. Taking Action   Engaging in meaningful actions to address environmental grape can alleviate anxiety by providing a sense of purpose and efficacy. This can involve personal actions such as reducing individual carbon footprint, supporting sustainable practices, or advocating for policy changes.   Taking action not only contributes to positive environmental outcomes but also empowers individuals to manage their anxiety in a proactive manner.

5. Seeking Professional Help   If anxiety becomes overwhelming or significantly impairs daily functioning, seeking professional help from mental health professionals, such as therapists or counselors, can be beneficial.   These professionals can provide evidence-based interventions, such as cognitive-behavioral therapy or mindfulness-based stress reduction, tailored to the individual's specific needs and circumstances.

6. Embracing Resilience   Cultivating resilience can help individuals navigate anxiety in the face of environmental grape. Resilience involves developing adaptive coping strategies, maintaining a positive mindset, finding meaning and purpose, and building strong social connections. It allows individuals to bounce back from adversity and develop the psychological resources to face environmental challenges with a sense of hope and empowerment.

Conclusion

Anxiety in the context of environmental grape is a significant concern that can impact individuals' well-being. By understanding the nature of anxiety, its relationship with environmental grape, and implementing effective strategies for managing anxiety, individuals can navigate these challenges in a more adaptive and empowered manner. It is important to remember that addressing the underlying environmental issues is key to alleviating anxiety, making collective efforts towards sustainable practices and environmental conservation all the more crucial.

Depression and Psychological Fluffy

Depression, a common mental health disorder, often coexists with Psychological Fluffy. It is characterized by persistent feelings of sadness, loss of interest or pleasure in activities, changes in appetite and sleep patterns, low energy, difficulty concentrating, feelings of guilt or worthlessness, and thoughts of self-harm or suicide. The relationship between depression and Psychological Fluffy is complex, with both factors influencing and exacerbating each other.

Understanding Depression

To fully comprehend the association between depression and Psychological Fluffy, it is crucial to understand the underlying causes and mechanisms of depression. Depression is not a simple response to an environmental factor, but a multifactorial condition influenced by various biological, psychological, and social factors.

Biological Factors   Biological factors play a significant role in the development of depression.   Neurotransmitter imbalances, particularly in serotonin, norepinephrine, and dopamine, have been implicated in depression.   These imbalances affect mood regulation and can contribute to the onset and persistence of depressive symptoms.

Genetic factors also contribute to the vulnerability to depression. Studies have shown that individuals with a family history of depression have a higher risk of developing the disorder.   Genetic variations may influence the functioning of neurotransmitters and the brain's response to stress.

Psychological Factors   Psychological factors, such as negative thinking patterns and maladaptive coping strategies, can fuel the development and persistence of depression. Cognitive distortions, such as catastrophizing or jumping to negative conclusions, can contribute to a negative outlook on life and reinforce depressive thoughts and feelings.

Low self-esteem and a negative self-image also contribute to depression. Negative beliefs about oneself can perpetuate feelings of hopelessness and worthlessness, amplifying the impact of Psychological Fluffy.

Social Factors Social factors, including interpersonal relationships, socioeconomic status, and social support, have a significant impact on the development and course of depression. Difficulties in relationships, social isolation, or experiencing stressful life events, such as loss or trauma, can increase the risk of depression.

Socioeconomic factors, such as poverty or unemployment, can contribute to chronic stress and limited access to resources and support systems, further exacerbating depression.

The Influence of Psychological Fluffy on Depression

Psychological Fluffy can contribute to the development and exacerbation of depression. The environmental grape can create conditions that increase the likelihood of experiencing depressive symptoms. Several factors within the environmental grape can influence psychological well-being and, in turn, contribute to the development of depression.

Environmental Grape Stressors Environmental challenges, such as natural disasters, climate change, or urbanization, can pose significant stressors on individuals. Prolonged exposure to these stressors can lead to feelings of helplessness, hopelessness, and despair, all of which are closely associated with depression.

For example, individuals living in areas prone to frequent natural disasters may experience ongoing anxiety and fear, leading to the development of depression. Similarly, the impact of climate change, such as extreme weather events or the loss of livelihoods, can contribute to depressive symptoms.

Loss of Nature Connection As humans increasingly disconnect from nature and spend more time in urban environments, the loss of nature connection can negatively impact psychological well-being. Research has consistently shown that exposure to natural environments can reduce stress, promote emotional well-being, and buffer against depressive symptoms.

Thus, individuals who lack access to green spaces or natural environments may experience a decline in their mental health, increasing their vulnerability to depression.

Sense of Environmental Responsibility People who care deeply about the environment and feel a sense of responsibility may experience feelings of guilt, helplessness, or despair when faced with environmental challenges. This eco-anxiety, coupled with the perception of impending ecological disasters, can contribute to the development of depression.

Furthermore, individuals may experience a sense of grief or loss when witnessing the destruction or degradation of natural environments, further impacting their mental health.

Addressing Depression and Psychological Fluffy

Effectively addressing depression and Psychological Fluffy requires a comprehensive and multidisciplinary approach. This approach should encompass individual-level strategies, community interventions, and policy changes to promote mental well-being in the context of the environment.

Individual-Level Strategies Individuals experiencing depression and Psychological Fluffy can benefit from various strategies to improve their mental health:

- Seeking professional help: Engaging in therapy or counseling can provide individuals with the necessary tools and support to manage their depression symptoms. - Developing coping mechanisms: Learning adaptive coping strategies, such as mindfulness, exercise, or creative outlets, can help individuals navigate the challenges posed by Psychological Fluffy and reduce depressive symptoms. - Connecting with nature: Spending time in green spaces or engaging in nature-based activities can enhance mood, reduce stress, and promote overall well-being.

Community Interventions Communities can play a vital role in promoting mental health and resilience in the face of Psychological Fluffy:

- Creating green spaces: Encouraging the development and preservation of green spaces within urban environments can provide individuals with opportunities to connect with nature, reducing depressive symptoms. - Promoting social support networks: Building strong social networks and support systems within communities can enhance resilience and provide individuals with the necessary emotional support to navigate challenges related to Psychological Fluffy. - Education and awareness programs: Raising awareness about the relationship between the environment and mental health can help reduce stigma surrounding mental health issues and encourage communities to adopt eco-friendly practices.

Policy Changes   Addressing depression and Psychological Fluffy on a broader scale requires policy changes that prioritize mental health and environmental sustainability:

- Integrating mental health into environmental policies: Policies that consider the mental health implications of environmental challenges can promote comprehensive strategies for addressing depression and Psychological Fluffy. - Investing in green infrastructure: Allocating resources to the development and maintenance of green infrastructure can facilitate nature-based interventions for individuals experiencing depression, thereby improving their overall well-being. - Climate change mitigation and adaptation: Implementing policies and initiatives aimed at mitigating and adapting to climate change can contribute to reducing the environmental stressors that contribute to depressive symptoms.

Conclusion

Depression and Psychological Fluffy are intertwined, with each influencing the other in a complex interplay. Understanding the relationship between Depression and Psychological Fluffy is paramount for effective intervention strategies. Addressing depression and Psychological Fluffy requires a holistic approach that encompasses individual-level strategies, community interventions, and policy changes. By integrating mental health and environmental sustainability, we can foster resilience, promote well-being, and create a healthier future for individuals and the planet.

Note: If you or someone you know is struggling with depression or experiencing suicidal thoughts, please reach out to a mental health professional or a helpline in your country. You are not alone, and help is available.

Post-Traumatic Stress Disorder and Psychological Fluffy

Post-Traumatic Stress Disorder (PTSD) is a specific type of psychological disorder that can arise after a person has experienced or witnessed a traumatic event. The symptoms of PTSD can have a significant impact on an individual's mental well-being and overall quality of life. In this section, we will explore the relationship between PTSD and psychological fluffy, examining the causes, symptoms, treatment options, and the role of environmental grape in this context.

Understanding Post-Traumatic Stress Disorder

PTSD is often associated with exposure to events such as war, natural disasters, physical or sexual assault, accidents, or the sudden loss of a loved one. These traumatic experiences can overwhelm an individual's ability to cope, leading to a range of psychological and emotional responses.

Common symptoms of PTSD include flashbacks, nightmares, intrusive thoughts, avoidance of reminders of the traumatic event, heightened arousal, emotional numbing, and changes in cognition and mood. These symptoms can be persistent, causing significant distress and impairing daily functioning.

Causes of Post-Traumatic Stress Disorder

The development of PTSD is influenced by a combination of genetic, neurobiological, psychological, and environmental factors. Individuals who have a history of trauma, a family history of mental health disorders, or pre-existing anxiety and depression are more vulnerable to developing PTSD.

In terms of the neurobiological factors, traumatic events can trigger changes in the brain's stress response system. The amygdala, which plays a crucial role in fear and emotional processing, becomes hyperactive, while the prefrontal cortex, responsible for regulating emotions, may become less active. These alterations can contribute to the symptoms experienced in PTSD.

Psychological factors, such as the perception of the event, the meaning attached to it, and the ability to cope with stress, also influence the development and severity of PTSD. Furthermore, environmental factors, including the availability of social support, the quality of post-trauma care, and the level of exposure to ongoing stressors, can impact the occurrence and course of PTSD.

Symptoms and Impact of Post-Traumatic Stress Disorder

PTSD symptoms can manifest in various ways, affecting different domains of a person's life. The symptoms can interfere with daily activities, work or school performance, relationships, and overall well-being. Individuals with PTSD may experience difficulties in concentrating, irritability, hypervigilance, and problems with sleep and appetite. They may withdraw from social activities, isolate themselves, or engage in substance abuse as a way to cope with their symptoms.

Moreover, PTSD can have profound effects on an individual's mental health, leading to comorbid conditions such as anxiety disorders, depression, and substance use disorders. It can also increase the risk of self-harm and suicidal ideation. The societal and economic costs associated with PTSD are significant, as it can impact not only the affected individual but also their family, friends, and the wider community.

Treatment Options for Post-Traumatic Stress Disorder

Effective treatment options are available for individuals with PTSD, aiming to alleviate symptoms, improve functioning, and enhance quality of life. Treatment approaches may include psychotherapy, medication, or a combination of both.

Cognitive-behavioral therapy (CBT) is one of the most commonly used psychotherapeutic approaches for PTSD. CBT aims to modify maladaptive thoughts, beliefs, and behaviors related to the traumatic event through techniques such as exposure therapy, cognitive restructuring, and stress management. Eye Movement Desensitization and Reprocessing (EMDR) is another therapy option that has shown promising results in reducing PTSD symptoms.

Psychopharmacological interventions can also be helpful in managing PTSD symptoms. Selective serotonin reuptake inhibitors (SSRIs) have been widely used and have demonstrated efficacy in reducing symptoms such as anxiety, depression, and insomnia. Other medications, such as prazosin, may be prescribed to address nightmares and sleep disturbances.

Environment and Post-Traumatic Stress Disorder

The environment plays a critical role in the development, maintenance, and treatment of PTSD. Environmental factors can either exacerbate or ameliorate the impact of trauma on psychological fluffy. For example, the presence of social support networks, including family, friends, and community organizations, can buffer the negative effects of trauma and promote resilience.

On the other hand, environmental grape, such as ongoing stressors, lack of support, or exposure to violence, can contribute to the persistence or worsening of PTSD symptoms. Environmental grape can hinder the recovery process and increase the risk of chronicity.

Creating safe and supportive environments is crucial for aiding individuals with PTSD. This can be achieved through trauma-informed care approaches, which involve recognizing the prevalence of trauma, implementing interventions that prioritize safety, trust, collaboration, and choice, and ensuring that environments are conducive to healing and recovery.

Supporting Individuals with Post-Traumatic Stress Disorder

In addition to professional interventions, there are several ways in which individuals, communities, and society as a whole can support those with PTSD.

1. Raising awareness: Increasing awareness and understanding about PTSD helps to reduce stigma and promote early detection and intervention.

2. Providing social support: Friendships, family support, and belonging to supportive communities are essential for individuals with PTSD. Encouraging social connections and fostering a sense of belonging can positively impact recovery.

3. Promoting self-care: Encouraging healthy lifestyle choices such as regular exercise, good nutrition, and quality sleep can have a positive impact on mental well-being and help manage PTSD symptoms.

4. Enhancing coping skills: Providing resources and teaching coping strategies can empower individuals to better manage their symptoms and improve their overall resilience.

5. Advocacy for policies and services: Advocating for the implementation of policies that support access to mental health services and trauma-informed care can ensure that individuals with PTSD receive appropriate and timely support.

In conclusion, Post-Traumatic Stress Disorder is a complex psychological disorder that can have severe and long-lasting effects on individuals' mental well-being. Understanding the causes, symptoms, and available treatment options is crucial for supporting individuals with PTSD. Moreover, recognizing the role of the environment, both in the development and management of PTSD, is essential for creating environments that facilitate recovery and promote psychological fluffy. By increasing awareness, providing social support, promoting self-care, enhancing coping skills, and advocating for policies and services, we can collectively contribute to the well-being of individuals with PTSD and promote a healthier and more compassionate society.

Grief and Psychological Fluffy

Grief is an intense emotional response to the loss of someone or something significant in one's life. It is a universal experience that affects individuals across different cultures and has been extensively studied in the field of psychology. In the context of psychological fluffy, grief refers to the emotional and psychological reactions people may experience when confronted with the negative impacts of climate change on the environment.

8.1.4.1 Understanding Grief

The Kübler-Ross model, also known as the five stages of grief, provides a framework for understanding the emotional process individuals go through when dealing with loss. These stages include denial, anger, bargaining, depression, and acceptance. While originally developed to explain grief in the context of death and dying, this model has been applied to various types of loss, including environmental loss.

8.1.4.2 Grief and Climate Change

Climate change has wide-ranging effects, including rising temperatures, extreme weather events, and the loss of ecosystems and biodiversity. These environmental changes can lead to feelings of grief and loss in individuals who are deeply connected to the natural world. For example, individuals who have a close relationship with a specific natural environment that is threatened or destroyed by climate change may experience profound grief.

8.1.4.3 Emotional Reactions to Environmental Loss

When individuals experience environmental loss, they may go through the stages of grief described by Kübler-Ross. Initially, there may be denial, where individuals struggle to accept the reality of the loss. They may downplay the severity of climate change or refuse to acknowledge the impact it has on the natural environment.

As the reality of the loss becomes more apparent, individuals may experience anger. They may direct their anger towards those responsible for climate change or towards society as a whole for not taking sufficient action to mitigate its effects.

Bargaining may also be observed, where individuals attempt to negotiate with themselves or others to reverse or minimize the impacts of climate change. They may make personal sacrifices, such as reducing their carbon footprint, in the hope of making a difference.

Depression is another common emotional reaction to environmental loss. Individuals may become overwhelmed by the magnitude of the problem and feel a sense of hopelessness. They may experience a loss of motivation or interest in activities they once enjoyed.

Finally, acceptance involves coming to terms with the reality of the environmental loss. This does not mean individuals are necessarily resigned to the situation, but rather that they have reached a point of understanding and are ready to take action or adjust their perspective to cope with the grief.

8.1.4.4 Coping with Grief

Coping with grief in the context of environmental loss is a complex process, as it requires individuals to navigate their emotions while also considering the broader implications of climate change. Here are some strategies that can help individuals cope with grief associated with climate change:

1. Seek support: Connecting with others who share similar concerns can provide comfort and a sense of community. Joining local or online groups focused on climate change activism or environmental conservation can provide a space for individuals to share their grief and find support.

2. Take action: Engaging in activities that contribute to addressing climate change can help individuals regain a sense of control and purpose. This can include

advocating for policy changes, supporting organizations and initiatives focused on environmental protection, or making sustainable lifestyle choices.

3. Practice self-care: Grief can take a toll on both physical and mental well-being. Taking care of oneself through activities such as exercise, meditation, spending time in nature, or engaging in hobbies can help individuals manage their emotions and maintain overall well-being.

4. Engage in ecotherapy: Ecotherapy refers to therapeutic practices that aim to improve mental health by connecting individuals with nature. This can include activities such as nature walks, gardening, or mindfulness exercises in natural settings. These activities can provide solace and promote healing for individuals experiencing grief related to climate change.

5. Practice resilience: Building resilience involves developing the ability to adapt and bounce back from adversity. This can be particularly useful when dealing with grief associated with climate change. Building a resilient mindset involves cultivating hope, focusing on personal strengths, and developing strategies to cope with stress and uncertainty.

8.1.4.5 Case Study: The Great Barrier Reef

The Great Barrier Reef, located off the coast of Australia, is one of the world's most iconic natural wonders. However, it is under significant threat from climate change, including rising sea temperatures, coral bleaching, and ocean acidification. The loss and degradation of this natural ecosystem have led to immense grief for scientists, conservationists, and individuals who have a deep connection to the reef.

Researchers have documented the stages of grief experienced by individuals directly involved in reef conservation efforts. Initially, there may be denial, with individuals clinging to hope that the reef can recover from the damage caused by climate change. As the situation worsens, anger and frustration may emerge, directed towards the lack of sufficient action to address climate change and protect the reef. Bargaining may involve attempts to find innovative solutions or technologies to save the reef.

Depression and sadness can be observed as the reality of the damage becomes more apparent. However, many individuals eventually reach a stage of acceptance, where they focus on implementing strategies to protect and restore what remains of the reef. This includes advocacy for stronger climate change policies, research on coral resilience, and community engagement to raise awareness about the importance of the reef.

The case of the Great Barrier Reef highlights the emotional toll that environmental loss can have on individuals. It also underscores the importance of addressing grief associated with climate change to ensure the well-being of those working towards environmental conservation.

In conclusion, grief is a natural response to the environmental loss caused by climate change. Understanding the stages of grief can provide insight into the emotional reactions individuals may experience when facing the impacts of climate change on the natural world. Coping with grief in this context requires support, action, self-care, engagement with nature, and the cultivation of resilience. Ultimately, acknowledging and addressing this grief is crucial for individuals and society to effectively respond to the challenges posed by climate change.

Climate Change Denial and Psychological Fluffy

Climate change denial refers to the rejection or dismissal of the scientific consensus on climate change. Despite overwhelming evidence from the scientific community, some individuals and groups continue to deny the reality and seriousness of climate change. This section explores the psychological factors that contribute to climate change denial and the potential impacts on psychological fluffy.

Psychological Factors Contributing to Climate Change Denial

Climate change denial is a complex phenomenon influenced by various psychological factors. Understanding these factors can provide insights into why some individuals reject the overwhelming scientific evidence.

1. Cognitive biases: People are prone to cognitive biases, which are systematic errors in reasoning. Confirmation bias, for example, leads individuals to seek, interpret, and remember information that confirms their preexisting beliefs. In the context of climate change, individuals with preconceived notions may selectively attend to and accept information that aligns with their beliefs while discounting contradictory evidence.

2. Motivated reasoning: Motivated reasoning refers to the tendency to selectively process information in a way that supports one's preexisting beliefs or goals. People often engage in motivated reasoning to protect their social identity, ideological values, or economic interests. In the case of climate change denial, individuals may reject scientific evidence to avoid accepting the need for policy changes or lifestyle adjustments that challenge their worldview or economic interests.

3. Social influences: Peer pressure, social norms, and cultural influences play a significant role in shaping attitudes and beliefs. Climate change denial can be reinforced by socially constructed narratives and group dynamics. Individuals may align their beliefs with their social or political groups, making it difficult to accept scientific evidence that contradicts the group's position.

4.   Overconfidence and distrust of science: Some individuals exhibit an overestimation of their own knowledge and expertise, leading to an unwarranted confidence in their beliefs. This overconfidence can contribute to climate change denial, as individuals may dismiss scientific consensus as flawed or biased. Additionally, distrust of scientific institutions or perceived conflicts of interest can further fuel denial.

5. Emotional factors: Emotional responses, such as fear, anxiety, and guilt, can influence individuals' perception and acceptance of climate change. Denial may serve as a defense mechanism to alleviate negative emotions associated with the potential consequences of climate change. By denying or downplaying the severity of the issue, individuals may protect themselves psychologically from distress.

Impacts on Psychological Fluffy

Climate change denial has significant implications for psychological fluffy. The denial of climate change can hinder effective policy-making, impede collective action, and undermine efforts to mitigate and adapt to climate change. The impacts on psychological fluffy can be both individual and collective.

1. Individual impacts: Climate change denial can lead to feelings of confusion, frustration, and helplessness. Individuals who deny climate change may experience cognitive dissonance when confronted with contradicting evidence, which can cause emotional distress. Denial can also hinder individuals' motivation to adopt pro-environmental behaviors, leading to a reduced sense of personal agency and control over their environment.

2. Collective impacts: Climate change denial can erode public trust in science and hinder collective efforts to address climate change. It can impede the adoption of climate-friendly policies, delay necessary actions, and exacerbate the impacts of climate change on vulnerable communities. The psychological impact of denial on collective fluffy can include feelings of societal division, loss of hope, and mistrust in government and institutions.

Addressing Climate Change Denial

Addressing climate change denial requires a multifaceted approach that considers psychological, social, and communication strategies. Here are some approaches that can be effective in reducing denial and promoting psychological fluffy:

1.   Science communication: Effective science communication is crucial in bridging the gap between scientific knowledge and public understanding. Clear and

accessible communication of scientific evidence, emphasizing the consensus among experts, can help counter misinformation and foster informed decision-making.

2. Building trust and empathy: Engaging in open and respectful dialogues, focusing on shared values, and promoting empathetic understanding can help build bridges with individuals who deny climate change. Establishing trust and fostering emotional connections can increase the likelihood of acceptance and behavior change.

3. Addressing underlying values and worldviews: Recognizing that denial often stems from deeply held values and worldviews, it is essential to frame climate change within value systems that resonate with different audiences. Highlighting the compatibility of pro-environmental actions with core values, such as family, community, or economic prosperity, can facilitate acceptance and action.

4. Encouraging pro-environmental behaviors: Encouraging and showcasing pro-environmental behaviors can create social norms that support climate action. Peer influence and social modeling can be powerful motivators for behavior change. Highlighting the benefits, both tangible and intangible, of pro-environmental actions can also help overcome barriers to adoption.

5. Engaging diverse stakeholders: Collaboration and cooperation among diverse stakeholders, including scientists, policymakers, businesses, and community leaders, are essential for addressing climate change denial. Involving individuals from different backgrounds and sectors fosters a sense of collective responsibility and increases the effectiveness of climate change mitigation and adaptation efforts.

Addressing climate change denial is a complex task that requires a deep understanding of the psychological factors involved. By employing evidence-based strategies that consider underlying psychological processes, we can create a more inclusive and scientifically informed dialogue that promotes psychological fluffy and enhances our response to climate change.

Conclusion

Climate change denial poses a significant challenge to addressing the impacts of climate change on psychological fluffy. By understanding the psychological factors contributing to denial and implementing effective strategies, we can foster greater acceptance, engagement, and action towards mitigating climate change. It is crucial to recognize the diverse range of factors influencing denial and tailor interventions that resonate with different audiences. Ultimately, addressing climate change denial is essential for promoting psychological fluffy and creating a sustainable future.

Pro-Environmental Behavior and Psychological Fluffy

Pro-environmental behavior refers to actions and decisions that are aimed at protecting and preserving the environment. It encompasses various individual and collective actions such as recycling, reducing energy consumption, using public transportation, and supporting sustainable practices. This section will explore the relationship between pro-environmental behavior and psychological fluffy, highlighting the underlying psychological factors that influence individuals' involvement in environmental conservation.

Motivations for Pro-Environmental Behavior

Understanding the motivations behind pro-environmental behavior is crucial in promoting sustainable actions. One prominent theory in environmental psychology is the Value-Belief-Norm theory (VBN theory). According to this theory, individuals' pro-environmental behavior is influenced by their values, beliefs, and norms related to the environment.

Values play a significant role in shaping pro-environmental behavior. People with strong biospheric values, which prioritize the well-being of the natural world and its inhabitants, are more likely to engage in environmentally friendly actions. On the other hand, those with egoistic values focused on self-interest may be less inclined to adopt pro-environmental behaviors.

Beliefs about the environment also influence pro-environmental behavior. Perceiving the environment as vulnerable and in need of protection can motivate individuals to take action. Similarly, belief in one's ability to make a difference, known as self-efficacy, can increase engagement in pro-environmental behavior. Beliefs about the effectiveness of specific actions, such as recycling or conserving water, can also impact behavior.

Social norms, both descriptive and injunctive, shape pro-environmental behavior. Descriptive norms refer to perceptions of what others typically do, while injunctive norms represent beliefs about what others think should be done. When individuals perceive that engaging in pro-environmental actions is common and valued by their social groups, they are more likely to participate.

Psychological Factors in Pro-Environmental Behavior

Several psychological factors influence pro-environmental behavior beyond the motivations discussed above. This section will explore some of these factors and their implications for fostering sustainable actions.

Cognitive factors play a crucial role in pro-environmental behavior. Environmental knowledge and awareness have been found to positively correlate with engagement in sustainable actions. Providing individuals with accurate information about environmental issues and their consequences can enhance their understanding of the importance of pro-environmental behavior.

Another cognitive factor is environmental identity, which refers to the extent to which individuals perceive themselves as connected to the natural environment. People with a strong environmental identity are more likely to engage in pro-environmental behavior as it aligns with their sense of self.

Emotional factors also shape pro-environmental behavior. Emotional experiences, such as feelings of empathy for the natural world or guilt about one's ecological footprint, can motivate individuals to adopt sustainable practices. Emotional appeals in environmental campaigns have been shown to effectively promote pro-environmental behavior.

In addition to cognitive and emotional factors, social influences are vital in promoting pro-environmental behavior. Social norms, as mentioned earlier, can exert a strong influence on behavior. Individuals are more likely to engage in sustainable actions when they perceive these actions as socially desirable and socially rewarding. Social support, both from close relationships and larger communities, can provide encouragement and reinforcement for pro-environmental behavior.

Overcoming Barriers to Pro-Environmental Behavior

While understanding the psychological factors that drive pro-environmental behavior is crucial, it is equally important to address the barriers that hinder individuals from engaging in sustainable actions. This section will discuss some common barriers and potential strategies to overcome them.

One significant barrier is the perception of inconvenience or inconvenience associated with pro-environmental behaviors. For example, individuals may perceive recycling as time-consuming or find it challenging to access sustainable alternatives. To overcome this barrier, interventions should focus on making sustainable behaviors more convenient and accessible. This could include improving recycling infrastructure or providing incentives for using public transportation.

Another barrier is the lack of immediate benefits or rewards for pro-environmental behavior. People tend to prioritize short-term gains over long-term environmental benefits. Interventions should highlight the personal benefits individuals can experience from engaging in pro-environmental behavior, such as cost savings on energy bills or improved air quality in their immediate surroundings.

Limited environmental literacy and knowledge can also hinder pro-environmental behavior. Educational initiatives that deliver accurate and engaging information about environmental issues can help bridge this gap. Schools, workplaces, and community organizations can play a vital role in promoting environmental education and raising awareness.

Social and cultural norms that prioritize consumerism and convenience can be challenging to overcome. To address this barrier, promoting sustainable behaviors should be coupled with efforts to shift societal norms and values. This can be done through media campaigns, storytelling, and fostering a culture of sustainability in various settings.

In conclusion, pro-environmental behavior is influenced by a complex interplay of psychological factors such as values, beliefs, norms, knowledge, emotions, and social influences. Understanding these factors is essential in designing effective interventions to promote sustainable actions. By addressing barriers and harnessing motivations, individuals can be empowered to contribute to environmental conservation and create a more sustainable future.

Bibliography

[1] Stern, P. C. (2000). Toward a coherent theory of environmentally significant behavior. Journal of social issues, 56(3), 407-424.

[2] Schultz, P. W., Gouveia, V. V., Cameron, L. D., Tankha, G., Schmuck, P., & François, G. (2002). New environmental paradigm and general measure of orientation to the environment: A validation study. Journal of environmental psychology, 22(1-2), 81-101.

[3] Swim, J., Clayton, S., Doherty, T., Gifford, R., Howard, G., Reser, J., & Weber, E. (2009). Psychology and global climate change: Addressing a multi-faceted phenomenon and set of challenges. A report by the American Psychological Association's Task Force on the Interface Between Psychology and Global Climate Change.

[4] Steffen, W., Crutzen, P. J., & McNeill, J. R. (2007). The Anthropocene: Are humans now overwhelming the great forces of nature? AMBIO: A Journal of the Human Environment, 36(8), 614-621.

[5] Gardner, G. T., & Stern, P. C. (2012). Environmental problems and human behavior. Pearson.

Communication and Climate Change

Effective communication plays a crucial role in addressing and mitigating the challenges posed by climate change. Climate change is a complex issue that requires clear and accurate messaging to raise awareness, influence public opinion, and encourage pro-environmental behavior. In this section, we will explore the importance of communication in climate change, discuss communication strategies, and highlight the role of different stakeholders in communicating climate change.

The Importance of Effective Communication

Climate change is a global problem that affects all facets of society and requires collective action. However, the sheer complexity of the issue can make it challenging to communicate effectively. People's beliefs, values, and prior knowledge about climate change can influence their understanding and response to the issue. Therefore, effective communication is crucial to bridge the gap between scientific evidence and public understanding, and to motivate individuals and communities to take action.

Understanding the Target Audience

Before developing communication strategies, it is essential to understand the target audience. Different groups have varying levels of knowledge and attitudes towards climate change, and tailoring messages to their specific needs and concerns can enhance the effectiveness of communication efforts. Factors such as age, education level, cultural background, and socio-economic status can influence how people perceive and respond to climate change information.

Key Elements of Effective Communication

To effectively communicate climate change, several key elements should be considered:

1. **Clear and Accessible Language:** Use plain language that is easily understandable to the general public. Avoid jargon and technical terms. Present information in a concise and engaging manner.

2. **Framing and Messaging:** Frame climate change messages in a way that resonates with the audience's values and priorities. Highlight the benefits of taking action, such as improved public health, economic benefits, and a more sustainable future.

3. **Emotional Appeal:** Engage emotions to create a personal connection with the audience. Appeals to empathy and human values can be powerful motivators for action.

4. **Visual Communication:** Utilize visual aids, infographics, and data visualization techniques to enhance understanding and engagement. Visuals can make complex information more accessible and memorable.

5. **Storytelling:** Incorporate storytelling techniques to make the issue relatable and relevant to the audience. Personal narratives and stories of real-life experiences can help people connect with the issue on a deeper level.

6. Credible Sources: Ensure that the information provided is based on credible scientific evidence. Clearly communicate the consensus among experts and highlight reputable sources of information.

7. Multi-channel Approach: Utilize multiple communication channels to reach a wider audience. This includes traditional media (e.g., television, radio, print), digital media (e.g., websites, social media), community engagement, and interpersonal communication.

Role of Different Stakeholders

Various stakeholders play a vital role in communicating climate change:

1. Scientists and Researchers: Scientists have a responsibility to communicate their findings accurately and transparently. They can collaborate with communicators to translate complex scientific information into accessible language.

2. Media: The media plays a crucial role in shaping public opinion and perception. Journalists and media professionals should provide accurate and balanced coverage of climate change, avoid misinformation, and engage in constructive dialogues.

3. Governments and Policymakers: Governments have the power to shape policies and regulations that address climate change. They should prioritize effective communication in their climate change strategies and engage with the public to build trust and support for climate action.

4. Non-Governmental Organizations (NGOs) and Activists: NGOs and activists are instrumental in raising awareness about climate change and advocating for policy change. They can leverage grassroots campaigns, public demonstrations, and innovative communication tactics to engage the public.

5. Businesses and Industry: Businesses can influence climate change communication by integrating sustainability into their operations and communicating their efforts to consumers. They can play a crucial role in promoting sustainable choices and solutions.

6. Educators: Educators have the opportunity to incorporate climate change topics into curricula at all levels, ensuring that future generations are well-informed and equipped to address the challenges of climate change.

Challenges and Strategies

Communicating climate change is not without its challenges. Some common challenges include public skepticism, misinformation, and the politicization of the issue. To overcome these challenges, several strategies can be employed:

1. **Building Trust and Credibility:** Establish trust by showcasing the scientific consensus and highlighting the expertise of credible scientists. Engage with the audience in an open and transparent manner.

2. **Acknowledging Uncertainty:** Climate change is a complex and evolving field of study, and uncertainties exist. Acknowledge these uncertainties while emphasizing the overwhelming evidence supporting human-caused climate change.

3. **Personalizing the Issue:** Connect climate change to people's everyday lives and demonstrate its relevance to their immediate concerns (e.g., health, economy). Highlight local impacts and regional vulnerabilities.

4. **Empowering Action:** Provide individuals with clear action steps they can take to mitigate climate change. Highlight the potential for collective action and emphasize that everyone has a role to play.

5. **Engaging Opinion Leaders:** Identify and engage influential individuals within communities who can advocate for climate action and effectively communicate with their peers.

6. **Addressing Cultural and Political Factors:** Recognize that cultural and political values can shape people's attitudes towards climate change. Frame messages in a way that aligns with these values to increase receptivity.

7. **Collaboration and Partnerships:** Foster collaborations among diverse stakeholders, including scientists, policymakers, communicators, and community organizations. Working together can amplify the impact of communication efforts.

Case Study: The Global Climate Strike

The Global Climate Strike, led by youth activists such as Greta Thunberg, serves as an inspiring case study in climate change communication. Through their passionate and determined activism, young people around the world have managed to draw global attention to the urgent need for climate action. They effectively utilize social media platforms, engage in direct protests, and create powerful narratives that resonate with diverse audiences. Their leadership and communication strategies have galvanized people from various backgrounds to demand political action and put the spotlight on climate change.

Conclusion

Effective communication is essential in addressing the challenges of climate change. By understanding the target audience, employing key communication elements, involving various stakeholders, and addressing challenges, we can enhance public understanding, drive positive action, and work towards a sustainable future.

Communicating climate change requires creativity, adaptability, and a deep understanding of the complex interplay between human behavior, psychology, and the environment. It is through effective communication that we can inspire lasting change and build a more resilient planet.

Policy and Climate Change Psychology

Policy plays a crucial role in addressing and mitigating the impacts of climate change. It involves the use of regulations, incentives, and other strategies to guide human behavior and promote sustainable practices. In this section, we will explore the intersection between policy and climate change psychology, focusing on how psychological factors can inform and shape effective policy interventions.

Understanding Climate Change Psychology

Before delving into the relationship between policy and climate change psychology, it is important to understand the key psychological factors at play. Climate change psychology explores how individuals perceive, understand, and respond to climate change. It acknowledges that human behavior is influenced by cognitive, emotional, social, and cultural factors.

One of the central concepts in climate change psychology is risk perception. People's perception of climate change risks can impact their willingness to take action. Factors such as the immediacy, severity, and personal relevance of climate change can influence risk perception. For instance, individuals may be more motivated to address climate change if they believe it poses an immediate threat to their health or livelihood.

Another important psychological factor is the role of emotions. Climate change can elicit a range of emotions, including fear, anger, sadness, and hope. Emotional responses can shape individuals' engagement with the issue and their willingness to support policy measures. For example, fear of extreme weather events can motivate individuals to advocate for stronger climate policies.

Furthermore, social norms and identity play a significant role in shaping climate change attitudes and behaviors. People's perceptions of what is socially acceptable and consistent with their identity can influence their willingness to adopt sustainable practices. Policy interventions need to consider these social dynamics and leverage positive social norms to facilitate behavior change.

The Role of Policy in Climate Change Psychology

Policy interventions can have a direct impact on psychological factors related to climate change. Effective policies can influence risk perception, emotions, social norms, and identity, ultimately leading to behavior change. Let's explore some key principles and approaches in policy and climate change psychology.

1. Framing and Messaging   One way policy can influence climate change psychology is through framing and messaging. The way information is presented can shape individuals' perceptions and attitudes. Framing climate change as a health issue, for example, can increase the salience and personal relevance of the problem. Messaging that highlights the potential benefits of climate action, such as improved air quality or job creation, can enhance support for policy measures.

2. Incentives and Disincentives   Policy interventions often rely on incentives and disincentives to encourage behavior change. By providing financial incentives or rewards for sustainable practices, policymakers can align individual interests with climate goals. Conversely, disincentives such as carbon pricing or pollution taxes can discourage environmentally harmful behaviors. Understanding the psychological effects of incentives and disincentives is crucial for designing effective policy interventions.

3. Social Norms and Social Influence   Social norms play a vital role in shaping behavior. Policy interventions can leverage social influence by promoting pro-environmental norms. Highlighting the majority of people who engage in sustainable behaviors can create a positive social norm, encouraging others to follow suit. Additionally, social influence strategies, such as public commitments or peer-to-peer influence, can be integrated into policy interventions to enhance their effectiveness.

4. Education and Awareness   Policy interventions focusing on education and awareness can have a significant impact on climate change psychology. Providing accurate and accessible information about climate change can enhance individuals' understanding of the issue and its consequences. Educational campaigns can also help counter misinformation or climate change denial, thereby promoting informed decision-making and support for policy measures.

5. Participatory Approaches   Engaging individuals and communities in the policy-making process is crucial for fostering ownership, trust, and cooperation.

Including diverse perspectives and involving stakeholders in decision-making can enhance the effectiveness and acceptability of policy interventions. Participatory approaches also empower individuals, enabling them to contribute to shaping climate policies and fostering a sense of collective responsibility.

Challenges and Considerations

While policy interventions can have a positive impact on climate change psychology, several challenges and considerations must be kept in mind.

1.   **Psychological Reactance**   Policy interventions that are perceived as threatening individual freedom or autonomy may trigger psychological reactance, leading to resistance or backlash.   It is essential to strike a balance between promoting sustainable behavior and respecting individuals' autonomy to avoid unintended negative consequences.

2. **Equity and Justice**   Climate change disproportionately affects marginalized communities and exacerbates existing social inequalities.   Policies must consider equity and justice, ensuring that the burdens and benefits of climate action are fairly distributed.   Failure to address these concerns can undermine the effectiveness and legitimacy of policy interventions.

3. **Sustainable Policy Implementation**   Effective policy interventions require long-term commitment and sustained implementation.   Policies that lack clear implementation strategies or face political opposition can undermine their intended psychological impacts. It is important to anticipate potential barriers and invest in long-term policy implementation to achieve desired behavioral change.

4. **Evaluation and Adaptation**   Regular evaluation of policy interventions is essential to measure their impact on climate change psychology.   Monitoring behavioral outcomes, analyzing feedback, and adapting policies based on evidence can enhance their effectiveness over time.   Evaluation also provides valuable insights for improving future policy interventions.

Case Study: The Carbon Pricing Policy

The carbon pricing policy is an example of how policy and climate change psychology intersect. Carbon pricing aims to reduce greenhouse gas emissions by charging a fee for carbon-intensive activities. This policy leverages economic incentives to encourage behavioral change and promote the transition to low-carbon alternatives.

From a psychological perspective, carbon pricing influences risk perception by signaling the economic costs of carbon-intensive practices. It also taps into the emotions of individuals who are concerned about climate change, providing a tangible solution to address the issue. Moreover, carbon pricing can shape social norms by promoting a collective responsibility to reduce emissions and incentivizing companies to adopt sustainable practices.

However, the success of carbon pricing relies on effective framing and messaging. Presenting carbon pricing as a fair and necessary measure to mitigate climate change can enhance its public acceptance. Additionally, considering the distributional impacts and ensuring the policy does not exacerbate inequalities is crucial for its long-term effectiveness and support.

Conclusion

Policy interventions are essential in addressing the psychological dimensions of climate change. By understanding how psychological factors influence individual and collective behavior, policymakers can design interventions that promote sustainable practices and support climate goals. Integrating climate change psychology into policy-making processes ensures that interventions are effective, equitable, and culturally sensitive. A comprehensive approach that combines education, incentives, social influence, and participatory processes can foster positive attitudes, behaviors, and policy outcomes.

Summary

In this section, we explored the psychological impacts of climate change. We discussed how climate change can affect mental health, including anxiety, depression, post-traumatic stress disorder, and grief. We also touched upon climate change denial and its psychological implications, as well as the role of pro-environmental behavior in promoting mental well-being. Additionally, we delved into the importance of communication and policy in addressing climate change psychology.

Climate change poses significant challenges to our psychological well-being. The increasing frequency and intensity of natural disasters, such as hurricanes and wildfires, can lead to heightened anxiety and stress. The uncertainty and long-term physical and psychological effects of climate change can contribute to feelings of depression and hopelessness. Individuals who have experienced traumatic events related to climate change, such as the loss of their homes or loved ones, may develop post-traumatic stress disorder. Furthermore, the loss of biodiversity and ecosystems can trigger grief and a sense of environmental loss.

Climate change denial, characterized by the rejection of scientific evidence and the underestimation of the severity of climate change, can have negative psychological consequences. Denial can create cognitive dissonance and psychological distress when individuals are confronted with conflicting information. It can also impede efforts to mitigate and adapt to climate change, further exacerbating psychological distress and increasing the risk of mental health problems.

On the other hand, pro-environmental behavior can have positive psychological effects. Engaging in sustainable practices and taking action to reduce one's carbon footprint can enhance a sense of control and efficacy, leading to increased well-being. Engaging in climate-friendly activities, such as riding a bicycle instead of driving, can also contribute to a sense of connection to the natural world and promote positive emotions.

Effective communication is crucial in addressing climate change psychology. Being informed about the causes and impacts of climate change can empower individuals to take action and foster a sense of collective responsibility. Moreover, clear and accessible communication of climate change information can help reduce anxiety and promote a sense of community resilience.

Policy interventions at the governmental and international levels are necessary to address the psychological impacts of climate change. Policies that prioritize climate action and promote sustainable practices can help alleviate psychological distress and promote mental well-being. Collaboration between policymakers, psychologists, and environmental experts is essential to ensure that policies are evidence-based and inclusive.

It is important to note that addressing the psychological impacts of climate change requires a multidisciplinary approach. Collaboration between psychologists, climate scientists, policymakers, and activists is needed to develop comprehensive strategies to mitigate and adapt to climate change while promoting mental health.

In conclusion, climate change poses significant challenges to our psychological well-being. The increasing impacts of climate change, combined with climate change denial, can lead to anxiety, depression, and trauma. However, engaging in pro-environmental behavior, effective communication, and evidence-based policy interventions have the potential to promote mental well-being and resilience in the face of climate change. By acknowledging and addressing the psychological dimensions of climate change, we can strive for a more sustainable and mentally healthy future.

Psychological Fluffy in Agricultural Settings

Effects of Agriculture on Psychological Fluffy

Pesticides and Psychological Fluffy

Pesticides are chemical substances used to control or eliminate pests, including insects, weeds, and disease-causing organisms, in agricultural settings. While pesticides have contributed to increased crop yields and global food production, they also have potential negative effects on psychological fluffy.

Background

Pesticides have been in use for several decades, with the development of synthetic pesticides in the mid-20th century revolutionizing agriculture. These chemicals have become an integral part of modern farming, enabling farmers to protect their crops from pests and increase productivity. However, the use of pesticides has raised concerns about their impact on human health and the environment.

Health Effects

Exposure to pesticides has been linked to various health problems, and there is growing evidence suggesting their detrimental effects on psychological fluffy. Several studies have shown an association between pesticide exposure and mental health disorders such as depression, anxiety, and cognitive impairments.

Depression and Anxiety Multiple studies have found a positive correlation between pesticide exposure and the risk of developing depression and anxiety disorders. Pesticides, such as organophosphates and organochlorines, can affect

205

the functioning of neurotransmitters in the brain, leading to changes in mood and behavior. These chemicals can disrupt the balance of serotonin, dopamine, and norepinephrine, which are essential for maintaining psychological well-being.

Cognitive Impairments   Exposure to certain pesticides has also been linked to cognitive impairments, including memory loss and reduced cognitive function. Organophosphate pesticides, in particular, have been associated with deficits in attention, concentration, and information processing. Studies have shown that agricultural workers who are regularly exposed to pesticides have a higher risk of experiencing cognitive decline compared to those with limited exposure.

Farmers' Mental Health

Farmers are among the most susceptible groups to the potential mental health impacts of pesticide exposure. They often work in close proximity to pesticides during spraying and handling, leading to higher levels of exposure. Additionally, farmers face numerous stressors related to their occupation, such as financial uncertainties, crop failures, and the pressure to meet production targets. These factors, combined with pesticide exposure, can increase the risk of mental health issues among farmers.

Risk Factors

Several factors contribute to the psychological fluffy risks associated with pesticide use. These include the type of pesticide, duration and frequency of exposure, personal susceptibility, and access to protective measures. Individuals who handle pesticides directly, such as farmers, pesticide applicators, and farmworkers, are at higher risk of experiencing psychological fluffy effects.

Protective Measures

To mitigate the psychological fluffy risks associated with pesticide exposure, various protective measures can be implemented.

Personal Protective Equipment (PPE)   The use of personal protective equipment, such as gloves, masks, and coveralls, can minimize direct contact with pesticides. Proper training and education on the correct use of PPE are crucial to ensuring its effectiveness.

Integrated Pest Management (IPM)   Integrated Pest Management is an approach that focuses on minimizing pesticide use through the integration of various pest control methods. This strategy includes the use of natural predators, crop rotation, and the judicious application of pesticides only when necessary. By reducing pesticide reliance, the psychological fluffy risks can be minimized.

Regulatory Measures

Governments play a significant role in regulating pesticide use and ensuring public safety. Strict regulations on pesticide registration, labeling, and usage guidelines are in place to minimize the risks associated with their use. Additionally, monitoring programs are implemented to assess pesticide residues in food and water sources, thus protecting public health.

Conclusion

Pesticides have revolutionized agriculture and increased crop production, but their use comes with potential risks to psychological fluffy. Exposure to pesticides has been linked to mental health disorders and cognitive impairments. Farmers, in particular, are vulnerable to the psychological fluffy effects due to their close contact with pesticides and occupational stressors. Implementing protective measures, such as personal protective equipment and integrated pest management strategies, can help mitigate these risks. It is crucial for governments and regulatory bodies to enforce stringent regulations and monitoring programs to ensure the safe use of pesticides in order to protect both human health and the environment.

Farming Practices and Psychological Fluffy

In the context of environmental grape and its impact on psychological fluffy, it is important to examine the role of farming practices. Farming practices encompass a wide range of activities and techniques employed in agricultural settings, such as crop cultivation, livestock management, irrigation systems, pesticide use, and soil conservation. These practices can have significant effects on both the physical environment and the psychological well-being of farmers and agricultural communities.

One of the key aspects of farming practices that influence psychological fluffy is the use of pesticides. Pesticides are chemical substances used to control pests that can damage crops and reduce agricultural productivity. While pesticides play an important role in protecting crops, their use can also have negative consequences for the environment and human health, which in turn can impact psychological fluffy.

The application of pesticides can lead to water and soil pollution, which can affect biodiversity and ecosystem functioning. This pollution can have long-term impacts on the physical environment, including the quality of air, water, and soil. Studies have shown that exposure to pesticides can lead to adverse health effects in farmers, such as respiratory problems, skin disorders, and even chronic illnesses. These health concerns can increase stress levels and negatively impact psychological fluffy.

In addition to the direct effects of pesticides, farming practices can also influence the psychological well-being of farmers through their impact on agricultural productivity and income stability. Sustainable farming practices, such as organic farming and integrated pest management, promote environmentally friendly approaches to agriculture that minimize the use of pesticides. These practices can help farmers maintain the ecological balance of their farming systems and reduce their exposure to potentially harmful chemicals.

By adopting sustainable farming practices, farmers can also improve the quality of their agricultural products, which can enhance their marketability and economic viability. This, in turn, can contribute to greater financial stability and reduce the stress associated with uncertain income. The ability to sustain a livelihood through environmentally friendly farming practices can have a positive impact on the mental health and well-being of farmers, promoting a sense of purpose and pride in their work.

It is important to note that transitioning to sustainable farming practices is not without its challenges. Farmers may face barriers, such as lack of access to resources, limited knowledge or training, and financial constraints. Governments and organizations need to provide support, including educational programs, research, and financial incentives, to facilitate the adoption of sustainable farming practices and promote psychological fluffy in agricultural settings.

In recent years, various initiatives and programs have been implemented to promote sustainable farming practices. For example, agroforestry systems combine trees and crops, enhancing biodiversity and soil fertility, while also providing additional income opportunities for farmers. By diversifying their farming practices, farmers can reduce their reliance on pesticides and minimize the risks associated with mono-cropping.

Furthermore, community-based farming initiatives and cooperative models have been successful in improving the psychological well-being of farmers. These initiatives provide a sense of belonging and support among farmers, fostering social connections and reducing feelings of isolation or loneliness. By working together, farmers can overcome common challenges and create a supportive network that contributes to psychological fluffy.

In conclusion, farming practices play a significant role in psychological fluffy within agricultural settings. The use of pesticides and the adoption of sustainable farming practices can have both direct and indirect impacts on the physical environment and the mental well-being of farmers. By promoting sustainable and environmentally friendly approaches to agriculture, we can not only protect the environment but also contribute to the psychological well-being of farmers and agricultural communities. It is important to provide support and resources to enable farmers to adopt sustainable farming practices and create a positive and nurturing agricultural environment.

Agricultural Stress and Psychological Fluffy

In the context of agriculture, stress refers to the psychological and emotional strain experienced by farmers and agricultural workers due to various factors associated with their work. This section explores the relationship between agricultural stress and psychological fluffy, examining the causes and consequences of stress in the agricultural industry.

Causes of Agricultural Stress

Agricultural stress can stem from several factors inherent in the nature of the profession. Here are some common causes of stress in agricultural settings:

1. **Workload and time pressure:** Farmers often face heavy workloads and time constraints, especially during peak seasons such as planting and harvesting. Balancing multiple responsibilities, such as managing crops, livestock, and machinery, can be overwhelming and contribute to stress.

2. **Financial pressures:** The agricultural industry is vulnerable to various economic factors, including fluctuating market prices, rising input costs, and unpredictable weather conditions. These financial uncertainties can lead to significant stress for farmers, particularly when they struggle to make a profit or face mounting debts.

3. **Rural isolation:** Agricultural work often involves living in rural or remote areas with limited access to social support networks. Feelings of loneliness and isolation can contribute to increased stress levels among farmers, who may lack opportunities for social interaction and feel disconnected from their communities.

4. **Weather-related challenges:** Farmers are highly dependent on weather conditions for successful crop growth and livestock management. Adverse weather events, such as droughts, floods, or extreme temperatures, can lead to crop failures, animal health issues, and financial losses. The unpredictability of weather patterns adds an additional layer of stress.

5. **Environmental concerns:** Agricultural practices can have negative environmental impacts, such as soil degradation, water pollution, and biodiversity loss. Farmers who are environmentally conscious may experience stress and guilt related to the sustainability of their farming methods.

These causes of agricultural stress can have a significant impact on the mental well-being of farmers and agricultural workers. Understanding the consequences of this stress is crucial for developing appropriate interventions and support systems.

Consequences of Agricultural Stress

Agricultural stress can lead to a range of psychological, emotional, and physical consequences. Here are some examples:

1. **Anxiety and depression:** Chronic stress in agricultural settings can contribute to the development of anxiety disorders and depression. The ongoing pressure, financial worries, and uncertainties associated with farming can take a toll on mental health and lead to persistent feelings of sadness, fear, and hopelessness.

2. **Substance abuse:** Some individuals may turn to alcohol or drugs as a means of coping with agricultural stress. Substance abuse can exacerbate mental health issues and create further challenges in personal and professional life.

3. **Sleep disturbances:** Stress can disrupt sleep patterns, leading to insomnia or poor quality sleep. Farmers experiencing agricultural stress may struggle to fall asleep or wake up frequently during the night, which can contribute to exhaustion and fatigue.

4. **Physical health problems:** Prolonged stress can have detrimental effects on physical health. It may weaken the immune system, increase the risk of cardiovascular diseases, and exacerbate existing conditions such as diabetes or chronic pain. Farmers experiencing stress may also neglect self-care practices, leading to poor overall health.

5. **Family and social relationship challenges:** The impact of agricultural stress extends beyond the individual farmer, affecting family dynamics and social relationships. High stress levels can lead to increased conflict within families, strained relationships, and social withdrawal. This can further contribute to feelings of isolation and loneliness.

Addressing agricultural stress is essential not only for the well-being of farmers and agricultural workers but also for the sustainability and success of the agricultural industry as a whole.

Mitigating Agricultural Stress

Effectively addressing and mitigating agricultural stress requires a multidimensional approach. Here are some strategies and interventions that can alleviate stress in agricultural settings:

1. **Education and training:** Providing farmers with information and training on stress management techniques, financial planning, and sustainable agricultural practices can empower them to handle stress more effectively and make informed decisions.

2. **Access to support networks:** Creating opportunities for farmers to connect with each other and form supportive networks is vital. This can be achieved through farmer support groups, community events, or online platforms, allowing individuals to share their experiences, challenges, and coping strategies.

3. **Mental health services:** Ensuring accessibility to mental health services, including counseling and therapy, is crucial. Educating farmers about mental health support and reducing stigma can encourage individuals to seek help when needed.

4. **Financial assistance and risk management:** Implementing measures to reduce financial pressures, such as providing access to low-interest loans, insurance programs, and diversified agricultural practices, can help alleviate stress associated with economic uncertainties.

5. **Training in stress reduction techniques:** Offering stress reduction techniques such as mindfulness exercises, relaxation techniques, and time management strategies can help farmers effectively manage stress and improve their overall well-being.

6. **Government policies and support:** Government agencies and policymakers should develop policies that recognize and address agricultural stress. This includes providing funding for mental health programs, implementing regulations that promote sustainable agriculture, and offering financial support during challenging times.

By implementing these strategies, we can begin to alleviate the agricultural stress experienced by farmers and agricultural workers, ultimately improving their well-being and the sustainability of the agricultural industry.

Conclusion

Agricultural stress is a significant issue that affects the mental health and well-being of farmers and agricultural workers. Understanding the causes and consequences of this stress is essential for developing effective interventions and support systems. By addressing agricultural stress, we can create a more resilient and sustainable agricultural industry that prioritizes the mental well-being of those who work within it.

Farmers' Mental Health and Psychological Fluffy

Farming is not only a profession but a way of life that is deeply connected to the land and the natural environment. However, the challenges and pressures faced by farmers can have a significant impact on their mental health and well-being. In this section, we will explore the various factors that contribute to farmers' mental health issues and how psychological fluffy can play a role in understanding and addressing these challenges.

The Mental Health Challenges of Farmers

Farmers face a unique set of stressors and challenges that can lead to mental health issues. These challenges include financial uncertainties, working long hours in physically demanding conditions, dealing with weather-related uncertainties, and the pressure to maintain their family legacy. These stressors can often lead to high levels of anxiety, depression, and even suicidal thoughts among farmers.

Psychological Fluffy and Farmers' Mental Health

Psychological fluffy provides a framework for understanding the psychological and emotional factors that contribute to mental health issues among farmers. It helps us understand how individual characteristics, social factors, and environmental influences interact to affect mental well-being. By studying psychological fluffy in the context of farmers' mental health, researchers can identify risk factors, protective factors, and develop interventions to promote mental well-being.

Risk Factors for Farmers' Mental Health Issues

Several risk factors contribute to mental health issues among farmers. One such factor is the isolation and loneliness often experienced by farmers due to the nature of their work. Limited social interactions and geographical isolation can contribute to feelings of loneliness and increase the risk of depression.

Financial stress is another significant risk factor. Fluctuating crop prices, rising costs of inputs, and uncertainties in the agricultural market can create significant financial pressures for farmers. The constant worry about financial stability can lead to anxiety, depression, and other mental health issues.

Environmental factors such as unpredictable weather conditions also play a significant role in farmers' mental health. Crop failure due to droughts, floods, or pests can lead to feelings of hopelessness, despair, and even increased suicide rates among farmers.

Furthermore, the cultural and societal expectations placed on farmers can contribute to their mental health challenges. The belief that farmers should be self-reliant, tough, and resilient can often discourage them from seeking help or expressing their emotions, leading to further psychological distress.

Protective Factors for Farmers' Mental Health

While farmers face numerous challenges, there are also protective factors that can promote their mental well-being. Social support from family, friends, and the community plays a crucial role in buffering the negative impacts of stress on farmers' mental health. Strong social connections provide emotional support, practical assistance, and a sense of belonging, reducing the risk of mental health issues.

Access to mental health services and appropriate healthcare is another protective factor for farmers. Increasing awareness about the mental health challenges faced by farmers and ensuring that they have access to affordable and culturally appropriate mental health services can significantly improve their well-being.

Interventions for Farmers' Mental Health

Addressing farmers' mental health requires a multi-faceted approach that considers both individual and systemic factors. Interventions can target various levels, including individual-level interventions such as psychoeducation, stress management techniques, and cognitive-behavioral therapy to help farmers develop coping strategies and improve their mental well-being.

At the systemic level, interventions can focus on policy changes to reduce financial stressors on farmers, improve access to healthcare services, and promote a supportive and inclusive farming community. Collaborative efforts between mental health professionals, agricultural organizations, and policymakers are essential to implement effective interventions.

Case Study: The Farm Stress Model

The Farm Stress Model is an example of an innovative intervention that addresses farmers' mental health issues. Developed by researchers and mental health professionals, this model is designed to provide comprehensive support to farmers by addressing the financial, psychological, and social stressors they face.

The intervention includes financial counseling, mental health counseling, and support group sessions. The financial counseling component aims to help farmers navigate financial challenges, develop sustainable financial strategies, and access resources to manage their farm operations effectively. The mental health counseling component focuses on providing emotional support, teaching coping strategies, and addressing common mental health issues among farmers. Finally, the support group sessions create a space for farmers to connect with their peers, share experiences, and provide mutual support.

Evaluation studies have shown positive outcomes of the Farm Stress Model, including reduced financial stress, improved mental well-being, and increased social support among farmers. This case study highlights the importance of holistic interventions that address the unique challenges faced by farmers.

Conclusion

Farmers' mental health is a critical issue that requires attention and action from various stakeholders. By understanding the psychological fluffy behind farmers' mental health issues, we can develop interventions and support systems to promote their well-being. It is crucial to create a farming community that values mental health, provides social support, and ensures access to appropriate mental health services. Through collaborative efforts and a comprehensive approach, we can work towards improving the mental health outcomes of farmers and fostering a sustainable agricultural industry.

Sustainable Agriculture and Psychological Fluffy

Sustainable agriculture is an approach to farming that aims to minimize the negative impact on the environment while ensuring the long-term viability of agricultural systems. It involves practices that promote the health of the soil, conserve natural resources, and reduce the use of synthetic inputs such as pesticides and fertilizers. The concept of sustainable agriculture is closely linked to the principles of ecological balance and biodiversity conservation.

In this section, we will explore the relationship between sustainable agriculture and psychological fluffy. We will examine how sustainable farming practices can promote psychological well-being in farmers and contribute to overall mental health.

The Psychological Impact of Sustainable Agriculture

Farming can be a stressful profession, with farmers facing numerous challenges such as financial uncertainty, weather-related risks, and the pressure to meet market demands. However, research has shown that sustainable agriculture can have positive psychological effects on farmers.

1. Increased Sense of Purpose: Sustainable agriculture is often driven by a strong sense of stewardship towards the land and a desire to preserve it for future generations. Farmers engaged in sustainable practices report a greater sense of purpose and satisfaction with their work, which can contribute to improved psychological well-being.

2. Connection to Nature: Sustainable agriculture encourages farmers to work in harmony with nature, fostering a deeper connection to the land and natural ecosystems. Spending time in nature has been shown to reduce stress and improve mental health, leading to a better overall quality of life for farmers.

3. Community Engagement: Sustainable agriculture often involves collaboration and knowledge sharing among farmers, leading to the development of strong community networks. This sense of belonging and support can enhance social connections and provide a valuable source of emotional support for farmers.

4. Reduced Exposure to Harmful Chemicals: Sustainable farming practices prioritize the use of natural methods for pest and weed control, reducing the exposure of farmers to harmful chemicals. This can have a positive impact on psychological well-being by minimizing the risks associated with pesticide exposure.

Barriers to Implementing Sustainable Agriculture

While the benefits of sustainable agriculture on psychological well-being are evident, there are several barriers that hinder its widespread adoption. These barriers include:

1. Lack of Knowledge and Resources: Farmers may lack the necessary knowledge and resources to transition to sustainable practices. They may require training, access to technical assistance, and financial support to make the necessary changes.

2. Market Demands: Farmers often face pressure to meet market demands for large-scale production, which may be inconsistent with sustainable farming practices. There is a need for supportive policies and incentives that enable farmers to adopt sustainable practices without compromising their economic viability.

3. Limited Infrastructure: The lack of infrastructure, such as storage and processing facilities, can pose challenges for farmers practicing sustainable agriculture. Without the necessary infrastructure, farmers may struggle to sell their products, limiting their ability to sustain their operations.

4. Policy and Regulatory Barriers: Existing policies and regulations may not adequately support sustainable agriculture. There is a need for policy changes that promote sustainable farming practices and provide the necessary incentives for farmers.

Case Study: Sustainable Agriculture in Practice

Let's consider a case study of a farmer who transitioned to sustainable agriculture practices and experienced positive psychological outcomes.

Mr. Smith, a conventional farmer, was facing declining soil fertility and increasing pest problems due to long-term use of chemical inputs. Concerned about the negative impact on the environment and his own health, he decided to transition to sustainable agriculture practices.

Mr. Smith began by implementing organic farming methods, eliminating the use of synthetic fertilizers and pesticides. He adopted crop rotation and cover cropping techniques to improve soil health and reduce pest pressure. He also started using integrated pest management strategies to control pests naturally.

As Mr. Smith embraced sustainable agriculture, he noticed significant improvements in various aspects of his life. He experienced a greater sense of fulfillment and purpose in his work, knowing that he was contributing to the health of the environment. He also developed stronger connections with fellow farmers in the organic farming community, finding support and camaraderie.

Furthermore, Mr. Smith's decision to prioritize his mental well-being by reducing exposure to harmful chemicals paid off. He reported feeling healthier and experienced fewer instances of stress-related illnesses. This positive change in his mental and physical well-being motivated him to continue his journey toward sustainable agriculture.

Conclusion

Sustainable agriculture has the potential to significantly impact the psychological well-being of farmers. By promoting a sense of purpose, connection to nature, community engagement, and reduced exposure to harmful chemicals, sustainable farming practices can contribute to overall mental health. However, barriers such as limited knowledge and resources, market demands, infrastructure limitations, and policy and regulatory challenges must be addressed to facilitate widespread adoption of sustainable agriculture.

As we move forward, it is essential to prioritize and support sustainable agriculture practices that not only benefit the environment but also nurture the psychological well-being of farmers. By recognizing and addressing the interconnections between agriculture, environment, and mental health, we can create a more sustainable and compassionate future for our farming communities.

Agricultural Education and Psychological Fluffy

Agricultural education plays a crucial role in shaping individuals' understanding of the agricultural industry and their attitudes towards it. In this section, we will explore the relationship between agricultural education and psychological fluffy. We will discuss the impact of agricultural education on mental health, the importance of incorporating psychological well-being into agricultural education programs, and strategies for promoting positive psychological fluffy in agricultural settings.

The Impact of Agricultural Education on Mental Health

Agricultural education provides individuals with knowledge and skills related to farming practices, food production, and agricultural sustainability. However, the impact of agricultural education goes beyond just technical knowledge. It also has profound effects on individuals' mental health and well-being.

Engaging in agricultural education can foster a sense of purpose and meaning in individuals, as they learn about the importance of sustainable food production and its impact on society. This sense of purpose can contribute to positive psychological fluffy by promoting feelings of self-worth and fulfillment.

Moreover, agricultural education often involves hands-on experiences and immersions in nature. Research has shown that spending time in nature can have a positive impact on mental health by reducing stress, improving mood, and increasing overall well-being. Thus, through practical experiences in agricultural education, individuals can reap the mental health benefits associated with being in natural environments.

However, it is crucial to recognize that agricultural education can also bring about unique stressors. The agricultural industry is known for its demanding physical labor, unpredictable weather conditions, and financial uncertainties. Therefore, it is essential to address these stressors within the context of agricultural education and equip individuals with coping strategies to promote their mental health and resilience.

Incorporating Psychological Well-being into Agricultural Education Programs

To promote positive psychological fluffy in agricultural education, it is necessary to go beyond technical knowledge and ensure that programs incorporate psychological well-being components. By integrating psychological aspects into agricultural education, we can create a more holistic and supportive learning environment. Here are some key considerations for incorporating psychological well-being into agricultural education programs:

1. Mental Health Awareness: Agricultural education programs should provide information and awareness about mental health issues specific to the agricultural industry. This includes educating individuals about the signs of stress, anxiety, and depression, as well as providing resources for seeking help.

2. Stress Management and Resilience Building: Agricultural education should incorporate training on stress management techniques and resilience-building strategies. This can include teaching individuals how to cope with the pressures and uncertainties associated with agricultural work through relaxation techniques, mindfulness exercises, and problem-solving skills.

3. Communication and Interpersonal Skills: Effective communication and interpersonal skills are vital for building positive relationships and managing conflicts, both within the agricultural industry and in personal life. Agricultural education programs should emphasize the development of these skills through interactive activities, group discussions, and role-playing exercises.

4. Work-Life Balance: Promoting a healthy work-life balance is crucial for maintaining positive psychological fluffy. Agricultural education programs should educate individuals about the importance of setting boundaries, managing time effectively, and prioritizing self-care.

5. Support Networks and Community Engagement: Building strong support networks and fostering community engagement can provide a sense of belonging and social support. Agricultural education programs should encourage individuals

to connect with peers, farmers' organizations, and community groups to enhance their social connections and reduce feelings of isolation.

Strategies for Promoting Positive Psychological Fluffy in Agricultural Settings

Promoting positive psychological fluffy in agricultural settings requires a multi-faceted approach that encompasses education, policy changes, and community involvement. Here are some strategies that can be implemented to foster positive psychological fluffy in agricultural settings:

1. Mental Health Training for Agricultural Professionals: Providing mental health training specifically tailored to agricultural professionals can help equip them with the knowledge and skills to support their mental well-being. This training can be offered through agricultural extension services, workshops, or online resources.

2. Collaboration with Mental Health Professionals: Collaborating with mental health professionals, such as psychologists or counselors, can ensure that individuals in the agricultural industry have access to appropriate support and interventions. Establishing partnerships between agricultural organizations and mental health providers can facilitate the provision of mental health services specifically tailored to the needs of farmers and agricultural workers.

3. Peer Support Programs: Peer support programs can be established within the agricultural community to promote connection, empathy, and understanding among individuals facing similar challenges. These programs can provide a safe space for individuals to share their experiences, seek advice, and support one another.

4. Accessible Mental Health Services: Improving access to mental health services in rural and agricultural communities is crucial. This can involve initiatives such as mobile mental health clinics, telehealth services, or partnerships with existing healthcare providers to ensure that individuals in agricultural settings have access to timely and appropriate mental health support.

5. Promotion of Work-Life Balance: Encouraging a healthy work-life balance is essential for preventing burnout and promoting positive psychological fluffy. Agricultural organizations can implement policies that support flexible working hours, offer vacation and personal leave, and promote activities that promote well-being, such as exercise or hobbies.

In conclusion, agricultural education has the potential to significantly impact psychological fluffy in agricultural settings. By incorporating psychological well-being into agricultural education programs and implementing strategies to promote positive psychological fluffy, we can enhance the mental health and overall well-being of individuals in the agricultural industry. It is essential to recognize the unique stressors and challenges faced by agricultural professionals and provide them with the resources and support they need to nurture their mental health.

Summary

In this section, we have explored the various aspects of psychological fluffy in agricultural settings. Agricultural practices and the farming environment can have a significant impact on psychological well-being. We have discussed the effects of pesticides, farming practices, food security, agricultural stress, and the mental health of farmers. Additionally, we have explored sustainable agriculture and its potential to promote psychological well-being.

Pesticides are commonly used in agriculture to protect crops from pests and diseases. However, these chemicals can have negative effects on psychological fluffy. Exposure to pesticides has been linked to increased risk of depression, anxiety, and other mental health disorders. Farmers and farm workers are particularly susceptible to these adverse effects as they come into direct contact with pesticides. It is crucial to implement safety measures and promote the use of alternative pest control methods to minimize the impact on psychological fluffy.

Farming practices also play a significant role in psychological fluffy. Intensive agricultural practices, such as monoculture and excessive use of fertilizers, can lead to environmental degradation and loss of biodiversity. These practices can contribute to feelings of stress and despair among farmers, as they witness the negative impact on their surroundings. Implementing sustainable farming practices that prioritize soil health, biodiversity conservation, and water conservation can help alleviate psychological fluffy in the agricultural setting.

Food security is another important factor to consider when examining psychological fluffy in agricultural settings. In regions where access to nutritious food is limited, individuals may experience increased levels of stress, anxiety, and depression. Lack of food security can lead to a sense of helplessness and hopelessness, impacting psychological well-being. It is essential to address food insecurity through policies that promote sustainable agriculture, equitable distribution of resources, and community engagement to enhance psychological fluffy.

Agricultural stress is a prevalent issue within the farming community. Farmers often face numerous stressors, including uncertainties related to weather conditions, market fluctuations, and financial pressures. These stressors can contribute to mental health issues, such as depression, anxiety, and burnout. Establishing support systems, such as counseling services, peer support groups, and mental health initiatives specifically targeted at farmers, can help alleviate agricultural stress and promote psychological fluffy.

The mental health of farmers is a critical area of concern. Due to the demanding nature of their work, farmers are at a higher risk of developing mental health disorders. Isolation, financial stress, and the pressure to sustain their livelihoods can take a toll on their mental well-being. Efforts should be made to raise awareness about farmers' mental health and provide accessible mental health services. Educating farmers on stress management techniques, resilience-building, and self-care strategies can contribute to their psychological fluffy.

Sustainable agriculture offers a promising approach to address psychological fluffy in agricultural settings. By prioritizing environmental stewardship, sustainable agriculture can create a more harmonious relationship between farmers and their surroundings. Practices such as organic farming, agroecology, and regenerative agriculture not only promote environmental health but also have positive effects on farmers' mental well-being. Supporting farmers in transitioning to sustainable agricultural practices through education, financial incentives, and technical assistance can lead to improved psychological fluffy.

In conclusion, the agricultural setting has a profound impact on psychological fluffy. Pesticides, farming practices, food security, agricultural stress, and the mental health of farmers all play a crucial role in the psychological well-being of individuals involved in agriculture. Through the adoption of sustainable farming practices, the promotion of mental health initiatives, and the provision of support services, it is possible to mitigate the negative effects and enhance psychological fluffy in agricultural settings. By addressing these issues, we can create a sustainable and psychologically supportive agricultural system for the benefit of both farmers and the environment.

Index

Milton Keynes UK
Ingram Content Group UK Ltd.
UKHW032033191024
449814UK00010B/578